# Nuclear Weapons and Conflict Transformation

This new volume explores what the acquisition of nuclear weapons means for the life of a protracted conflict.

The book argues that the significance of the possession of nuclear weapons in conflict resolution has been previously overlooked. Saira Khan argues that the acquisition of nuclear weapons by states keeps conflicts alive indefinitely, as they are maintained by frequent crises and low-to-medium intensity violence, rather than escalating to full-scale wars. This theory therefore emphasizes the importance of nuclear weapons in both war-avoidance and peace-avoidance. The book opens with a section explaining its theory of conflict transformation with nuclear weapons, before testing this against the case study of the India–Pakistan protracted conflict in South Asia.

This book will be of much interest to students of strategic studies, international relations and Asian politics and security.

**Saira Khan** is at the University of British Columbia, Canada.

# Asian security studies

Edited by Sumit Ganguly and Andrew Scobell
*Indiana University, Bloomington and US Army War College*

Few regions of the world are fraught with as many security questions as Asia. Within this region it is possible to study great power rivalries, irredentist conflicts, nuclear and ballistic missile proliferation, secessionist movements, ethnoreligious conflicts and inter-state wars. This book series publishes the best possible scholarship on the security issues affecting the region, and includes detailed empirical studies, theoretically oriented case studies and policy-relevant analyses as well as more general works.

# Nuclear Weapons and Conflict Transformation

## The case of India–Pakistan

**Saira Khan**

LONDON AND NEW YORK

First published 2009
by Routledge
2 Park Square, Milton Park, Abingdon, Oxon, OX14 4RN

Simultaneously published in the USA and Canada
by Routledge
270 Madison Avenue, New York, NY 10016

*Routledge is an imprint of the Taylor & Francis Group, an informa business*

Typeset in Times New Roman by
Keystroke, 28 High Street, Tettenhall, Wolverhampton
Printed and bound in Great Britain by
Biddles Digital, King's Lynn, Norfolk

*British Library Cataloguing in Publication Data*
A catalogue record for this book is available from the British Library
*Library of Congress Cataloging in Publication Data*
Khan, Saira.
Nuclear weapons and conflict transformation : the case of India-Pakistan / Saira Khan.
p. cm. – (Asian security studies)
Includes bibliographical references.
1. Nuclear arms control. 2. Conflict management. I. Title.
JZ5665.K53 2008
355.02'170954–dc22
2008009167

ISBN10 0–415–37507–X (hbk)
ISBN10 0–203–89176–7 (ebk)

ISBN13 978–0–415–37507–8 (hbk)
ISBN13 978–0–203–89176–6 (ebk)

To my beloved son, Andaleeb

# Contents

# Figures

# Acknowledgments

This book could not have been written without the generous support of many individuals. The idea for the book came from a discussion I had with Mark Brawley on my view of nuclear weapons as deterrents in the India–Pakistan protracted conflict, making it stable. He asked me, "Will the conflict never end?" This question inspired me to investigate the history of the India–Pakistan conflict and understand both the positive and the negative effects of nuclear weapons acquisition. Thus the book owes much to Mark Brawley. Thanks to T. V. Paul for inspiring me and supporting my endeavor to publish the book with Routledge. Special thanks to Sumit Ganguly, who showed special interest in the project and strongly encouraged me to publish it. Thanks to him also for his constructive comments as a discussant of a paper focusing on the basic thesis of this book, which I presented at the International Studies Association Convention in Los Angeles. Without thanks to Michael Brecher for broadening my horizon of thinking about crisis, conflict, and war, this acknowledgment section would be incomplete. His graduate course at McGill, his books on the subject, and each discussion I had with him since my graduate years at McGill, helped me to think and rethink about the triangular relationship between protracted conflicts, crises, and wars. He has never failed to discuss with me any of my projects despite his busy work schedule and I thank him especially for his support and assistance all the way.

During the research work I received enormous help from a number of people. My sincere thanks are due to the former Prime Minister of India, I. K. Gujral, for giving his precious time to discuss with me the possibilities of a peaceful South Asia. Thanks also for his extremely useful comments on South Asian security and politics, and especially for sharing his personal experiences as the Prime Minister of India in the context of the India–Pakistan conflict and nuclear weapons acquisition. His expectation of a prosperous South Asia in the future has encouraged me to take this study further and explore the possibilities of how the seemingly intractable India–Pakistan conflict could be terminated, the focus of the last chapter of this book. My deepest thanks go to K. Subrahmanyam for sharing with me his useful insights on the subject. Special thanks also go to K. K. Nayyar, Muchkund Dubey, S. K. Singh, K. Santhanam, General V. K. Srivastava, and Uday Bhaskar for giving me their time and sharing with me their views on the subject at a time when India was faced with one of its most serious crises and they were all engaged in policy-making discussions. Thanks are also due to Brahma Chellaney, Amitabh Mattoo, Raj Chengappa, Savita Pande, R. R. Subramanian, P. Sahadevan, Bhavani Sen Gupta, P. R. Chari, and S. D. Muni for their constructive comments on the topic. Very special thanks go to Air Commodore Jasjit Singh for never failing to discuss my projects with me and for sharing his views on the India–Pakistan conflict. I would like to thank Aga Shahi, Mushahid Hussain, and Shireen Mazari for their very useful thoughts on the topic. Special thanks to Niaz Naik for sharing with me his personal experience of the behind-the-scenes diplomacy India and Pakistan launched in secret. His analysis and comments helped me not only by informing me of the diplomatic endeavor when very few people knew about it but also by showing me that India and Pakistan both wanted to attain peace through diplomacy when war was no longer an option. Special thanks to Pervaiz Iqbal Cheema, Nasim Zehra, Rasheed Khalid, Matiur Rahman, and Khalid Mahmud for their thought-provoking comments. My thanks are overdue to Khalilur Rahman and Najam Rafique – two important people who introduced me to many important strategists and policy-makers in India and Pakistan respectively. Thanks are also due to Farooq Sobhan, Mostafa Faruque, and Gaddam Dharmendra for their analysis of the India–Pakistan conflict. Special thanks to Ambassador Q. A. M. A. Rahim, the former Secretary General of the South Asian Association for Regional Cooperation, for his very insightful comments on the conflict and SAARC.

Special thanks to Andrew Humphrys, an editor at Routledge, for bearing with my delays in submitting the manuscript and helping me through the process of writing the book. It was a delight to have him as my editor. Thanks also to the editorial staff of Routledge for bringing this book to press.

A generous research grant was provided by the American University in Cairo for field research in India and Pakistan. The book thus owes much to the AUC.

I have benefited enormously from the kindness of colleagues and friends while researching and writing this book. While I am unable to mention names, I most sincerely thank them all.

My greatest debts are to my family. My deepest abiding gratitude goes to my mother Nargis Khan for her constant prayers which have helped me to lead a productive life. I pay special tribute to my late father, Shafiullah Khan, the memory of whose unbounded love gives a new meaning to my life every day. Sincere thanks to my husband Jalal for his support and for accompanying me to India and Pakistan during periods of heightened tension in the region. I cannot thank my son Andaleeb enough for his encouragement, support, and help while I was writing the book. I would like to thank him especially for helping me with the figures. Without his loving presence in my life this book and much else would not have come to pass. It is with great pleasure that I dedicate this book to Andaleeb.

# Introduction

The proliferation of nuclear weapons is one of the most pressing problems in world politics today. After the United States first gained possession of nuclear weapons toward the end of World War II, four countries followed it in acquiring these devastating weapons, making the nuclear club a group of five major states. After China tested a nuclear weapon in 1964, the Nuclear Non-Proliferation Treaty (NPT)[1] was established in 1970 to prohibit other states from acquiring these destructive armaments. It was expected that China would be the last nuclear state in the world. However, in 1974, India, a non-signatory to the NPT, detonated its peaceful nuclear device, alarming the international community, especially the five nuclear states. As a result, the nuclear states adopted a more cautious approach to supplying nuclear materials that can have dual use. The Indian nuclear test was a catalyst for the creation of the Nuclear Suppliers Group (NSG)[2] in 1975. While concerted efforts by the nuclear powers were underway to control the spread of nuclear weapons, India, Pakistan, and Israel were suspected of serious steps toward developing nuclear weapons in the 1970s and 1980s. Although the focus was on these three states because they had shown interest in acquiring nuclear weapons clandestinely and refused to join the NPT, by the 1980s a number of other states, namely Iraq, Iran, North Korea, South Korea, and Taiwan, were also suspected of developing these weapons. With the end of the cold war, Belarus, Kazakhstan, and Ukraine – the three countries that had inherited nuclear weapons from the former Soviet Union – also became causes of concern for the international community in its efforts to contain proliferation. As these countries had shown signs of wanting to aquire nuclear weapons, scholarly works on the subject began to concentrate on what makes states proliferation prone. Studies revealed that the motivations for acquiring nuclear weapons derive from systemic, domestic, and individual factors. A hierarchy of motivations was established and proliferation cases were analyzed against these causal factors. Studies revealed that security was the primary driving force for most states' tendency to proliferate. Scholarly debates revolved around the consequences of nuclear proliferation, especially whether or not nuclear deterrence – the main cause of proliferation – works. One of the most important reasons for proliferation – the existence of protracted conflicts – was ignored by most proliferation scholars. With the exception of the states that inherited nuclear weapons from the former Soviet Union and eventually renounced them, states responsible for proliferation have been engaged in some form of protracted conflicts. Research on the connection between protracted conflicts and proliferation was, thus, invaluable.[3] Similarly, it was pertinent to probe the consequences of proliferation for these protracted conflicts. In other words, if protracted conflict states proliferate to enhance security through deterrence, how does that impact the overall conflict relations? Proliferation scholars never probed this significant research question, neither did conflict scholars.

In the domain of conflict studies, research focused mainly on conflict management, resolution, transformation, and termination, producing a range of rich, significant, and valuable works. Management, resolution, transformation, and termination of conflicts of different types have been investigated and studied by scholars. Inter-state and intra-state conflicts obviously have different root causes, requiring different management, resolution, transformation, and termination mechanisms. Scholarship has established that tools and strategies employed to resolve one kind of conflict cannot be used to solve other kinds. Additionally, within each type of conflict, cases are different, requiring different resolution mechanisms. Interestingly, the role of the possession of nuclear weapons in conflict resolution has been overlooked by scholars. Although states engaged in conflicts tend to acquire nuclear weapons, no one has investigated what happens to a conflict once the states involved gain possession of these weapons that are expected to increase their security. Thus, while conflict scholars have provided multiple perspectives on how to manage, resolve, or transform conflicts, proliferation scholars have probed why states acquire nuclear weapons and whether or not the acquisition of such devastating weapons makes deterrence effective in the specific context. This study moves beyond these questions to understand what the acquisition of nuclear weapons means for the life of a protracted conflict.

The study explores when and under what conditions a protracted conflict moves to a level of almost indefinite protraction arguing that this happens with the acquisition of nuclear weapons by the states in question. It maintains that crises are embedded in each protracted conflict and their escalation to war depends on the nuclear status of the adversaries. Pre-nuclear states generally manage serious crises through full-scale wars, while nuclear adversaries tend to use violent clashes or low–medium-intensity violence as crisis management tools. In the past war tended to be the ultimate instrument employed by states to bring an end to conflicts. As war no longer remains a tool for the termination of protracted conflict in a nuclear environment, other mechanisms must be used. Means such as peace initiatives and diplomatic negotiations can be effective only if the conflict is not in crisis. Unfortunately, the deterrent effect of nuclear weapons creates a no-war situation, but heated crises and low–medium-intensity violence continue and often become more common due to the low probability of escalation to war. Given frequent crises and continuing low–medium-intensity violence – a protracted conflict changes its nature in such a way that it may remain alive indefinitely. As dialogue becomes usual between the states in conflict in periods of calm, perhaps as a result of external pressure, they learn to live in an environment which encourages cooperation on non-controversial issues with positive-sum results and benefits to parties, and discourages dealing with the more controversial and zero-sum issues that exacerbate the conflict. The relationship is beset with hatred and suspicion, owing to its crisis-prone environment. Not only does this transform the conflict, but the opposing states become comfortable with the transformation.

The project underscores the relevance of nuclear weapons to both war avoidance and peace avoidance. Underpinning this idea is the assumption that peace can only be achieved through war avoidance and crisis avoidance. Its aims are the following:

1  to demonstrate that every protracted conflict encompasses several stages: a beginning, upsurge or escalation, de-escalation, and termination. Although a conflict can be triggered for a variety of reasons, escalation, de-escalation, and termination are strongly influenced by the acquisition of nuclear weapons;
2  to clarify that although the absence of war constitutes some form of peace, crisis management techniques — such as violent clashes and low–medium-intensity violence – can continue to jeopardize peace between states in conflict;
3  to highlight that a conflict is likely to be protracted when the two parties acquire nuclear weapons, a unit-level attribute, unless there is a serious change in an actor attribute such as leadership or political/economic capability, or a situational attribute, such as third-party intervention to terminate the conflict;
4  to explain why standard definitions of crisis, which include heightened probability of war, need to be changed for nuclear weapons states;
5  to show that cooperation on simple non-controversial, positive-sum issues may lead to permanent non-cooperation on zero-sum territorial issues.

The possession of nuclear weapons by India and Pakistan has changed the pattern of the relationship between crisis, conflict, and war in South Asia. In the first three decades of the two states' independence, crises escalated to war on three occasions. Since 1971 or so they have not waged war. The 1986–7, 1990, 1999, and 2001 crises substantiate the belief that serious crisis may not escalate to all-out war. A similar crisis in 1965 was managed by war in pre-nuclear South Asia. However, these frequent crises during the nuclear period also confirm that peace between the two countries is unlikely. Peace initiatives, such as the Lahore Peace Process of 1999 and the Agra Summit of 2001, could not prosper, owing to the eruption of serious crises in the conflict setting. In the absence of war, but given the existence of further crises, the level of hostility rises for an extended period and paths to conflict termination remain unexplored, protracting the conflict indefinitely. This change becomes institutionalized when states learn to cooperate on non-complicated issues but refrain from addressing the more difficult root cause of their conflict, making excuses for absence from any discussions or presenting preconditions for such discussions and learning to live in a crisis- and violence-prone environment.

## Significance and implications

The rationale for this study is that although much scholarly attention has been given to the consequences of nuclear proliferation, the focus has generally been on the concept of deterrence. It is now pertinent to understand the effects of deterrence on the life of a protracted conflict. This study makes a substantial contribution to both proliferation and conflict literature by examining the consequences of nuclear weapons acquisition for protracted conflicts.

The study has significant theoretical and policy implications:

1   Realism, which upholds in maximizing state security through military capabilities, fails to explain why states face insecurity for extended periods following the acquisition of the most advanced weaponry – nuclear weapons.
2   Deterrence, a debated paradigm, plays an important role in preventing wars between protracted conflict states when they acquire nuclear weapons. However, by deterring wars and thereby generating further crises, nuclear weapons acquisition jeopardizes comprehensive stability between two states in conflict.
3   Peace theorists need to understand peace as a function of absence of war and crisis; crisis theorists need to redefine crisis by excluding war in the case of nuclear weapon states; conflict theorists need to understand the word "transformation" comprehensively – both positively and negatively.
4   Although proliferation scholars argue that states often acquire nuclear weapons for security enhancement, a state may be more insecure in its long-term relations with a protracted conflict adversary as a result of possessing such weapons. Nuclear weapons, ultimately, may have limited ability to give a state comprehensive security.

Among others, the primary policy recommendation of this study is that major powers need to create a propitious environment for states to terminate their intractable conflict. The transformed India–Pakistan protracted conflict could be terminated with the help of a facilitator, a third party; without this help, a congenial environment for conflict resolution may never be created by the two states in their frequent crisis-prone confrontations.

## Methodology

Two important criteria determined the research approach of this study: (1) the state of the literature on the association between protracted conflict and nuclear proliferation, which is essentially under-theorized; and (2) the question under investigation. A causal explanation is provided, which is mostly absent in the literature. The India–Pakistan case study was selected because the two parties did not have nuclear weapons for the first half of their protracted conflict and do possess them in the second half. This is useful and makes a single case study more powerful because of the existence of within-case variance. In-depth case studies also enable intensive analysis by which critical variables or causal relationships can be found.

The research for this study has been conducted through primary materials as well as secondary sources on the sixty-year conflict between India and Pakistan. Primary field research was conducted in December–January 2001–2, a time when a serious crisis with the propensity to escalate to conventional/nuclear war had just erupted between the two nuclear states, and in April 2003, when the two parties were about to initiate the dialogue that is ongoing at the time of writing in 2007. Interviewing key decision-makers and strategic analysts has been an integral part of the field research.

The book is divided into two parts and has ten chapters. The first part is theoretical. Chapter 1 discusses studies on conflict transformation. This is followed by a chapter that assesses scholarship on proliferation and the consequences of nuclear weapons acquisition. The third chapter lays out the theoretical framework of the book. It offers a theory of how nuclear weapons can transform a conflict. Part II is a case study of the India–Pakistan protracted conflict. The theoretical study is tested against this case study. Chapter 4 portrays the history of the India– Pakistan protracted conflict. The next chapter assesses the causes of the introduction of nuclear weapons into the conflict setting. Chapter 6 outlines and discusses all the crises and wars between the adversaries when they both had conventional capabilities only. The following chapter looks at all the crises between the two during the period after the acquisition of nuclear weapons, none of which escalated to war. Chapter 8 presents the array of peace initiatives taken by both countries, all of which failed to produce positive results. Chapter 9 shows how the conflict essentially changed to a state of indefinite protraction as a result of the absence of war and existence of more crises or constant violence in the conflict setting. The two parties learned to live in that environment by holding dialogues – under external pressure – for cooperation on non-controversial issues while ignoring the core problem. A final chapter assesses the potential for conflict termination. It discusses when and under what conditions the conflict is likely to be terminated. It analyzes the roles of actor attributes – leadership and political/ economic factors – and situational factors – the role of external powers, especially the US – in changing the conflict relations in a positive manner. The conclusion provides a summary of the book and explains how it contributes to the understanding of conflict transformation as a result of nuclear weapons. It discusses the findings of the study, assessing how far the India–Pakistan case study supports the theory presented in this book. Additionally, it presents some significant theoretical and policy implications of the research and encourages further research on the subject.

# Part I
# Theory

# 1 Studies on conflict transformation

Conflict scholars have studied the management, resolution, termination, and transformation of conflicts. Although the first of these three efforts/strategies pertaining to conflicts have different meanings, conflict transformation essentially entails all three. Management, resolution, and termination are all different types of conflict transformation. A conflict is transformed primarily when there are signs of a changed relationship between the states in conflict. The changed relationship may be better or worse for the parties concerned. This new relationship may be short-lived or enduring. A conflict between states starts when they have opposing or incompatible desires or goals; management, resolution, transformation, and termination are steps/processes/strategies in the history of a conflict. This chapter discusses previous scholarship on these strategies relating to conflicts, and demonstrates the absence of research on the linkage between nuclear weapons acquisition and conflict transformation. It also highlights the idea that conflict transformation may be negative, in contrast to the positive aspects portrayed by existing studies.

## Conflict management

Conflict management is a term used to describe a "situation where a conflict continues but where its worst excesses are avoided or mitigated. Conflict management would, in particular seek to avoid or terminate violence between parties."[1] Thus, conflict management is often sought when some form of conflict control is necessary but complete resolution seems impossible. In cases of resolution-resistant or even protracted conflict, it is possible to manage the situation in ways that make it more constructive and less destructive.[2] The ultimate aim of conflict management is to intervene in ways that make the ongoing conflict less damaging to all contending parties. For example, peacekeeping forces can calm a situation and, thus, manage a conflict. However, such endeavors can never resolve the conflict but only provide temporary solutions. D. Bloomfield and Ben Reilly define conflict management as

> the positive and constructive handling of difference and divergence. Rather than advocating methods for removing conflict [it] addresses the more realistic

question of managing conflict: how to deal with it in a constructive way, how to bring opposite sides together in a cooperative process, how to design a practical, achievable, cooperative system for the constructive management of difference.[3]

Conflict management is also often achieved by strategies of mutual deterrence.[4] Thus, changes in the attributes of the participants can manage a conflict. The acquisition of nuclear weapons can be used to manage conflicts through deterrence. That this does not, however, resolve the conflict is one of the primary under-standings of the present book. William O. Staudenmaier states that technology was a pivotal

factor in the breakup of classical strategy and the assumptions underlying the great power system. Nuclear armed superpowers found it difficult to fight each other in wars, even over vital interests, because of the uncertainties and risks associated with potential escalation to nuclear war and because of the catastrophic consequences should it occur. For superpowers, the use of force became more subtle in situations short of war – what is frequently called coercive diplomacy or crisis management.[5]

He further argues that such warfare is "characterized by its strong political and diplomatic content, its use of limited means in measured ways and the close control of strategic (and very often tactical) options by civilian policymakers."[6] Scholars have also studied conflict termination through general or limited nuclear war. According to the Soviet view, in the cold war years "a general nuclear war would constitute an 'end of the line' clash of the two contending social systems, communism and imperialism, in which imperialism and the capitalist system would collapse and expire."[7] Soviet political and military leaders in the 1970s and 1980s repeatedly insisted on the impossibility of victory in nuclear war. They only believed in social victory.[8] Thus, these devastating weapons are instrumental simply in managing conflicts, not in terminating them.

Interestingly, while some kind of calm in a conflict is generally expected when one speaks of conflict management, in international politics conflicts are also often managed by crises and wars; thus, these are called conflict management techniques or tools. The impacts of crises and wars are different, but there exists a commonality. Both transform the conflict in some way. The relationship becomes better or worse at the end of a crisis or war. War may end a conflict and, where it does not, the relationship between the contending parties may become worse than it was before the war. This is a salient proposition of the present study and is discussed in chapter 3, the theoretical chapter.

## Conflict resolution

Conflict resolution is a highly challenging approach to the analysis of the causes and solutions to conflict situations. Conflict resolution is sought in the hope of finding a compromise that will work for the opposing parties to a conflict, even if only in the short run. Conflicting parties redefine their relationships in such a way that they can realize their ultimate goals without conflict or in such a way that their goals do not conflict. Conflict resolution is defined by Thomas Saaty and Joyce Alexander "as the search for an outcome that, at a minimum, represents for some participants an improvement from, and for no participants a worsening of, their present situation."[9] This essentially means a degree of change in the relationship between the participants. Attempts to resolve conflicts change their dynamics, whether or not the resolution itself is successful.[10] Peter Wallensteen notes that conflict resolution is concerned with purposefully seeking grounds of commonality between the contending parties, whereas conflict transformation refers to a change in the relationship between the parties. This change in relationship occurs through conflict resolution, but it can also occur should one party totally defeat the other. This means that in both cases conflict transformation has occurred.[11] Interestingly, although conflict transformation theorists differ in terms of how they conceptualize and comprehend transformation, there is one commonality in their views. They all agree that transformation is "the impact of the conflict resolution process on parties, relationships, and institutions beyond immediate issues under dispute."[12] This shows the strong connection between conflict resolution and transformation. That said, conflict resolution almost always remains an ideal type in the dictionary of conflict termination against which actual diplomatic outcomes are judged. Conflict termination occurs when the underlying sources of the conflict are removed. While this remains the major understanding in the realm of conflict termination, conflict settlement does not mean conflict termination, although the two terms are often used interchangeably. A conflict may be settled if one party to the conflict wins, which essentially means the defeat or submission of the other party. This has been the traditional settlement of conflict. However, new leaders may agree on an arrangement for the settlement of their conflicts. Sometimes arbitration may be a conflict settlement tool; if the parties are satisfied with the outcome of the settlement, the conflict may be terminated. Once a conflict is terminated, parties go back to the pre-conflict relationship. This, again, depicts a transformation of the conflict. The point is that successful or unsuccessful conflict prevention, management, resolution, or termination witnesses a change in the relationship between the parties, and, thus, transformation of the conflict.

## Conflict transformation

The goal of peace research and conflict research has always been transformation. Quincy Wright eloquently states what environment may constitute peace.

> The attribute conducive to peace is neither that popularity attributed to the ostrich, which denies the possibility of war, nor that of the cynic, who considers war inevitable, but that of the rational man, who appraises the opinions and conditions tending to war and the direction of human effort which at a given point in history might prevent it.[13]

Although peace is strongly connected to transformation, during the cold war the idea of transformation was rarely used in most peace and conflict research studies, but this changed as the cold war ended.[14] The idea of transformation was then widely acknowledged and used. In 1991 R. Vayrynen argued that a "dynamic analysis of conflicts is indispensable: the study of their resolution in a static framework belies social reality. . . . Conflicts are continually transformed even if efforts to resolve them have not made any visible progress."[15] He further asserted that many protracted "conflicts of interests or values" are likely to find solutions "through the process of transformation."[16] He discussed transformation of actors, issues, rules and norms, and structures involving themes of integration and isolation. He analyzed internal changes in the actors and the emergence of new actors, changes in the agenda of conflict issues, modification of the rules governing a conflict, and changes in the entire structure of the relationships and power distribution. He examined these dimensions of transformation against conflicts in for example, South Africa, Afghanistan, Haiti, and Colombia, and the intifada in Palestine, and concluded that transformation can be imprecise and its consequences hard to predict. In a work written a few years later, Vayrynen argued that transformation may be a better option than resolution in a complex conflict situation. However, he also warned that because of its attractiveness and easy applicability, where it is all about "general improvement of society," the drive to mitigate the conflict is lost. He argued that one should focus on the root causes of conflict that are amenable to solution.[17] There are several problems with his work. First, although he focuses on the factors that may trigger conflict transformation, he does not incorporate actor attributes such as the possession of power capabilities or the interactive conflict management mechanism/strategy of deterrence that could transform a conflict. In other words, he does not make the connection between the good intention of conflict management and the unintended consequence of conflict transformation through indefinite protraction. Second, he does not consider the typology of conflict transformation – short-term transformation and indefinite transformation; consequently, he cannot identify which kind of factor change is good in the realm of transformation and which is not. Third, although he makes a strong point in stating that transformation can be indeterminate and its consequences unpredictable, and the root causes of conflicts must be addressed, he fails to show how to focus on those root causes of conflicts that are amenable to solution.

In similar vein, J. D. Leatherman *et al.* argue that "conflict transformation depends on containing escalatory processes over the short term, while altering the underlying structural conditions over the long term."[18] They state that

> the limitations of diplomacy to achieve durable peaceful outcomes to contemporary conflicts and to prevent others from turning violent, means there needs to be innovation in traditional ideas and practice. We need to go beyond the containment of violence and negotiation, to transform social injustices, perceptions, cultural tensions, deep rooted hatred and issues of institutional legitimacy.[19]

However, it is unclear from their work how the underlying structural conditions of conflicts are to be changed. Additionally, the reasons for transformation and whether or not transformation is good for the overall conflict are not addressed by these and other scholars. This demonstrates the need for further research on this line of thinking.

J. P. Lederach comments that a "transformation approach recognizes that conflict is a normal and continuous dynamic within human relationships . . . conflict brings with it the potential for constructive change."[20] He sees peace-building as a long-term transformation of a war system into a peace system, inspired by a quest for the values of peace and justice, truth and mercy. Peace-building is, therefore, seen as a structural process. He widens his understanding of conflict by drawing peace-building resources from wider society. He, like other conflict resolution theorists, discusses when, under what conditions, and by which actors intervention is appropriate, and of what type. In the realm of intervention, although it is believed that facilitation is appropriate at the initial stage of a conflict and coercion may be necessary when conflicts are more deep-rooted and mature, he argues that efforts may be made to avoid coercive intervention.[21] However, other scholars believe that even in the initial stage, facilitation may not be a preferred option for conflict resolution. As R. Kraybill notes, the "idea of transformation implies that facilitators bring an agenda to situations of conflict,"[22] which, Stephen Ryan believes, is problematic because there is no consensus on "what value system/peace tradition is to be preferred."[23] Others argue that conflicts can be resolved only by addressing the roots of the problem and creating new solutions which parties may not have thought of and which are generally facilitated by third parties. It is believed that parties can move from zero-sum destructive patterns of conflict to positive-sum constructive outcomes.[24] Thus, previous scholarship on whether or not intervention is appropriate remains inconclusive. These scholars fail to recognize that when conflicts are seemingly protracted indefinitely owing to a no-war no-peace situation, the time may be ripe for third-party facilitation, not intervention.

Stephen Ryan contends that

> all approaches to conflict transformation begin with an optimistic assumption that a sustainable peace can be created out of violent and destructive conflict. Beyond this there may be differences in emphasis and phraseology, but several common features start to emerge that should allow us to construct an identikit picture. The most significant features appear to be: innovative thinking, an emphasis on deep and wide-ranging change, an understanding that conflict is dynamic and can be an agent of positive conversion, a focus on empowerment and sensitivity to indigenous culture, an awareness that this is a long process where quick fixes are not going to work, and an emphasis on working at all levels of society.[25]

Using Edward Azar's argument, he further states that

> the persistence of what Azar . . . termed protracted social conflicts made analysts aware of the limitations of conventional approaches to conflict

settlement. Some bitter conflicts appear to be so immune to existing tried and tested approaches to peace that only a radical change seems likely to jolt the parties out of their destructive interactions. From a traditionalist perspective protracted conflicts often appear to be unresolvable. This may breed fatalism and cynicism, but for some it is also a stimulus to explore more radical approaches.[26]

The problem with Ryan's work is that he, like most scholars, draws a connection between conflict transformation and sustainable peace. This essentially means that the aspect of negative transformation is overlooked in the study. Additionally, Azar's study focuses on protracted conflicts that are simply long-running and seemingly unresolvable. It does not examine the impact of the presence of nuclear weapons on a protracted conflict, making it get more intractable and making radical approaches to conflict resolution even more pertinent.

The usefulness of the introduction of radical approaches to conflict resolution is also stressed by other prominent scholars. Johan Galtung links transformation to transcendence, which he describes as something "new, sui generis, usually unexpected" and the result of creative thinking.[27] Along the same lines of creative and radical thinking, D. Francis states that if the conflict transformation approach is to work, it must address the limitations of the resolution approach and "must have something radical to offer in conflicts where power asymmetry is not incidental but of the essence."[28] In a similar vein, A. Tidwell notes that conflicts are dynamic and transformation remains a key element in the conflict process, which is why the field of conflict transformation is receiving prominence. Thus, he states that a large number of theorists seem to be "rejecting the notion of conflict resolution as such, and instead writing about conflict transformation. . . . A major contribution to date is the recognition that conflicts are dynamic and that they cannot be spoken of as if they were immobile."[29] Interestingly, the primary problem of these studies is that although their authors speak of the dynamic process of a conflict so as to highlight the aspect of conflict transformation, they do not address the typology of the mobility of a conflict.

William O. Staudenmaier introduces a model entitled the Strategic Rational Conflict Model, arguing that

> the input into the system is some type of political dispute . . . that cannot be resolved without the use of military force or the threat of its use. . . . It is important to identify those critical elements that might lead the decision-maker to choose a military solution over a diplomatic one. Some of these considerations are: Is the war aim one of deterrence or compulsion? If there is an asymmetry of interest or power, who does it favor? What are the decisionmaker's views on the utility of war? What are the probabilities and consequences of success and failure? . . .
>
> The output of the systems model is some type of resolution of the political issue that caused the conflict. The focus of the output segment of the model is

the policymaker's decision either to quit or to continue the war. . . . After the policymaker compares the political, economic and social costs of the war, he rationally chooses from alternatives that range from escalation to surrender. . . .

The conversion from input to output in the strategic-rational model is accomplished by selecting a strategy that will resolve the political issue for which military force is being used. The strategic choice is between classical and modern strategy. Classical strategy, which is aimed at the destruction or neutralization of the enemy's armed forces, is in the great power tradition of Clausewitz, Jomini, Mahan and Corbett. Modern strategy, on the other hand, is a quite different affair because its target is the enemy's society or social order. At one extreme, it includes general nuclear war and strategic air bombardment and, at the other, revolutionary guerrilla warfare and politically inspired terrorism. Its advocates span the spectrum from the American nuclear strategists and Giulio Douhet to Mao Tse-Tung and Yasser Arafat. Obviously, it is a manifestly important decision to choose between these two general types of strategy. . . .

Finally, it is also possible that the political disputes cannot be resolved by using military force; or perhaps, as so often happens, new issues will arise during hostilities that plant the seeds for subsequent wars. In either case, the system is closed by entering these new or unresolved issues into the new cycle of the model.[30]

What is intriguing about this model is that while the author introduces four scenarios, covering when the use of military force is likely, when surrender is a possibility, when a strategy can resolve the political issue at stake, and finally when the continuous emergence of new issues means that political disputes may remain unresolved by the use of military strength, he does not study actor attributes such as the acquisition of non-conventional weapons that may come in the way of conflict resolution.

With regard to the process of conflict transformation, scholars also present differing opinions. Conflict transformation theorists believe that contemporary conflicts require more than theorizing or identifying a win-win solution. The very structure of parties and relationships may be embedded in a conflictual pattern that extends beyond the particular site of conflict, implying that everything and everyone connected to the conflict needs to be transformed. To Hugh Miall, conflict transformation is the "process of engaging with and transforming the relationships, interests, and discourses, and, if necessary, the very constitution of society that supports the continuation of violent conflict."[31] Where this is the case, mediation by outside powers plays a lesser role in conflict transformation. Clements argues that

conflict transformation should incorporate a wide cross-section of political decision-makers, citizens, aid and development agencies, religious organizations, and social movements. Too often, in the past, conflict transformation has been conceptualized largely as a political problem. It has to be cast as a social and economic problem as well if structural change is to occur.[32]

Saaty and Alexander believe that parties should not be over-hasty in attempting to resolve a conflict. Everything takes time and conflict transformation is no exception. They state that

> in a conflict the participants will, in general, have conflicting objectives and desires and the so-called best outcome will almost certainly fall short of each party's desired outcome, in the view of that party. How can we persuade each party to cease pursuing its own goals to the limit and to accept the compromise solution? The most distinctive attribute of humans is their ability to reason and analyze. It is particularly necessary that people in conflict should use reason, since there may be interests at stake; to hold one's ground without the use of reason is to inhibit progress. We need to introduce more reason and less intransigence into our methods of conflict management. . . . Reason alone does not lead directly to agreement. The initial step is often the acceptance of a broader framework for the conflict; such a framework should show some possible benefits to the parties. In other words, we often need to take time to engage in foreplay before we can embark on the resolution of a conflict.[33]

Here, too, scholars comprehend that with reason, rational effort, and adequate time, conflicts should be able to undergo positive transformations. Unfortunately, this reasoning cannot be applied to the most intractable conflicts where the warring parties acquire weapons of mass destruction, especially nuclear weapons.

## Conflict termination

Scholars have identified factors that could lead to conflict termination and have struggled to understand the value of each such factors in ending conflicts. It has, however, always been difficult to generalize factors conducive to conflict termination across cases. In world politics every conflict is different and this variety makes it difficult to reach a general conclusion on the tools that will terminate conflicts. The general categories of inter-state and intra-state conflicts each includes a variety of different examples. Thus inter-state conflicts may or may not be protracted, between two parties, between proximate states, between asymmetric parties, in the regional or the global system, between major and minor powers, and between blocs. This variety makes it even harder to build a universal theory of conflict resolution/termination. Even theorists focusing on only one type of conflict, such as protracted conflict or enduring rivalry, have not been able to provide a theory of conflict termination that can be generalized across the conflict type. The reason is simple: each conflict, even within the same category, is unique, and conflict resolution techniques must be correspondingly different. For example, although the Iran-Iraq and India–Pakistan conflicts are enduring, bilateral, territorial, and between proximate states, the mechanisms that may terminate one could not be used to resolve the other. The regional context of each case is different; so are the great power interests. The conflict domains are also dissimilar and are different in terms of the support they receive from their immediate neighborhood and from extra-regional states. Steven Spiegel states that "the endless variety of states and the infinite variations in their relations make any given situation appear to be unique."[34] Stuart Thorson asserts that not all conflicts are easily resolved and not all are susceptible to traditional or even alternative dispute resolution mechanisms.[35] He introduce a category of intractable conflicts, defined as ones that cannot be resolved.[36] Although this may be an unrealistic definition, it does make it clear that intractable conflicts are extremely difficult, if actually impossible to resolve. Consequently, strategies that successfully terminate one conflict may not resolve another, even one with overt similarities. However, there are some general factors that help to introduce a thaw into most, if not all, conflict cases that fall into the same category. Cooperation in a relationship is a product of a combination of these factors. However, cooperation is not enough to resolve a conflict, even though it may have a strong potential to create an atmosphere conducive to conflict termination. Conditions likely to generate cooperation have received inadequate attention from conflict scholars, even though some form or degree of cooperation precedes conflict resolution and the nature and durability of cooperation determine the prospects of conflict termination.

Using systemic and state-level factors, Gary Goertz and Paul F. Diehl argue that for an enduring rivalry to end, political shocks – systemic or state-level – are required. They posit that dramatic systemic changes, such as world wars and changes in the distribution of power, or state-level changes, such as a civil war in one party, could be instrumental in ending the rivalry.[37] These determinants have impacted world politics, and some protracted conflicts have indeed ended in the aftermath of dramatic systemic shocks – for example, the protracted conflict in South Africa ended after the ending of the cold war and multi-regional protracted conflicts ended after World War II. However, it is worth noting that Goertz and Diehl do not define other precipitating factors of conflict termination. In other words, even though they conclude that shocks are necessary conditions for conflict termination, they are somewhat vague as to what other factors might help in resolving a conflict. They do not regard these shocks as necessary and sufficient conditions. This begs the question: What is a sufficient condition? This remains one of the major problems of using their analysis of conflict termination. On account of this unexplained gap, they are unable to elucidate why many protracted conflicts, such as the Arab-Israeli conflict and the India–Pakistan conflict, have survived the end of the cold war. Additionally, the state-level shock of the civil war in Pakistan in 1971 did not end its national rivalry with India, even though the Pakistani state had disintegrated and there was tremendous disparity in the bilateral power configuration. On the contrary, the India–Pakistan conflict intensified in the aftermath of the civil war, as a result of which an independent Bangladesh was created with Indian help. The theory may be more useful for understanding a thaw in a conflict than for conflict termination.

While systemic elements and state-level shocks are important in the dynamics of conflict resolution, the individual decision-making level is also an important factor. Janice Gross Stein argues that images of the enemy must change if any progress is to be made on conflict resolution. She states that this change may be very difficult to achieve because such images are "deeply rooted and resistant to change, even when one adversary attempts to signal a change in intent to another."[38] She believes, however, that these embedded images of the enemy may change if they are contradicted by information coming in "large batches" rather than in bits and pieces.[39] She further argues that time can help to change images, lessons can be learned from past mistakes, and leaders may be motivated to change the image of the enemy for domestic political and economic considerations.[40] Although a leader's political agenda may provide a motive for changing the image of the enemy, it may not be enough to initiate a conflict resolution process if the environment is not conducive to the endeavor. A. B. Vajpayee, Indian Prime Minister from March 1998 to May 2004, always stressed the importance for South Asia of focusing on the South Asian Free Trade Agreement (SAFTA) and on regional economic prosperity. But this has never been enough to change the image of the enemy, Pakistan. For most of his term of office Vajpayee accused Pakistan of supporting terrorists in South Asia and providing assistance to cross-border terrorism, a change that most Indian leaders have made repeatedly since the 1980s when terrorism became a feature of the India–Pakistan conflict. Three wars in South Asia may have made India and Pakistan war-weary and may have made them learn from their past mistakes, but they have not made the rivals renounce policies likely to provoke war such as the mobilization of heavy forces along the international border after the attack on the Indian Parliament. However, the enemy's image may change if and when it is contradicted by a substantial body of information. Once a stream of such information starts coming in, it becomes increasingly difficult for any leadership to ignore, and the new data may help to facilitate the process of conflict resolution. When General Pervez Musharraf started to make promises to crack down on terrorists in January 2002, this did not receive much attention from the Indian side. However, when he fulfilled some of those promises in 2003, it became clear that his intentions were good and initiating a new peace process began to look possible. Stein simply focuses on domestic incentives or the failure of coercion in the past that could induce a leader to accept a change in the image of the enemy state and, ultimately, move to resolve a conflict. She never explicitly states under what other conditions such concessions would be made by the enemy. In other words, when would the contradictory information arrive? Additionally, she never considers how cooperation should be launched and what happens to a conflict once cooperation has started on less controversial issues. Nor does she discuss the impact of recurrent crises on the changed images that could have mitigated the conflict.

As well as pinpointing factors that may be instrumental in resolving or terminating conflicts, a number of scholars have investigated the processes or strategies that facilitate conflict resolution. The Graduated Reduction in International Tension (GRIT) strategy, advocated by Charles Osgood, is one strategy that helps to bridge the gap apparent in Stein's work. According to GRIT, one of the parties to a conflict announces its intention to take some conciliatory moves designed to reduce tension and then implements those moves. Words are followed by deeds. This is done regardless of whether the other side decides to reciprocate.[41] The other side is invited to reciprocate and is likely to follow the lead of the first state, but the decision is entirely its own. No negative consequences will follow non-reciprocation unless the other side takes advantage of the conciliatory moves made by the first state. If it does, the initiator is likely to respond in kind.[42] Osgood cautions that the initiator should not impair its defense capacity by its conciliatory actions in case the second state exploits the situation.[43] The peace research community's examination of how intractable conflicts can be de-escalated is particularly relevant to conflict resolution, and the GRIT strategy has been influential in the field. Experimental studies agree that strategies like GRIT, which involve a series of conciliatory initiatives taken by one side independently of the other's actions, are more effective than strategies requiring reciprocation directly and immediately.[44] Other scholars believe that GRIT has been an effective tool in peacemaking, under certain conditions, when applied to protracted conflicts.[45]

This strategy can help to change the image of an enemy and can also be instrumental in paving the way to conflict resolution through friendly gestures. It is little used, however, because it is too utopian, especially where there is protracted conflict between states that do not trust each other and where mutual hatred is embedded. Although one of the parties has to take the initiative at some point for any conflict to thaw, this first step is very difficult to take, especially when a relationship has always been troubled. In other words, although a reduction of tension is obviously a function of leadership initiatives, other factors are also needed. This is because leaders are unlikely to be motivated to take such initiatives – even if they have political incentives, are war-weary, have learned from past mistakes, or want to make their mark before leaving office. Leaders have more difficulty in taking conciliatory steps on their own initiative when conflicts are protracted. For example, it would be extremely difficult for a Pakistani president to persevere in friendly unilateral action towards India in the absence of any positive response from the Indian side. Pakistan's policies have always been geared to Indian actions and reactions, and this pattern is difficult, if not impossible, to change. While France and the US – a non-protracted conflict pair – disagreed over the war on Iraq and their relationship was bitter for much of 2003, it was not difficult for one of the parties to improve the relationship when the question of post-war reconstruction of Iraq emerged. This illustrates the difference between a protracted and a non-protracted conflict. What is primarily missing from the GRIT strategy is the factor that pressures one of the parties to start a series of conciliatory initiatives without thinking about the repercussions. Also, GRIT cannot be utilized for conflict resolution. It never spells out how and under what conditions it can be used to resolve a protracted conflict. Ultimately, it is a strategy that may be employed by states simply to deal with soft issues, not with the root cause of a conflict.

Other scholars assert that cooperation is the key to conflict resolution. States must demonstrate their willingness to resolve conflicts, which is often done through dialogue and other cooperative gestures. Susan Heitler observes that conflict resolution occurs "only when both sides share a willingness to pursue mutually optimal solutions,"[46] through a process that is also characterized by talk and generally cooperative behavior.[47] Given that conflict resolution is a function of cooperative behavior, scholars have presented optimal cooperation strategies to advance the process.

Robert Axelrod shows that cooperation can be started by players who are prepared to reciprocate. However, there are two key prerequisites: cooperation must be based on reciprocity and must look forward to the future. He argues that "once cooperation based on reciprocity is established in a population, it can protect itself from invasion by uncooperative strategies."[48] In a world where defection is always an attractive option, a state cannot protect its interests by undertaking unilateral measures unless its rival responds in kind; reciprocal cooperation is essential. Thus, reciprocity is a primary condition for cooperation to work. Looking forward to the future means that state leaders must expect to meet again for significant discussions. Consequently, Axelrod proposes a tit-for-tat strategy for players who cooperate wherein cooperation is the first move and then each state does exactly what its counterpart does. He argues that the theory is robust because it is "nice, provocable, forgiving, and clear."[49] This may sound good, but it is important to emphasize at least two important problems that may arise if this theory is used in a protracted conflict situation. First, this is a utopian approach as far as protracted conflicts are concerned because no state will be willing to be the first to initiate cooperation without knowing how the other party will respond and without assurance of reciprocation. Second, the strategy may be useful where non-security issues or soft issues are concerned but not in the context of security or strategic issues. Most importantly, Axelrod never clearly states how the strategy can help states ultimately to resolve their outstanding disputes or terminate their conflicts. Thus, this theory, even if used by states in a protracted conflict, only provides an understanding that they may cooperate in certain situations, but never addresses what this cooperation ultimately does to the conflict itself – something that the present study intends to do.

A number of scholars study mediation as a problem-solving mechanism in conflicts. Conflicts are often managed as well as resolved by third parties. The role of a third party is that of a moderator keeping records and guiding discussions. Parties involved in a conflict are unlikely to have sufficient knowledge either of the sources of their conflictual relationship or of the options available to resolve them. "A problem-solving approach to conflict resolution as applied to particular situations requires, therefore, a most knowledgeable and skilled 'third party.'"[50] Saaty and Alexander note that mediators and arbitrators are often

> "buffers who can convey a most agreeable attitude in explaining the tough line
> or opening position of each party. Most conflicts are greatly helped by the
> presence of a third party or organization called in to assist. The mediators'

concern of balancing and creating a fair result should outweigh their strict concern for impartiality; the mediators must be careful that their impartiality would not lead them to play into the hands of the stronger party.[51]

This does not mean that parties to the conflict should be indifferent to the conflict resolution processes. John Burton states that "experience shows that there must be full participation by the parties in any process dealing with conflicts that are deep-rooted for the process to be acceptable and effective"; and some form of direct communication between the parties is essential, which is "unlikely without the assistance of a third-party."[52] This underscores the significance of a third-party mediator in the process leading to conflict resolution. However, the expected neutrality of conflict resolution is premised on the assumption that a third party has no vested interest in the outcome of an intervention and only works for some sort of resolution between the parties. It is important to note, however, that mediation often addresses only the surface issues as presented by the parties, instead of identifying the deeper motivations underlying the issues.[53] Although these are significant points, effective third-party involvement is a function of proper timing and the conflicting parties' approval. One of the most significant points missing in all this is that great powers may be compelled to intervene, even as facilitators, when they see the possibility of a major crisis escalating into nuclear war. Thus, this gravest danger could bring a great power into a conflict, whether the parties approve of this or not. The US engagement in the India–Pakistan conflict when serious crises erupted after the two sides introduced nuclear weapons is an illustration.

Most political disputes are settled peacefully since international conflicts are "controlled by treaty, custom or law, alliances, bilateral and multilateral agreements and international organizations, all of which help to moderate the more aggressive tendencies of nations."[54] However, William O. Staudenmaier states that "frequently, these conflict measures fail when sovereign nations collide over what each believes to be a vital interest, making peaceful resolution of the dispute through negotiation unlikely."[55] A number of scholars believe that the success of conflict resolution strategies thus depends on whether or not actors are focusing mainly on the most significant issues. Saaty and Alexander present the Analytic Hierarchy Process. This is an appealing

> decision theory for conflict resolution because it combines opposed elements in a series of pairwise comparisons arranged hierarchically. All conflicts require tradeoffs for their successful solution. At the heart of the process, participants agree upon the major issues involved in a conflict even if one participant adopts an issue as of prime importance diametrically opposed to another issue held by another participant. The process does not require perfect consistency for an outcome but realistically allows a degree of inconsistency not to exceed approximately 10 percent. . . . Disputants can express an intensity of preference for opposing positions and still achieve a degree of resolution through the process without producing a high degree of

inconsistency. . . . Using the process, disputants must express weighted preferences among at least several issues or goals; in these pairwise comparisons among many rather than one issue or goal, their intransigence becomes diffused (resolved). . . . The hierarchical aspect of the Analytic Hierarchy Process forces the actors in a conflict to distinguish between goals and subgoals, thereby avoiding wasting time fighting over trivial issues.[56]

Along the same lines although not mentioning hierarchy of issues, Keith A. Dunn states, "when we fail to articulate clearly what our goals and objectives are, it is hard to image how the 'system' can generate succinct, well-defined operational strategies to achieve desired conflict termination ends."[57] While issues may or may not be salient, sometimes they intertwine as a conflict becomes intractable and it is then very difficult to create a hierarchy of issues. In the India–Pakistan conflict, although Kashmir is the central territorial issue that needs to be addressed, the religious dimension is embedded in this protracted territorial problem, making the conflict ethno-religious in addition to being territorial.

## Inadequacies of conflict transformation scholarship

Studies on how conflicts are generally managed, resolved, terminated, and ultimately transformed are valuable if peace is to be achieved in this conflict-prone world. However, it is interesting to note that although scholars have discussed factors that transform conflicts through the process of conflict management, resolution, and termination, studies have not been done on the indefinite transformation of conflicts. It is also interesting to see that most conflict transformation theories concentrate either on the causes and evolution of conflict or on the emergence and maintenance of peace-building capacity. They fail to integrate an understanding of how preventors and causes of conflict interact. The theories are also unclear as to whether or not conflict transformation is synonymous with conflict management and resolution or whether these two approaches should or can be differentiated from conflict transformation. Hugh Miall argues that conflict transformation draws on many familiar concepts of conflict management and resolution and thus "it is best viewed not as a wholly new approach, but rather as a re-conceptualization of the field in order to make it more relevant to contemporary conflicts."[58]

While factors on different levels of analysis have been put forward to explain what might trigger conflict transformation through the process of management, resolution or termination, the interactive attribute of the acquisition of nuclear weapons by conflicting states and its impact on conflict transformation have not been examined by scholars. Drawing on the second criticism of Vayrynen's work, it is worth noting that there is consensus among scholars on the normative aspect of transformation. All studies seem to imply that transformation has virtues because it is a consequence of conflict settlement, management, or resolution, which are all strategies designed to attain some form of peace – whether sustainable or not. This book departs from this traditional line of reasoning to demonstrate negative, as opposed to positive, transformation. Although Ryan mentions negative transformation in his work, his understanding of it is entirely different from what this study portrays. Ryan argues that during a violent conflict,

> a number of negative transformations take place at the structural, inter-cultural and individual level. As a result, around the conflict there develop excrescences that cocoon the parties and trap them in a set of destructive behaviors and mind sets. These will not go away just because elites sign a piece of paper at the conference table, though the ending of the violence may help to reduce the impact of these "residues of violence." However, this will only happen if the peace process is able to meet the perceived needs of all groups. . . . Far from promoting security, a peace process might promote insecurity, in which case some of these processes might become more stronger.[59]

He further states, "understanding the dynamics of violent conflict and the nature of the 'residues' it leaves behind also gives us some clues about what issues transformation work should concentrate on in the immediate aftermath of violence."[60] While Ryan is interested in exploring the negative consequences of a peace process which does not address the concerns of all parties involved, this study advocates the idea that transformation itself can be negative to the extent that parties may not be able to establish a peace process.

Two points need to be noted. First, none of these seemingly important conflict resolution/termination theories probe the impact of the acquisition of nuclear weapons on conflict resolution or termination, even though the possession of nuclear weapons by states in conflict creates strategic parity among them, which might be conducive to conflict resolution and/or termination. Second, these theories do not draw a connection between the acquisition of nuclear weapons and the transformation of the nature of a protracted conflict, which is the goal of this study. Conflicts may be precipitated, intensified, resolved, or even transformed by changes in the environment or by changes in the attributes of the conflicting states. The environment may be changed by an increase or decrease in the number of participants in the conflict or through modification of the capabilities of the parties. Although in the short term the basic capabilities do not change, the regime or the leadership may suddenly be replaced and military capabilities may rapidly be increased by outside assistance. Capabilities themselves affect the roles played by the government in conflict management. "Deterrence, conflict avoidance or management, arms control, shows of strength, military mobilizations, alliances, and diplomatic consultations are all political-military activities or actions."[61] They impact conflicts and their possibilities of resolution. Consequently, the present study moves beyond the questions raised by conflict scholars, and addresses what the acquisition of nuclear weapons means for the nature of a protracted conflict. The primary concern is to explore when and under what conditions a protracted conflict may be drawn out to an almost indefinite extent. Before moving on to the theoretical framework of the book, it is pertinent to point out that even proliferation scholars have not conducted research on the puzzle this study investigates. To that end, the next chapter revisits previous scholarship on nuclear proliferation.

## Summary

This chapter has studied previous scholarship on conflict transformation to demonstrate the lack of academic work on establishing and understanding the connection between the acquisition of nuclear weapons by states in conflict and the transformation of such conflicts by prolonging them indefinitely. This study aims to fill this lack. The chapter also establishes the fact that conflict transformation, as understood by the theorists, has been conceptualized as a positive aspect in the history of a conflict. This study deviates from that understanding and argues that conflict transformation can also be negative, another area requiring further research.

# 2 Ramifications of nuclear weapons acquisition

The acquisition of nuclear weapons has received enormous attention from international security scholars and experts. Since the detonation of US atomic weapons in 1945, the development and testing of the atomic bomb by the Soviet Union, and the development and progress of the doctrine of nuclear deterrence, the general interest of these scholars has been to understand why states acquire nuclear weapons and to examine the consequences of nuclear weapons acquisition. In the next few decades, when the number of states joining the nuclear club was increasing, scholars primarily focused on what motivates states to acquire nuclear weapons. This became a more serious research question when Israel was suspected of clandestinely developing nuclear weapons ready for assembly at short notice in the late 1960s, and when India detonated its peaceful nuclear device in 1974. In an effort to stop proliferation of nuclear weapons, understanding why states want to acquire them became important. Consequently, the first stage of scholarship focused on the motivations for acquiring nuclear weapons. As motivations were identified and explained, and theories tested against actual events, it was concluded that a good number of states might be interested in acquiring nuclear weapons; stopping production of the capability became significant. With this aim in mind, some scholars worked on how to arrest proliferation, discussing and critically analyzing security regimes for this purpose. Thus, a second stage of research studied non-proliferation security regimes. In a third stage, efforts were made to understand the consequences of nuclear weapons acquisition, what this study is concerned with. Some scholars have been deterrence optimists – believing that deterrence works when states, global or regional, go nuclear – while others have been deterrence pessimists – believing that deterrence may not always work and accidents can easily happen in a nuclear environment. Interestingly, some scholars have argued that deterrence is only effective between the original proliferators, that is the nuclear states. Yet others believed that both groups of scholars – optimists and pessimists – may have logic on their side since there may be a stability/instability paradox as states acquire nuclear weapons. As the cold war ended, some scholars began to emphasize non-traditional threats instead of threats emanating from state actors, placing terrorists at the center of the investigation. The greatest fear has been that if terrorists gain access to nuclear technology or non-conventional weapons of mass destruction, they would be likely to use them.

In an effort to stop this from happening, rogue states were identified which were suspected of having connections with terrorists or of being willing to help them to acquire these weapons. Thus studies focused on rogue states' propensity to proliferate and the likely ramifications of nuclear weapons acquisition by non-state actors. Within this context, scholarship attempted to understand the nuclear black market, including, for example, the Russian black market and that created by rogue scientists like A. Q. Khan, the key nuclear scientist of Pakistan.

Apart from the causes of proliferation, almost all research pertaining to nuclear proliferation dealt with the consequences of nuclear weapons acquisition in some form or another. While some studies focused simply on security regimes or nuclear black markets, the goal was to stop proliferation because its consequences are grave. Similarly, even though a lot of research after the end of the cold war has been devoted to rogue proliferation, regional proliferation, and weapons in the hands of terrorists, the studies have also looked at the reasons why these actors should not have nuclear capability – meaning the focus has always been on the serious consequences of state and non-state actors going nuclear. Only in the past few decades has a new group of scholars focused on more specific consequences of proliferation – namely, stability/instability in regional contexts – and has proved the functional limitations of nuclear deterrence on specific levels. It is important to highlight that a large number of these research projects produced descriptive works and simple case studies, while only a handful of them involved theoretical work that was tested against real-life events. In a nutshell, although the consequences of nuclear proliferation have constituted a major research topic for a large group of scholars and they have dealt with the ramifications of weapons proliferation, all very important and significant for proliferation studies, none of them have investigated the implications of nuclear weapons acquisition for the conflicts that states are engaged in. This is the primary concern of this study. A major limitation of the previous studies is that even when analyzing the causes of nuclear proliferation none of them looked at the impact of protracted conflict.[1] This means that the concept of protracted conflict was absent, and therefore the consequences of nuclear proliferation on such conflict have likewise not been part of the research. Given this lack, the purpose of this chapter is to discuss various studies that were conducted on proliferation, especially the consequences of proliferation, and to highlight the inadequacies of these studies in understanding one major consequence: the further protraction of a protracted conflict as a result of the acquisition of nuclear weapons. The study is a follow- up of the stability/instability paradox because it tries to understand what stability/instability does to the conflict/adversarial relationship. From that perspective, the study picks up from where some scholars dealing with the consequences of proliferation left off.

## Triggers for proliferation

The first stage of scholarly investigation into proliferation aimed to comprehend why states go nuclear: what motivates them to take the nuclear path? Interestingly, although the five declared nuclear states made it clear that all other states aspiring to possess nuclear weapons would be considered proliferators, and thus a dichotomy between the nuclear haves and have-nots was created, with respect to the incentives to proliferate, all proliferators – vertical and horizontal – were treated in the same way. This means that incentives or motivations to acquire nuclear weapons were the same for both groups of states. Identifying the motivations was essential for a clear understanding of why some states may need nuclear weapons while others do not. The motivations studied by scholars comprise a combination of military, political, economic, and leadership concerns, which can be grouped into three categories – systemic, state, and individual actor – in accordance with the levels of analysis framework of International Relations. Under each of these categories are specific motivations. For example, quest for security, seeking regional hegemony, gaining international prestige and obtaining bargaining advantages fall into the systemic category of motivations. Domestic turmoil, economic motivations, public opinion, scientific/technological momentum, and bureaucratic politics fall into the state category, and the attitudes and beliefs of individual leaders are factors in the individual category.[2] Most of these motivations are self-explanatory and do not require detailed clarification. National security has been the basic driver of the decisions pertaining to nuclear weapons. All vertical and horizontal proliferators so far have wanted to acquire nuclear weapons for security purposes. However, other motivations may have come into play in the decision. For example, it is believed that the struggle for regional hegemony may have driven both Iran and Iraq to strive to acquire nuclear weapons. States with status inconsistency may desire nuclear weapons to raise their international prestige; for example, India, a country that should have had a seat in the UN Security Council because of its power capabilities. It is often argued that North Korea may have gone nuclear to improve its bargaining position vis-à-vis the west. In some cases, such as Argentina after the Falklands War, a state may have tried to divert domestic attention from internal turmoil by obtaining nuclear weapons. Since nuclear weapons are cost-effective, it is often believed that states suffering economic hardship, but requiring heavy security which they are unable to maintain with costly conventional weapons, may be proliferation prone, for example Pakistan in the aftermath of the 1971 war. It is also argued that populations may motivate their leaders to go nuclear, although this is not borne out by case studies. Rather, public opinion is often molded by leaders. With respect to India, research has been conducted on the scientific/technological momentum that could have set the state on a nuclear path. A country that was backward at the time of the industrial revolution was unwilling to remain backward in the nuclear revolution when it had the potential to move forward. Science and technology have been among India's assets and scientists have been proud to show off their skills. With respect to Pakistan, a lot has been written about the military's desire for a nuclear state. This argument was not given much value because nuclear weapons are non-usable, and the military generally does not like to waste defense funds on such weapons. Leaders are, of course, important decision-makers on nuclear weapons, but as leaders change so do their aspirations. Thus, it is hard to draw general conclusions from leaders motivations. The only systemic motivation that has received universal acceptance by scholars and policy-makers alike in the realm of proliferation is security, primarily because states facing security threats require nuclear weapons for deterrent purposes and deterrence has been the only function of nuclear weapons since the first two detonations in Hiroshima and Nagasaki in 1945 by the US.

## Security regimes to prevent proliferation

After the Chinese nuclear detonation in 1964 brought a fifth member into the nuclear club, concern focused on how to keep nuclear weapons possession limited to these five powers, the US, the USSR (as it then was), Britain, France, and China. To this end, the Nuclear Non-Proliferation Treaty (NPT) was drafted, signed, and ratified by almost every state in the world, with the exception of Israel, India, Pakistan, and Cuba, although the latter signed it about four decades later. After India's detonation of a nuclear device, the Nuclear Suppliers Group (NSG) was created to stop the supply of nuclear materials to countries aspiring to acquire nuclear weapons. Eventually, other security regimes were also created with similar intentions. These include the Comprehensive Test Ban Treaty (CTBT) and the Fissile Material Cut-off Treaty (FMCT).

Scholarly works focusing on these security regimes were mostly descriptive and policy oriented. Most of them highlighted the purposes of these non-proliferation initiatives, their flaws, and ways of improving them with a view to attaining a world without further proliferation. While the first aim of the NPT was to stop horizontal proliferation and the second was to allow the transfer of nuclear technology to non-nuclear states for peaceful purposes under the aegis of the International Atomic Energy Agency (IAEA), the third was to stop further vertical proliferation with a view to moving towards total nuclear disarmament. To track the progress made by the NPT toward achieving its goals, Article 8 called for a review of the Treaty every five years. Structurally, the NPT was always flawed by the dichotomy it created between the nuclear haves and have-nots. This division was not acceptable to many states even if they ultimately signed the Treaty. Unlike other security regimes such as the Chemical Weapons Convention (CWC), opened for signature in 1993, or the Biological Weapons Convention (BWC), opened for signature in 1972, the NPT cannot escape this criticism. Other controversies surrounding the NPT were that three countries – India, Israel, and Pakistan – refused to sign it, that the Treaty allowed for virtual proliferation, that there were inadequate enforcement mechanisms, that states were allowed to withdraw from the Treaty on ninety days' notice, and that the nuclear club was not accountable for its nuclear policies to the regime.[3] Additionally, although the NPT received universal endorsement from states in the international system, three countries violated it to varying degrees: Iraq in the 1980s, even though it did not succeed in going nuclear; North Korea from the 1990s when it probably built its nuclear weapons, which is why it had to leave the Treaty at a later date; and Libya until 2003, although it was unable to develop a bomb and ultimately gave way to western pressure. Iran is also suspected of violating the NPT, for which it faces sanctions.[4] With the end of the cold war, a number of scholars have criticized the NPT on the grounds that it was drafted for a world that no longer exists. More recently, scholarship has focused on how to deal with the three non-signatories which are in reality key regional nuclear states. Additionally, concern was aroused by the fact that North Korea has opted out of the Treaty.[5] The primary recommendation was that if the NPT is to be relevant in the present international context, it will have to be totally overhauled. Andy Butfoy writes,

> Universal membership of the NPT is much less likely. Technically it can only come about if the treaty is rewritten to bring Israel, India and Pakistan on board as "legitimate" nuclear weapons states, or if they dismantle their nuclear arsenals and join up as normal members. Neither seems likely. Expanding privileged membership of the nuclear club to Israel could provoke a walk-out of the NPT by Muslim states like Egypt and Iran, which are unlikely to accept an international treaty which institutionalizes their strategic inferiority to Israel.[6]

In the context of North Korea, the belief is that granting any kind of legitimacy to its nuclear weapons would be "a clear reward for the most blatant bad behavior."[7] Thus, the salient question is: Is there a universal way to deal with these states or should each be dealt with differently?

The CTBT, which bans nuclear tests, was opened for signature in 1996. This Treaty would not only have been instrumental in stopping proliferation by states, it was also designed to help control vertical proliferation, which would be held back by a ban on tests. But it could not come into force even though a large number of states ratified it. According to most scholars, the main problem pertaining to the CTBT is that after signing it, the US walked away from it on the grounds that it was not verifiable; the US maintained it might need to conduct nuclear tests for safety and national security considerations.[8] Thus, most scholarly works dealing with the CTBT have essentially focused on the US and the Treaty's failure to come into force and become instrumental in controlling further proliferation by all states concerned.[9] Similarly, the FMCT, which bans the production of highly enriched uranium and plutonium for weapons use while allowing the production of nuclear energy, was also unsuccessful due to Washington's non-commitment to it. According to the US, even the FMCT is unverifiable, and thus is useless as a non-proliferation measure,[10] a notion strongly debated by scholars.

In the context of the success of the nuclear arms control regimes, Stephen J. Cimbala states,

> International arms control regimes met with only partial success in the 1990s in expediting a favorable climate for non-proliferation. Although the U.S. won indefinite extension of the Nuclear Non-Proliferation Treaty (NPT) in 1995, the Clinton administration fell short of persuading the U.S. Congress to endorse the Comprehensive (CTB) Test Ban Treaty opened for signature in 1996. In addition, non-signatories to NPT like India could still argue that the

nuclear great powers had mostly failed to deliver on their original commitment to downsize their engorged arsenals of long range nuclear force. This complaint against the U.S. and other established nuclear powers was not without legal or logical merit, but it was unlikely to find strategic or political traction in the foreign offices of the acknowledged nuclear states.[11]

With regard to these measures against proliferation and their use against three countries, Sidney D. Drell and James E. Goodby contend that the international community has learned two lessons from the clandestine nuclear weapons programs of North Korea, Iran, and Iraq: first, covert efforts are successful temporarily, mostly because monitoring of nuclear proliferation and nuclear weapons-related activities is extremely demanding and difficult; second, that "unless nuclear proliferation issues are addressed as integral parts of the broad security context in which these issues arise, proliferant countries sooner or later will try to slip out of any constraints that temporarily limit their nuclear ambitions."[12] As part of their policy recommendations for attaining a world free of nuclear proliferation, they assert that

> the Non-Proliferation Treaty must be bolstered with other actions. These include U.S. reductions in nuclear weapons; continuing non-use tradition; reducing the salience of nuclear weapons in the U.S. military strategy; continuing the moratorium on underground nuclear tests of nuclear weapons and ratifying the Comprehensive Test Ban Treaty (CTBT).[13]

With a view to highlighting the loopholes of the NPT and the IAEA, Jed C. Snyder states that although the Treaty was primarily designed to prevent the transfer of nuclear material to non-nuclear states, it

> does not prohibit NPT states from receiving and accumulating sensitive fissile material (that is, plutonium or enriched uranium) as a component of a peaceful research effort subject to IAEA safeguards. The problem is that the recipient state defines for itself what is peaceful or military-related. This allows and even encourages NPT states to acquire the capability to produce nuclear weapons materials without violating the Treaty. In sum, NPT states may use the Treaty to pursue what in fact are non-peaceful ends.[14]

Additionally, the IAEA is limited in the sense that it does not have the power to investigate beyond a narrowly defined parameter. For example, the IAEA safeguards failed to detect the clandestine activities at Osirak in Iraq.[15] Libya's nuclear ambitions revealed in 2003 and South Korea's admission in 2004 that it had conducted experiments to enrich uranium some years previously and did not report the fact are clear examples of the IAEA's inspection flaws or limitations.[16] Other scholars focus on the export control mechanism and argue that export controls – which involve efforts to prevent the illicit sale of controlled items such as nuclear weapons and associated materials, equipment, and technologies from countries that possess them – are important "long-term challenges requiring continuous attention and development to address the changing domestic and international environment," which do not receive adequate attention.[17] These scholars also argue that in the post-cold war world, the US and Russia are not cooperating between themselves for non-proliferation purposes as they did during the cold war. Russian missile and nuclear exports to Iran became a contentious issue between the US and Russia in the 1990s and 2000. Other major problem areas were Russia's nuclear exports to India, lack of intelligence-sharing on illicit trafficking in nuclear material, and the lack of cooperation on South Asian, Middle Eastern, and North Korean security issues.[18] There was always a tendency on the part of the US and Russia to emphasize economic and political considerations over non-proliferation efforts. Thus, the goal of attaining a non-proliferated world has not been achieved.

## Optimists and pessimists on nuclear deterrence

Nuclear weapons are the most powerful and destructive weapons devised by humans. Since the introduction of nuclear weapons, scholars and policy makers have attempted to convey the power of these weapons in terms of their destructive capacity with a view to dissuading states from wanting to acquire them. The development of the fusion or hydrogen bomb added a whole new dimension to these types of weapons. Their destructive power is limitless, yet the production and installation of very large weapons may be of dubious value. The easiest option for the scholars was to show how useless these weapons are because of their non-use in battlefields. The non-use of these weapons has made them simply deterrents. Therefore, any state willing to pay the enormous cost involved in acquiring nuclear weapons would have to be satisfied with the fact that they are simply for deterrence, and that this is the only value of nuclear weapons. "If you want peace, prepare for war" is the motto of deterrence strategy. Nuclear weapons made deterrence all the more significant.[19] Bernard Brodie conceptualized nuclear weapons as "absolute weapons."[20] Nuclear strategists understood deterrence as the possession of sufficient capability to inflict unacceptable damage on a potential aggressor. Deterrence theory is based on the assumption that states are the primary actors in world politics, that they are rational actors able to base their decisions on cost-benefit calculations, and that the possession of weapons, the threats, and the intention to retaliate when attacked are all credible. Deterrence will not work if any of the above assumptions are unfulfilled.[21]

Thus nuclear weapons are primarily deterrent weapons, yet some scholars are doubtful whether deterrence could work under all circumstances. Examples from the cold war, in particular the Cuban Missile Crisis, proved that even the US and the Soviet Union could not guarantee that deterrence would always work. Also, accidental use was always a possibility. In the 1960s most analysts believed that with respect to world stability, "wide nuclear diffusion would be gravely disruptive. It would increase the likelihood of the use of nuclear weapons both by accident and by deliberation."[22] In 1977 Lewis Dunn argued that "a proliferated world is likely to be a nasty and dangerous place, entailing threats to the security and domestic well-being of virtually all nations and posing a serious possibility of a longer-term decay of global political order."[23] More recently Scott Sagan, in an extensive and intensive debate with Kenneth Waltz, has shown how military organizational behavior has led to major problems in meeting three salient requirements of stable nuclear deterrence – prevention of preventive war during periods of transition when one side has a temporary advantage, the development of survivable second-strike forces, and avoidance of accidental nuclear war – by the nuclear states and argued that similar problems would emerge in new nuclear states.[24] He argued that if Pakistan had acquired nuclear weapon, before India tested its own, the military in Pakistan would have favored waging a preventive war. He supported his argument by the evidence which revealed that even democratic India's military had considered launching a preventive war against Pakistan's Kahuta nuclear facility in the early 1980s.[25] As for the survival of second-strike nuclear capabilities, Sagan had no factual evidence to prove his point but argued that the intelligence services of both India and Pakistan had been able to uncover each other's secrets. He stated that there is "difficulty of keeping knowledge about 'secret' operations away from one's adversary."[26] He further argues that accidents and unauthorized use of nuclear weapons are functions of, among other things, less government control over nuclear weapons, more reliance on the military organizations that cannot maintain discipline, and financial constraints on maintaining the nuclear structure.[27] He provides examples of Pakistan and India again to substantiate his points, although he could not prove that nuclear accident or unauthorized use has ever happened in either case. On the other side of the debate, Waltz argues that preventive attacks are unfeasible because only a small number of nuclear weapons are required for deterrence, military officers are not more "reckless" or "war-prone" than their civilian counterparts, and weak states can build secure second-strike forces and "they guard them with almost paranoiac zeal."[28] Thus Waltz's views are optimistic and he believes that all states – rich or poor, developed or underdeveloped, democratic or non-democratic – should be able to successfully use the strategy of deterrence as long as they possess nuclear weapons.

To reiterate, scholars generally agreed that the value of nuclear weapons lies in their deterrent power; questions were raised as to whether or not this notion is universally applicable. Some argued that volatile regional states are more vulnerable and may end up using nuclear weapons intentionally or inadvertently. Thus, there emerged a division between deterrence optimists and deterrence pessimists. Optimists, such as Waltz and his followers,[29] believed that deterrence would be successful in all cases where states acquire nuclear weapons. Unconditional pessimists, such as William Potter and his associates, believed that deterrence may not be successful even by the original nuclear states. Potter stated, "To the extent that a deterrence relationship characterizes US-Soviet relations, it is probably more delicate than stable and represents a theoretical goal not yet violated rather than a description of the actual relationship."[30] Conditional pessimists such as Sagan and other scholars[31] believed that nuclear deterrence is most likely to be unsuccessful in regional cases.

Stephen Cimbala adds a fourth group to portray a more realistic proliferated world and provides policy recommendations to address it. He highlights four distinct groups: pro-proliferation pandemicists, pro-proliferation selectivists, anti-proliferation systemists, and anti-proliferation incrementalists.[32] The first group of scholars believe that more nuclear states could actually make the world more stable and that new nuclear states are not necessarily more accident prone than older ones. The second group think that these weapons should not be in the hands of rogue states and terrorists or even entities that may have grievances against the existing international system. If they were, it could be seriously destabilizing for the existing order. Only if owned by states that support "peaceful resolution of disputes and among whom a stable security community exists, nuclear weapons do not harm and may reinforce stability." The third group consists of scholars who believe that no further ownership of nuclear weapons is good for stability. Less is always better and further proliferation must be stopped by all means; and states which have nuclear weapons must roll back their capabilities. Finally, the last group believe that proliferation may not be stoppable, so the United States needs to check those states that are would-be proliferators and that pose serious security threats to the US and its allies as well as to its interests overseas.[33] Although these divisions seem reasonable on the basis of the scholarly works that exist, no accident has occurred in the nuclear realm between the declared nuclear states or regional nuclear states such as India and Pakistan. Even rogue nations have shown enough restraint and caution in handling their nuclear capabilities. Thus, the classifications presented by scholars are merely abstract assumptions without any case study to back them up. The pessimistic views, in particular, may be considered precautionary warnings only.

## Accepting both optimism and pessimism

While not accepting the exact reasons for the disagreements on the linkage between stability and nuclear weapons acquisition, some scholars believe that in the case of all proliferators, vertical and horizontal, there can be both stability and instability. The acquisition of nuclear weapons creates a stability/instability paradox.

In general, security scholars have paid serious attention to the issue of stability and instability in the context of the cold war. The long peace that prevailed between the two superpowers during the cold war became a major research puzzle for scholars in the post-cold war era. Some have argued that the long peace between the two superpowers was a function of the absence of wars.[34] Others argued that peace had a chance to prevail on account of the proxy wars waged by the superpowers in different regions.[35] Some conflict theorists argued that wars were replaced by crises, and that the frequent eruption of crises generated instability instead of stability.[36] Stability has been inadequately defined to mean the "absence of wars" between adversaries. Michael Brecher and Jonathan Wilkenfeld questioned John Lewis Gaddis' assumption that absence of war equals stability.[37] First, there were proxy wars during the cold war. Second, crisis itself is an indicator of instability. Crisis has specific links to systemic instability. Therefore, stability should not refer simply to absence of wars. To them, global instability was high throughout the long peace. Glenn Snyder, on the other hand, has convincingly argued that there was a stability/instability paradox in the east-west protracted conflict.[38] In Snyder's analysis, stability at the strategic level of conflict – the result of mutual assured destruction (MAD) – leads to instability at the lower levels of conflict. Due to the MAD, states were able to engage in conventional conflicts for limited gains without having to worry about whether these small wars would spiral out of proportion. The key question to resolve is whether or not the stability/instability paradox could function in situations where MAD does not exist but states possess nuclear weapons. Two points need to be understood. First, Snyder's thesis was primarily meant to explain the cold war, when MAD prevailed, and it was not meant to be and may not be applicable in cases where MAD does not exist. Second, his focus was on the proxy wars of the superpowers in the regional spheres, not direct lower-level conflicts between them. When scholars began to employ the stability/instability paradox in the regional cases, especially in the India–Pakistan conflict, when analyzing the instability aspect they referred to crises in the conflict setting. Although the basic assumption that stability on the strategic level could lead to instability on the lower level holds good, what is problematic is the comparison of the US-Soviet protracted conflict with the India–Pakistan conflict. The US and the former Soviet Union had satellite states and they fought proxy wars against each other in the regions. India and Pakistan do not have spheres of influence and thus proxy wars are fought between them in their own territories. There is no indirect war in this case. They confront each other in crises, violent acts, and war – limited or not. Thus, a comparative study of the two cases is methodologically incorrect.

The pivotal scholarly interest was to understand whether or not South Asia was, is, and will be stable in the post-proliferation period and whether or not Snyder's stability/instability paradox theory could be applied in the India–Pakistan case. As tensions and crises between India and Pakistan had intensified in a nuclearized subcontinent, lower-level instability in a generally stable South Asia was evident. Given this, South Asian scholars paid serious attention to the stability/instability paradox. However, their findings have been somewhat mixed. In 2001, Sumit Ganguly stated that the stability/instability paradox will hold in South Asia for the foreseeable future that is until one of the parties has sufficient first-strike capacity to launch, against the other.[39] In 2002, Jeffrey W. Knopf claimed that "flare-ups in South Asia since the Indian and Pakistani nuclear tests of 1998 indicate the continued relevance of Glenn Snyder's 'stability/instability paradox.'"[40] Along the same lines, Lowell Dittmer argued that resort to violence in South Asia was a product of the "fear of escalation to the nuclear level."[41]

By contrast, others have been skeptical about using the stability/instability paradox to understand the ongoing violence in the region. Paul Kapur, for example, argued that this violence is the result of a strategic environment where nuclear escalation remains a possibility if a limited Indian-Pakistani conventional confrontation turns into a full-scale war.[42] Moving beyond the notion of the intentional spiraling of a limited conventional war into a full-scale war and underscoring the possibility of accidental wars, Michael Krepon argued that although India and Pakistan have experienced several crises but carefully avoided conventional war, nuclear risk reduction measures must be put in place to avoid any inadvertent war.[43] In similar vein, Feroz Hassan Khan stated, "any limited or low-level conflict now carries with it the threat of escalation and nuclear inadvertence."[44] There is no doubt that the research questions and findings are interesting and invaluable. However, it is important to note that in the realm of proliferation, scholars have not moved beyond these stereotypical questions. What is missing in all of this is a study that traces the relationship between nuclear weapons acquisition and the life of a protracted conflict, or the consequences of the stability/instability paradox for the conflict.

This study derives its importance from the inadequacies of the previous scholarship on the ramifications of nuclear weapons acquisition for conflicts. Despite the amount of scholarly attention given to the consequences of nuclear proliferation, the endeavors have generally revolved around the concept of deterrence. It is pertinent to look at the impact of either stability or instability, or the paradox, which are all functions of nuclear weapons acquisition, on the development of a protracted conflict. It is necessary to understand what the acquisition of nuclear weapons does to the relations between the parties to the conflict. Not only have proliferation scholars[45] ignored this salient question, but even protracted conflict scholars have neglected the connection between proliferation and conflict transformation, which is crucial to understanding why some protracted conflicts continue indefinitely while others are resolved or terminated. While Brecher, Wilkenfeld, Edward Azar, and others have examined the issues that trigger protracted conflicts and have, in general, probed the necessary and sufficient conditions that protract a conflict, others have developed theories on the management, resolution, and termination of conflicts.[46] But neither they nor any other conflict scholars have studied the consequences of nuclear proliferation for protracted conflicts. This study therefore plans to make a substantial contribution to both the proliferation and the conflict literature by examining the impact of nuclear weapons acquisition on protracted conflicts.

## Non-traditional security threats

Although terrorism is not a new phenomenon in international politics, terrorist activities were infrequent in the cold war years. Terrorism has been on an upswing since the end of the cold war. There are many definitions of terrorism but no universally accepted one. The most commonly used definition is that "terrorism is the illegitimate use of force to achieve a political objective when innocent people are targeted."[47] According to the US government, terrorism is "premeditated, politically motivated violence perpetrated against noncombatant targets by sub-national groups or clandestine agents, usually intended to influence an audience."[48] In essence, terrorists use violence to instill fear among the targeted society and demoralize it.

While terrorism is an international security problem and apparently unconnected to the proliferation problem, these non-traditional security threats have disrupted efforts to achieve non-proliferation and stability in the world. The reasons are quite obvious. First, in the realm of proliferation, states are the primary actors which must be stopped from proliferating; therefore any new actor arriving on the stage of international politics gives grounds for further worry about proliferation. Second, as mentioned above, states proliferate primarily because they want to obtain a deterrent capability and the primary use of nuclear weapons is to deter adversaries. This objective is not the main aim of terrorists who want to obtain nuclear weapons. Their objective is to use nuclear weapons, which essentially means that deterrence does not work with non-state actors. "Terrorists have no state to lose and, therefore, cannot be effectively deterred by the threat of retaliation."[49] This means that if terrorists have nuclear weapons they will not hesitate to use them, and this is a cause for concern. To stop this happening, the international community is attempting to ensure that these non-state actors do not have access to weapons of mass destruction. With that aim in mind, the US has targeted rogue states to stop them from obtaining nuclear weapons and having the chance to hand them on to non-state actors such as terrorists. Rogue states have been the main focus because it is believed that they have one thing in common with terrorists: they hate the United States and would do anything to hurt the American people in order to bring about changes in US policies affecting themselves. The United States has identified seven rogue states: Iraq (before March 2003), Iran, Syria, Libya (until the US and Libya resolved their dispute and the latter renounced its nuclear ambition), North Korea, and Cuba.[50] Today, the US still defines Iran, Syria, and North Korea as problem states that need to be under surveillance and prevented from transferring these devastating weapons to terrorists. Because terrorists are not easy to find, and it is believed that they cannot operate without financial, military, economic, and logistical support from state actors, states suspected of helping them are in the sights of the international community, especially the US.

Scholars have conducted extensive research on nuclear proliferation by rogue states and its consequences, these states' propensity to spread nuclear weapons to non-state actors, and what that would mean for the stability of the international system,[51] In most scholarly works it has been argued that rogue states would not hesitate to pass these weapons to terrorists because they have a common enemy, the US, as stated before. Highlighting the conditions under which this could happen, Stephen Cimbala states that an

> Iran caught up in revolutionary upheaval between contending factions of modernizers and mullahs, and already in possession of nuclear weapons, could witness a power struggle that leads to unauthorized delegation of nuclear command authority and/or illicit transfer of nuclear weapons to third parties allied to one faction or another. The third parties could include terrorists.[52]

Once they have acquired nuclear weapons, because terrorists have no state/territory to worry about they will use them, most scholars believe. Thus, Cimbala writes,

"Terrorists do not usually have a singular 'address' or central command post, the destruction of which can guarantee the nullification of their striking power."[53] Moreover, unlike state actors, terrorists are not accountable to anyone, and they would not have proper or effective control of their nuclear weapons due to the structure of the transnational terror groups.[54] Studies on rogue nuclear proliferation have also been conducted that propose policy recommendations for the US to contain these renegades and prevent outlaw states from having access to these weapons. Recommendations include: identifying allies who also consider these states as rogues and want to contain them; not making inflated threats so that rogues do not obtain international attention or regard developing nuclear weapons as the best strategy to drag the US into regional security issues; combining deterrence and reassurance, so that rogue states gain some form of security from not going nuclear; and maintaining adequate defense capabilities to address rogue threats, if required.[55] Most of these policy recommendations have been employed by the US in varying degrees at different times to prevent rogue states from acquiring nuclear weapons.

## Nuclear black market

In addition to the anxiety for the international community caused by the possibility of rogue states acquiring nuclear weapons and transferring them to non-state actors, there is also the growing fear that nuclear proliferation will result from nuclear black markets. Even rogue states could obtain these weapons through this route. Although this is not a new-found concern, it became serious after the end of the cold war, with the disintegration of the former Soviet Union and, more recently, with the discovery of the Pakistani rogue nuclear scientist A. Q. Khan's proliferation activities. The dissolution of the Soviet Union in 1991 aroused doubts pertaining to the ability of the newly independent state to effectively control the storage, transportation, and export of fissile materials and nuclear warheads. One of the greatest fears was the "selling out scenario,"[56] which meant that if control over the Soviet nuclear complex was lost, then a black market for nuclear technology could emerge, with large-scale dissemination of first-hand knowledge about weapons production.[57] In 1991 William C. Potter stated, "If you are in the market for a fast-breeder reactor, enriched uranium, a little heavy water, or even 'peaceful nuclear explosives,' Moscow is the place to shop."[58] An international media campaign branded Russia as the source of nuclear smuggling throughout the 1990s. Although the terms nuclear smuggling and theft are used interchangeably, smuggling means the illegal export of fissile material or nuclear warheads from the territory of a nuclear facility whereas theft is the illegal act of taking these things from the facility. Nuclear theft is possible for a number of reasons, namely poor physical protection of facilities, insufficient safeguards, unrestricted movement around the facilities, and inadequate detectors.[59] The easiest way for a terrorist or non-state actor to obtain nuclear capability would be through theft or illegal purchase.[60] Because these possibilities aroused serious proliferation concerns, scholars have devoted much time to laying out policy recommendations designed to stop these illicit activities that threaten global security.[61] With respect to rogue scientists who have helped states to proliferate, A. Q. Khan's name stands out. His network, described as a Wal-Mart of nuclear proliferation, apparently reached North Korea, Libya, and Iran, among others.[62] If scientists help those hoping to acquire nuclear weapons, no security regime or export control mechanisms in the world can contain proliferation. This is the main reason why so much has been written on nuclear scientists and their role in proliferation. Cimbala writes that

> states seeking a nuclear start-up can save enormous amounts of time and money by turning to experts in and out of government for help, and the knowledge how to fabricate nuclear weapons is no longer as esoteric as it was in the early days of the atomic age.[63]

The three proliferation concerns – by rogue states, proliferation terrorists gaining access to nuclear weapons, and nuclear black markets – are connected in the sense that rogue states can transfer nuclear materials to terrorists, and both–states and terrorists–can obtain the materials and know-how to build nuclear weapons or acquire bombs through nuclear black markets. Studies focusing on these three intertwined problems have been concerned about the incentives, processes, and consequences of nuclear weapons acquisition. Their research questions have not generally meant examining the connection between nuclear weapons and conflicts. However, they could have incorporated this connection since rogues states–North Korea, Iran, Iraq, and Syria–have all been engaged in protracted conflicts. Protracted conflicts as factors encouraging proliferation, and the further intract-ability of such protracted conflicts in consequence of proliferation, could have been investigated and analyzed.

## Summary

This chapter aimed to provide a review of the studies conducted in the realm of proliferation so as to demonstrate what is absent in the literature and what needs to be studied. It explains that despite rich scholarship on incentives to proliferate, non-proliferation regimes, proliferation concerns, and the positive and negative consequences of proliferation for new and old proliferators, studies have not been conducted on the linkage between nuclear proliferation and protracted conflict. This topic is essential since all proliferators in the world have been involved in some form of protracted conflict. The ramifications of proliferation for protracted conflicts represent a crucial area for research. Consequently, the next chapter presents a theoretical framework demonstrating the linkage between nuclear weapons acquisition and the indefinite continuation of a protracted conflict.

# 3   Elucidating conflict transformation with nuclear weapons

The management, resolution, transformation, and termination of conflicts have been studied by conflict scholars, and the motivations for developing nuclear weapons and the implications for global or regional stability have been investigated by proliferation scholars. These have been discussed in chapters 1 and 2 respectively. As stated in the previous two chapters, this study moves beyond these problems to address what the acquisition of nuclear weapons means for the life of a protracted conflict. The central objective is to understand when and under what conditions a protracted conflict moves to a level of almost indefinite protraction. Why a protracted conflict becomes intractable is analyzed in this chapter.

Before presenting the main arguments of the study, it is pertinent to define and comprehend three primary terms that are used throughout the book. The dependent variable, *protracted conflict transformation*, encompasses three words that require elucidation. Although the word *conflict* could have a variety of meanings, in this study it means "conflict of interest" between two or more states. Conflict is, thus, a hostile relationship where two or more states are in dispute as a result of their views on certain issues. This also means that the book does not consider war as a conflict. War is a conflict behavior[1] and/or a crisis management tool, which involves the most acute form of violence.

> A conflict is produced by a clash of cultures, a disharmony of interests, a disparity of perceptions – all of which result in the inability of the parties to accept separately and together the environment they live in. The immediate context of any conflict is created by the attributes and the interactions of the parties.[2]

Conflicts may or may not be protracted, depending on a number of factors. Edward Azar gives a general definition of protracted conflicts as:

> hostile interactions which extend over long periods of time with sporadic outbreaks of open warfare fluctuating in frequency and intensity. They are conflict situations in which stakes are very high. . . . While they may exhibit some breakpoints during which there is a cessation of overt violence, they may linger on in time and have no distinguishable point of termination.[3]

This study defines a *protracted conflict* as a high conflict situation between two or more states that endures for decades without termination points, in which a number of crises are embedded, and where war remains a higher-than-normal probability, owing largely to the territorial nature of some of these conflicts.[4] A protracted conflict may be managed, resolved, transformed, or terminated, as stated on p. 9. Management of a conflict refers to avoiding or terminating violence between parties. A conflict is resolved when the root problems that triggered it are solved and it can be terminated. A conflict is settled when the inner causes are suppressed. In such a case, the conflict may also be terminated, but it may start again at some point in the future. A conflict is *transformed* when there are signs of a changed relationship between the states involved. The relationship between the parties that existed from the eruption of the conflict may have changed for the better or the worse. The primary concern of this study is to comprehend the transformation of a conflict. Thus, conflict transformation related to the continuation of a protracted conflict is the dependent variable of the study. This means that while conflict transformation is generally seen by scholars as a positive aspect of any conflict process, this study considers it in a negative sense because of the focus on its sense of indefinite continuation. The object is to understand the causal connection between the independent variable, acquisition of nuclear weapons, the intervening variables – absence of wars and presence of frequent crises – and the dependent variable, conflict transformation leading to the prolongation of a protracted conflict. The effects of the independent variable and intervening variables are analyzed in the study to shed light on why some protracted conflicts drag on indefinitely while others do not or may be resolved or terminated.

The primary hypothesis of the book is: Protracted conflict transformation is a function of the absence of war and presence of crisis, which are products of nuclear weapons acquisition by the states in conflict. With an in-depth analysis, which follows, the study underscores the following:

- Most states engaged in protracted conflicts over territorial issues are nuclear proliferation prone in order to avoid war.
- The impacts of nuclear weapons acquisition are war avoidance and peace avoidance.
- Peace is a function of war avoidance and crisis avoidance.
- Protracted conflict, that is, hostile relations between two or more states, is transformed and protracted due to peace avoidance, a function of frequent crises.

## Analyzing the life-cycle of a protracted conflict

Every protracted conflict has a four-phase life-cycle which encompasses its beginning, escalation/intensification, de-escalation, and cessation. Each phase has its own characteristics and is influenced by a number of variables/factors. Also, each phase invariably impacts the others. In other words, phases are interconnected in a protracted conflict. Generally, each phase has to be gone through in order to reach the cessation stage in a protracted conflict, although exceptions to this have occurred. These points need to be elucidated further.

Although generally two states in conflict will need to go through all three phases to reach cessation, a conflict may erupt into war, meaning that it skipped the first stage and started with escalation/intensification. However, there is always a very short period of crisis before escalation and that period sets the stage of the conflict. Additionally, there are bound to be issues in dispute, causing hostility for some time before the situation deteriorates. This means that no country can really skip the initial stage of a conflict. Every conflict involves a number of crisis situations, each of which goes through several stages of its own.[5] With the escalation of each crisis, the conflict intensifies. However, when the crisis de-escalates, the conflict may not necessarily de-escalate; de-escalation means the conflict is about to be terminated – which does not necessarily happen when a crisis de-escalates. There are different degrees of intensification – high, medium, and low – in the escalation phase of a conflict. Given a high degree of intensification, severe crises leading to war occur. An arms race intensifies the escalation phase. In a medium degree of intensification, low–medium-intensity crises and violent military action short of full scale war occur frequently. Arms races generally continue during this phase. A low degree of intensification means an ongoing crisis de-escalates or terminates, or if a new crisis erupts it is unlikely to have the propensity to be very violent. A low level of violence – such as border skirmishes, bombings, and shelling – may characterize the conflict. These three degrees represent the escalation/intensification stage of a conflict, meaning that it is not close to being de-escalated. De-escalation occurs with third-party mediation, or when leaders take initiatives to come to a compromise due to domestic political pressure or economic difficulties. It can also be a function of one state winning a war in the escalation stage and the losing state surrendering. Where this happens, the next stage, cessation, is primarily a function of conflict settlement instead of conflict resolution. Thus, in such a case, de-escalation is a product of conflict settlement and not conflict resolution. Cessation of a conflict represents a stage where peaceful relations between the contending parties have been established due to the de-escalation of the conflict. In other words, cessation is the outcome of the de-escalation phase and demonstrates that the de-escalation was well founded and has been consolidated. It must be noted here that cessation means that the conflict has been permanently terminated. Parties to the conflict may or may not be happy with the termination process, but the point is that the conflict has been terminated. States are expected to establish friendly diplomatic and political relations after a protracted conflict has been terminated. Although a new conflict may start due to the dissatisfaction of one of the parties with the result of a previous conflict settlement, as long as peace is institutionalized for a protracted period, usually for twenty-five years, and there is no war between the parties for a decade or so,[6] the protracted conflict has been terminated.

In sum, the four phases of a conflict involve the following:

- *beginning* – triggering factors/issues (setting the conflict stage)
- *escalation/intensification* – crises and wars, arms races (nuclear/conventional);

Degrees of intensification are: high, medium, and low:

- A high degree of intensification means serious crises and wars occur, accompanied by arms races.
- A medium degree of intensification means low–medium-intensity crises, causing severe and violent military action short of full-scale war, erupt frequently. Arms races continue during this phase.
- A low degree of intensification involves violence such as border skirmishes, bombings, and shelling; crisis de-escalation and/or termination processes.

- *de-escalation* – product of agreements, compromises, settlements, third-party mediation, and leadership initiatives; it could also be a function of war, meaning victory by a state
- *cessation* – end of conflict with peaceful relations.

Figure 1 illustrates the four-phase life-cycle of a protracted conflict.

A protracted conflict between two or more states may start over territorial, economic, religious, or ideological issues. One of the first things to note is that a conflict does not become protracted if the issue in dispute is insignificant and compromise is easily reached. Because of the importance of some issues, the contending states cannot come to a compromise or solution, making the conflict intractable. Protracted conflict cases indicate that these erupt over different kinds of issues, some of them perhaps intertwined, so that it is difficult to identify the primary and the secondary causes. Additionally, a conflict may start over one issue, and then spill over to other domains of interaction; consequently the new issues also become integral parts of the conflict. Thus, once the issues are intertwined, it is difficult to highlight the primary problem and concentrate on dealing with it, ignoring the others. Issues are also important because they are often linked to the escalation of a crisis to war. Not all issues will prompt contending states to wage wars to settle their differences. Contentious and territorial issues are more likely to trigger wars,[7] whereas most non-territorial issues may not trigger major crises or wars. John Vasquez states that rivals that have territorial disputes are more apt to go to war with each other at some point in their history than those that do not have territorial disputes. Hence, rivals that do not go to war are likely to be those without territorial disputes.[8] Because of the tangible and intangible value of territory, the expected utility of fighting for it increases even if the probability of success appears to be low. The Arab-Israeli wars and the India–Pakistan wars are examples of territorial issues being the primary causes of war between contending states. However, many issues have triggered wars and others have not, and it may be impossible to pinpoint the necessary and sufficient conditions for a war. Once a conflict starts, a zero-sum mentality prevails between states and they begin to focus on the idea of relative gains in the relationship. Each state wants to be more powerful than the other. Depending on the sphere, global or regional, one state may be inclined to dominate the other's sphere. In the global sphere, the United States and the Soviet Union acquired nuclear weapons and power not only for

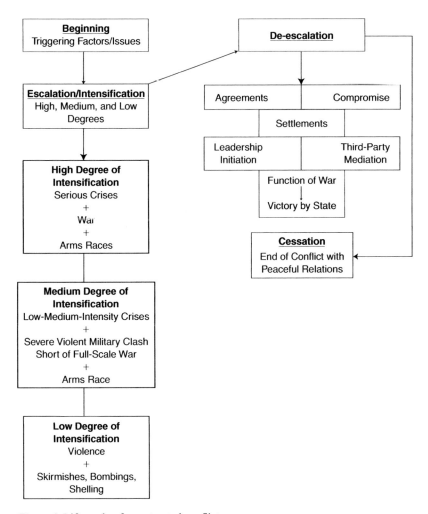

*Figure 1* Life-cycle of a protracted conflict

mutual assured destruction (MAD) but each also wanted to have more security and territorial dominance than the other. The ultimate purpose was to dominate the world. While that may not be the case in the regional spheres, lust for regional hegemony may prevail in those theaters as well. Additionally, proximate states are more prone to waging wars when they have territorial issues to fight over. Proximity may not only create the issue over which the adversaries confront each other but also makes the option of war possible. Proximate states with territorial issues at stake have been known to be more prone to crisis escalation and war.[9] Where the issues continue unresolved, proximate protracted conflict states with territorial issues at stake are likely to be proliferation prone due to the need to avoid war in a relationship where it appears unavoidable due to the nature of the conflict.

India and Pakistan are examples of proximate states with territorial issues at stake which have gone nuclear to avoid wars in the conflict setting.[10]

States make efforts to prevent inter-state wars through, among other strategies, deterrence, arms control, domestic political and economic reforms, interdependent trade, preventive diplomacy, mediation, and arbitration. Although most of these options are employed by states to avoid wars, protracted conflict states that have fought frequent wars against their adversaries are unlikely to make use of any of these strategies apart from deterrence. For example, none of these strategies were utilized by protracted conflict belligerents such as India–Pakistan, India-China, North Korea-South Korea, among others. The hostility surrounding the conflict prevents the adversaries from focusing on bilateral interdependent trade or from using preventive diplomacy to facilitate agreements to resolve disputes that trigger wars. Consequently, domestic political reforms or economic restructuring may not be attractive options for such states to employ for war avoidance and they are unlikely to embrace the theory of democratic and trading states not fighting wars. Deterrence is the most attractive strategy for such states that are both weary[11] and fearful of war in the conflict setting. Thus, they are more likely to consider the strategy of deterrence to prevent wars. However, nuclear deterrence is preferred to conventional deterrence. The universe of protracted conflicts proves this point. All of the states involved – regional or global – have either acquired or made efforts to obtain nuclear weapons or have been under the nuclear umbrella of other states for deterrence purposes.

A protracted conflict is escalated if crises, war, and violence occur in the conflict setting. The intensification phase could be high, medium, or low depending on the crisis or level of violence in the conflict relationship. Where a war erupts between the parties, the conflict reaches a high intensification phase. The three wars of 1947, 1965, and 1971 between India and Pakistan are examples of high intensification phases of the two countries' protracted conflict. Where low–medium-intensity crises and violence erupt frequently and there is no full-scale war, a medium intensification phase has been reached. All crisis situations since the introduction of nuclear weapons in the India–Pakistan conflict are examples of low–medium-intensity violence. Finally, where a crisis has just erupted or has been de-escalated, or low-level violence prevails in the conflict, a low intensification phase has been reached. When the Brasstacks crisis had just erupted in 1986 and when it was ending due to Indian and Pakistani troop withdrawal in 1987, the conflict was in a low intensification phase. The ongoing violence in Kashmir since 1989 is also indicative of a low intensification phase of the India–Pakistan conflict. Interestingly, both high and low intensification phases have the propensity to reach the de-escalation phase, leading to the cessation of the conflict. Wars, which represent a high intensification phase, ending with winners and losers, may terminate a conflict. On the other hand, in a low intensification phase where a crisis has just abated or been triggered, but violence is not on the surface, an atmosphere conducive to mediation with a view to mitigating the conflict, or to the parties coming to the negotiating table by themselves, may arise. This is a significant point which needs to be highlighted because it means that these two kinds of intensification are closely connected to the de-escalation and cessation phases and may have positive ramifications for the conflict. Also, their existence may not protract the conflict indefinitely. The point about wars needs further explanation. It means that if a war occurs in a conflict, although it constitutes a high intensification period, it does not last indefinitely. Thus, enemy states may resolve their problems once the dust of war settles if they deem it necessary. Similarly, the beginning and the de-escalation of a crisis are periods which are not long term and when violence is not severe; rivals may settle their differences after these periods are over. On the contrary, the medium intensification stage of a conflict is the worst of the three phases due to the presence of several crisis situations in the conflict setting. Suspicion and hatred increase and endure, making it difficult for the parties to trust each other and come to the negotiating table to resolve the conflict. The intensification stage is the most critical since it is this stage that decides the fate of the conflict. More precisely, the adversarial experiences in this phase become the primary reasons that either keep the conflict alive indefinitely or stop it from moving on to the next phase.

Some protracted conflicts are resolved, while others continue for indefinite periods. The resolution of a conflict depends on whether or not a protracted conflict is able to progress through the other stages of its life-cycle, namely escalation and de-escalation. Once a conflict advances from the escalation to the de-escalation phase, it is likely that it will be terminated. But the de-escalation phase is the most difficult to complete because it means that the parties have been able to sort out their differences through their own initiatives or through third-party mediation, neither of which is easy in the case of long-running conflicts involving a lot of intertwined issues. It is more difficult to complete the phase when the parties in conflict have acquired nuclear weapons because the probability of war may become virtually non-existent, generating more crises in the conflict setting and creating an environment which is not conducive to the parties mitigating the conflict through their own initiatives. There is no example in the history of international relations of two nuclear states waging a direct war against each other.[12] Thus, as states in conflict acquire nuclear weapons, one of the main de-escalation tools, war, can no longer be used for conflict termination. Hans J. Morgenthau remarked, "Nations active in international politics are continuously preparing for, actively involved in, or recovering from organized violence in the form of war,"[13] meaning war is an integral part of international politics. Crisis scholars portray an even stronger connection between protracted conflicts, crises, and wars. According to Michael Brecher, inter-state crises that occur during a protracted conflict are more likely than others to escalate to violence and war.[14] Thus, protracted conflict states are more war prone than non-protracted conflict states. However, conflict and crisis scholars do not address a central question which is essential for understanding the connection between protracted conflicts and wars. Do all protracted conflict states wage wars? If not, then this begs another question: When are protracted conflicts likely to be war prone? Theorists who believe in the value of nuclear deterrence argue that states in protracted conflicts that do not have nuclear weapons may become involved in traditional, full-scale wars. Conversely, protracted conflict states with nuclear weapons are unlikely to wage traditional wars due to the mass destruction that nuclear weapons can cause. Other measures to prevent inter-state wars include promoting arms control measures, reforming the domestic political and economic apparatus in states, developing an open international economy, strengthening international institutions for promoting norms and cooperative security relations, focusing on preventive diplomacy, and engaging in mediation and arbitration. However, none of these measures can assure a no-war situation in the relationship, as the possession of nuclear weapons can. Following the acquisition of nuclear weapons by states engaged in protracted conflict, wars become generally unlikely. This cannot be said of any of the other factors that may also be instrumental in preventing wars. Nuclear deterrence is absolute deterrence.[15]

> Nuclear war, in the minds of many, can have no utility at all; the only useful function of nuclear weapons is to deter the use of other nuclear weapons. While one cannot unequivocally state that conventional war aimed at the destruction of the enemy army has completely lost its utility to resolve political disputes, the evidence seems to be pointing in that direction.[16]

In the context of the east-west rivalry of the cold war, it has been argued that

> advancing technology, particularly the fusion of the thermonuclear warhead to the supersonic intercontinental ballistic missile, however, has made certain forms of war dysfunctional. A hegemonic war between the superpowers and their allies would seem to be an event of very low probability, but the catastrophic consequences of which would be so great that the superpowers are justified in taking military precautions to insure that it does not occur.[17]

In line with this argument, where states in protracted conflicts acquire nuclear weapons and create a no-war situation they fall into a trap where war can no longer end the conflict they are engaged in. One of the mechanisms to terminate their conflict has become unusable or obsolete. The parties realize this and try to look for alternatives that could be used to attain their goals. Each party still has the same intention of ending the conflict by achieving its own objectives. Each still views the conflict as a zero-sum game and still wants to gain as much as possible through other mechanisms that are still available.

In the absence of war, alternatives are searched for. Crises are the easiest alternatives to wars in a conflict setting. One can argue that crises precede wars and wars are integral parts of crises, as stated before. This means that war makes the conflict reach its high intensification stage and a war is a crisis management mechanism. Although it is theoretically correct that wars are part of crises and crises precede wars, in real life where wars cannot erupt crisis becomes the alternative. Crises occur more frequently in the conflict setting, causing further destabilization. (This will be discussed in detail on pp. 51–2.) However, the important point is that wars do not occur in the conflict, so conflicts between nuclear-armed states cannot be terminated with the waging of war. This does not imply that wars are the only means of terminating conflict or that wars always do terminate conflicts. History provides many examples of wars terminating a protracted conflict. World War I and World War II represent the most spectacular examples of long-running conflicts which were terminated by war. Nevertheless, not all wars end protracted conflicts. In the history of their conflict, India and Pakistan have fought three wars, two of them over the root cause of the protracted conflict, Kashmir, yet the conflict was nowhere near being terminated with the cessation of the wars. Similarly, several wars fought between the Arabs and the Israelis have not brought an end to the Arab-Israeli protracted conflict. The point to underscore is that wars are tools that can be used to end a conflict. One of the parties to the conflict wins the war and attains its goals, and the root cause of the conflict is resolved in favor of the winning side; or the loser gives in to the pressure of the winning side; or both parties come to the negotiating table to end the conflict because they are war-weary or see no alternative to negotiation. Thus, though devastating and undesirable for the human casualties they cause, wars have a positive attribute in that they may be instrumental in terminating conflicts. However, war, a primary crisis management tool, cannot be used to in protracted conflicts between nuclear states because of the devastating nature of nuclear weapons, the use of which may mean total annihilation.

Figure 2 depicts the ideal connection between nuclear weapons acquisition and conflict termination.

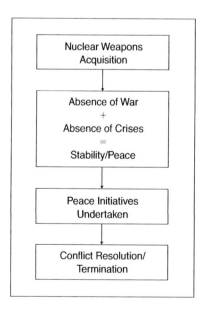

*Figure 2* Nuclear weapons and the ideal flow of events

## Negative impacts of nuclear weapons possession

States acquire nuclear weapons to deter their adversaries from launching an attack against them, but this acquisition is the reason why conflicts move to a level of indefinite protraction. This is the irony and primary paradox of nuclear weapons acquisition. It is somewhat similar to the security dilemma in which one state increases its level of security in order to feel secure, but ultimately it is never secure because it provokes its rival to increase its level of security which in turn makes it more insecure. Protracted conflict states are impelled to acquire nuclear weapons to keep the conflict relationship stable – to deter wars. Although they may attain that goal, nuclear weapons acquisition keeps the protracted conflict alive for an indefinite period. Although the rivals are secure on one level, in that they do not have to worry about war, they are insecure all the time in that they are in a crisis-prone environment, cannot bring peace to the relationship, and are unable to terminate the conflict due to the atmosphere that is not conducive to conflict resolution. Thus, security on one level generates insecurity on the other and total peace and security become remote possibilities.

Glenn Snyder, in a fascinating way, has argued that there was a stability/instability paradox in the east-west conflict due to the acquisition of nuclear weapons. His paradox claims that when two nuclear rivals face one another, their nuclear weapons cancel each other out, allowing lower-level conventional conflicts to occur.[18] According to this theory, the superpowers should have fought lower-level conventional wars. In reality, they did not wage any lower-level bilateral conventional wars but did pursue proxy wars in Asia, Africa, and Latin America. Superpower stability has been a product of the no-war situation that existed throughout the cold war. The fear of nuclear escalation played a major role in preventing conventional wars at all levels. However, crises, which Snyder calls "surrogates for war," had replaced war. He states that crises' "systemic function is to resolve without violence, or with only minimal violence, those conflicts that are too severe to be settled by ordinary diplomacy and that in earlier times would have been settled by war."[19] Here his argument seems to create a link between the absence of war and the presence of crisis. He believes that crisis has replaced war in the nuclear realm. He does not deny the fact that stability includes absence of war and that crisis indicates instability, which basically means that he incorporates Brecher and Wilkenfeld's indicators of stability and instability in his stability/instability paradox. Thus he seems to bridge the gap between the scholars who considered absence of war to be equivalent to stability and those who objected to that definition. In sum, the impacts of nuclear weapons acquisition are war avoidance and peace avoidance because peace is a function of not only war avoidance but also crisis avoidance, which is unlikely in a conflict featuring nuclear weapons.

Stability must incorporate absence of war (large-scale, small-scale, limited, conventional, and nuclear) and absence of crisis (heated, non-violent, violent) in its definition. An inter-state war must be defined not only to include 1000 or more battle deaths,[20] but also crossing an internationally recognized border between sovereign states. Conflict scholars contend that crisis involves a threat to basic values, time pressure for response, and heightened probability of war.[21] The International Crisis Behavior (ICB) Project defines an international crisis as: (1) a change in type and/or an increase in intensity of disruptive interactions between two or more states, with a heightened probability of military hostilities; this, in turn, (2) destabilizes their relationship and challenges the structure of an international system.[22] Others have defined it differently, but have included the "war probability" aspect. On war probability in a crisis situation, Glenn Snyder and Paul Diesing write:

> The centerpiece of [the] definition is "the perception of a dangerously high probability of war" by the governments involved. Just how high the perceived probability must be to qualify as a crisis is impossible to specify. . . . [It] must at least be high enough to evoke feelings of fear and tension to an uncomfortable degree.[23]

Brecher and Wilkenfeld consider "heightened probability of war" as a necessary condition of crisis. They state that

> this probability can range from virtually nil to near certainty. For a crisis to erupt, however, perception of war likelihood need not be high. Rather, it must be qualitatively higher than the norm in the specific adversarial relationship. This applies both to states for which the "normal" expectation of war is "high" and to those for which it is "low".[24]

In any case, they include war as an integral part of a crisis, but in a nuclear situation this is inapplicable. Crisis now must be defined differently. Although acute threat to basic values and time pressure for effective response constitute the basic features of a crisis, the probability of war is almost nil between nuclear states. There must be two definitions of crisis – for non-nuclear adversaries and for nuclear states. While the existing definition of crisis could be used for non-nuclear adversaries, for nuclear adversaries "heightened probability of war" must be replaced by "heightened probability of heated and low–medium-intensity violence short of actual war." Finally, instability should incorporate the presence of crisis and war, and the absence of peace initiatives, in any conflict.

By absence of war, does one mean absence of any war, or of large-scale war, low-intensity war, or limited war? The definitions could have major implications on the stability/instability paradox. Additionally, does crisis indicate instability in a conflict relationship? If it does, then even when countries do not have wars, crisis could still generate instability. Therefore it is also important to find out the necessary and/or sufficient condition(s) for stability. If "absence of war" is a necessary condition for stability, then "absence of war" always precedes stability, but stability does not always occur in the "absence of war," since "absence of war" on its own may not be sufficient to generate stability. For the present discussion, "absence of crisis" is also a necessary condition of stability. Furthermore, what is the relationship between crisis and war among nuclear adversaries? It has been argued that where countries acquire nuclear weapons, wars are avoided due to the fear of nuclear escalation. Here the concern is to find out which wars are avoided – nuclear, conventional, or both? If all kinds of wars are avoided due to the possession of nuclear weapons, does crisis still occur? If it does, is it because of the absence of war? In other words, is crisis a replacement of war? Also, when a study focuses on stability/instability, does it deal with the overall protracted conflict setting? Do studies try to find out whether or not the protracted conflict itself is stable? Is it the absence of war or the presence of peace in a conflict relationship that indicates stability? These are extremely important questions to consider for understanding the degree of stability/instability that prevails in a conflict relationship. It is impossible to neglect these questions because crisis, conflict, and war are intertwined and "stability" or "instability" is a function of this intertwined relationship.

In sum where adversaries have nuclear weapons, the following questions must be addressed:

- Will a nuclear war be avoided?
- Will a conventional war be avoided?
- Will any war, even a limited war, be avoided?
- Is low-intensity or medium-intensity violence not war?
- Will crises be avoided?
- Is it because war is avoided that crisis has a tendency to erupt?
- Will a foreign policy crisis not turn into an international crisis?
- Will the protracted conflict remain stable?

This study argues that all wars – nuclear, conventional, and limited-aims – will be avoided when states in conflict acquire nuclear weapons, as was the case in the India–Pakistan conflict after nuclear weapons came into the picture. It also argues that war is an acute form of violence in which 1000 or more battle deaths are expected and where a regular military force that is of sufficient intensity/magnitude crosses the internationally recognized border between the adversaries to inflict catastrophic defeat on the opponent. Low–medium-intensity violence, which the conflicting parties could use to attain limited territorial gains, does not fall into the category of war. According to this definition, the violence between India and Pakistan over Kargil in 1999 remained a crisis only. This study claims that nuclear weapons acquisition generates more crises in the conflict setting because escalation to war is unlikely, as the stability/instability theorists believe. The frequent eruption of serious crises in the nuclear period in the India–Pakistan conflict demonstrates the value of this line of reasoning. However, it may often happen that a foreign policy crisis does not turn into an international crisis when low-intensity violence is initiated by one of the parties to a conflict. This is the case if the party faced with this new threat does not respond with similar menacing actions that could be perceived by the first party as a threat to its values. The consequences of such foreign policy crises are grave because the hostility level is elevated as a result of continuing hatred and suspicion. India remains a striking example of a state which is often faced with foreign policy crises resulting from Pakistan's threatening behavior and which does not turn these situations into international crises by undertaking similar threatening action against Pakistan. The low-intensity violence that continues in Kashmir is also a proof of this. The Kashmir Legislative Assembly attack, which triggered a foreign policy crisis for India, did not turn into an international crisis because India did not counterattack or take threatening action against Pakistan. Finally, the India–Pakistan conflict is permanently unstable, being crisis prone and violence prone in a nuclear context.

It now becomes essential to make a connection between absence of war and presence of crisis in the development of a conflict. If absence of war breeds presence of crisis, how does this situation impact the overall protracted conflict? A protracted conflict may be frozen[25] at any stage of its life-cycle if both sides have nuclear weapons. There is limited understanding between the sides when this is the case. Arms races may continue at a high level, creating more discomfort for both parties. Each continues to distrust the other as more technological innovations enter the military realm. However, a protracted conflict is generally frozen in its second stage. Direct confrontation remains likely, but not in a formal and declared mode. Consequently, states continue to use various means to strengthen their position as regards their territorial or other claims, but without direct recourse to war. War becomes a remote possibility and crises occur more frequently. Attacks and counterattacks become more common, taking forms including guerrilla strategies, terrorism, and proxy attacks. In the absence of war, rivals resort to violence of different degrees and crises are provoked to achieve some of their goals. This is generally the primary strategy of the weaker of the powers in a conflict. In asymmetric conflicts, the initiator of a crisis may derive significant benefits if its attacks hold an element of surprise. It may obtain "an early advantage in terms of upsetting the status quo, and if that advantage can be converted into a long-lasting politico-military *fait accompli*, the materially weaker party can gain politically, if not militarily."[26] The dissatisfied and revisionist state generally tries to challenge the status quo through different forms of violence, even though it may not be able to alter it in the end. With the acquisition of nuclear weapons a conventionally weak revisionist state is encouraged "to challenge the territorial status quo through aggressive conventional behavior."[27] Additionally, the crisis initiator expects to attract the attention of the international community, especially the US, and make it intervene and/or pressure the opposing side, which is obviously stronger, to negotiate. The external power is likely to intervene because where nuclear weapons are present there is the possibility that they might be used inadvertently or even intentionally in desperation. The "risk of escalation to nuclear war reopens the possibility that a demonstration crisis will lead to forceful diplomatic intervention by the international community, most notably the United States."[28] These factors motivate the revisionist state to provoke serious and violent crises in the conflict, there being no potential of escalation owing to the presence of nuclear weapons.

In a protracted conflict where adversaries possess nuclear weapons, the escalation phase generally becomes chronic, with frequent crises which may be extremely heated and warlike. Such situations can often be worse than war, in which hostility reaches a peak for a limited period and then becomes somewhat muted as the war ends even if the conflict continues. When low–medium-intensity crises erupt every now and then, hostility continues for a very long time and is hard to end. This not only leads to more animosity and mutual hatred at the inter-state level, the societies are also seriously affected by the continuous state of rivalry and fighting. The resulting animosity becomes part of the national psyche or national culture, and is hard to change in the absence of dramatic reversals in the political leadership of the opposing state, signaling a modification of hostile policies. No one can deny the grave consequences of a war and its implications on the relationship between the adversaries, the societies, the regions, or the world, but generally wars do not continue for protracted periods. Parties in conflict may consider negotiating at different levels after a war ends. Human nature is to forget the past and move on to make a better future. This is equally applicable to nation-states. Wars are fought, but they soon come to an end. There are protracted wars in the history of world politics such as the 1980–8 Iran-Iraq war, but this is an exception. In most cases wars are fought with specific aims and are short-lived. For example, all three India–Pakistan wars have been short-lived, the last, in 1971, having been two weeks long. New wars may start, but this takes time for financial, military, political, and diplomatic reasons. In the interim contending parties or even third parties may negotiate to resolve the conflict. Even if negotiations do not take place, parties have time to let past wounds heal. Crises, on the other hand, may continue for longer periods than wars because they cost less in financial, military, and political terms. Additionally, as one crisis ends, another may easily erupt. This, again, is because of the low cost involved in triggering a crisis compared to a war. The destructive impacts of wars bring a positive contribution to the conflict, making another war in the near future unlikely on account of the possible consequences. Although a crisis is generally less destructive in concrete terms, unless it involves a war, its destructiveness, even if not apparent all the time, affects every aspect of a conflict. A proper environment is a primary prerequisite for conflict de-escalation. There is little room for negotiation in a crisis-prone environment. A positive security climate is essential not only for conflict resolution but also to come to any level of understanding and reconciliation, these being impossible in a heated crisis environment.

Where serious crises – heated and violent – continue, there can be no stability in a protracted conflict. The east-west protracted conflict was not stable during the Cuban Missile Crisis, which has been described as representing the high point of the cold war. The South Asian situation is no different. Protracted conflict may be stable or unstable depending on the frequency and severity of its crises and on the peace initiatives taken by the adversaries. Absence of war is only one of the indicators – the others being absence of crisis and the presence of a peace process – of stability in a protracted conflict setting. Absence of war is only a necessary condition of stability in a protracted conflict, but not a sufficient one. From this perspective and because war is only one of several crisis management techniques used by states, absence of crisis seems to be the most important requirement of protracted conflict stability. Thus, every war reflects a state of crisis, but every crisis does not reflect a state of war. This point is significant because it means that absence of crisis is the key to protracted conflict stability. As long as peace is not achieved at the conflict level owing to severe crises, a protracted conflict is likely to continue.

While two countries which have nuclear weapons may then start a protracted conflict, history shows no illustration of this other than the US, which had nuclear weapons before the east-west protracted conflict started. In most cases, especially regional cases, countries have acquired nuclear weapons after starting a conflict. Countries that have had nuclear weapons find it difficult to make peace with one another, whereas non-nuclear states have been more accommodating. Nuclear weapons have no relationship with the wish to be accommodating. In other words, the weapons may be simple acquisitions, but it is the impact of the acquisitions that makes parties confident about maintaining non-war crises. Most countries want to be accommodating, but frequent crises create a negative environment for accommodation, as stated before. The east-west protracted conflict would not have been terminated if the former Soviet Union had not had economic troubles making it unable to keep up with the pace of the arms race with the US. The point is that internal weakness within the Soviet Union compelled it to come to terms with the US. Many argue that the Intermediate Range Nuclear Forces Treaty (INF) of the 1980s indicates that both Gorbachev and Reagan realized that with nuclear weapons no end to the conflict was in sight. However, the Soviet Union would never have abandoned its superpower status had it not been for its economic and political problems. A unit-level factor was weakened and that triggered the termination of the intractable conflict. While system-level protracted conflicts have also been frozen by the acquisition of nuclear weapons, their case is very different from regional conflicts, especially as regards the proximity of the regional rivals. Most protracted conflict states at the regional or the subsystemic level have proximate rivals, and a crisis may easily erupt along their joint borders. Often even the central governments are willing to undertake certain risky border adventures in the hope that war will not ensue. These situations create mounting hostility in the relationship.

What is the connection between absence of crisis and conflict termination? Conflicts are terminated through resolution processes and peace initiatives. For peace initiatives to be undertaken by parties engaged in a conflict, periods of calm are required. Where peace initiatives are undertaken, if they are to be institutionalized, the calm must endure. This lasting calm brings a remarkable decrease to hostility and builds trust and confidence among the parties. Lasting peace may come through these important confidence-building measures. Recurrent crises, which are common in a nuclear environment, are unfavorable for building any degree of trust between the parties. Chronic suspicion does not augur well for building peace. Trusting the opposing state is difficult if a crisis erupts after a peace process is initiated because it creates the feeling that "trust can invite betrayal."[29] No matter who initiates a crisis, the parties go back to their hostile behavior and paths to conflict termination remain unexplored owing to the frequent low–medium-intensity violence that besets the conflict. Whatever gains the parties have made through their peace process, and would make by consolidating it, disappear with the eruption of a new crisis. It is pertinent to understand that "building peace requires building trust, even among states that have few reasons to have confidence in one another."[30] New outbursts of anger, frustration, and subsequent violence in different forms surround the conflict, making it hard for the parties to reconsider the fact that they are structurally determined rivals. Moreover, rivals learn to develop new strategies to confront each other in this crisis-prone environment and get accustomed to frequent violence in the conflict setting. Well-established doubts about commitments voiced by a former enemy inhibit "mutually beneficial collaboration and encourage[s] defensive non-cooperation."[31] States find it difficult to rebuild their relationship because insecurity persists. All these factors create an environment that is not congenial to peace. The absence of new rounds of peace initiatives, the result of the non-conducive environment, transforms the conflict, prolonging it indefinitely. While great powers interested in defusing crises in a nuclear environment may pressure the parties to hold dialogue and settle their differences bilaterally, this is instrumental in drawing out the protracted conflict yet further. The parties learn to cooperate on non-controversial, positive-sum issues, such as trade, communications, and culture, and do not deal with their most crucial and complex bilateral problems. Thus they get accustomed to a situation of simultaneous cooperation and non-cooperation in a violence-prone and crisis-prone setting. The question then is: Can this situation change and can the conflict be resolved?

Figure 3 (opposiet) illustrates the actual connection between nuclear weapons acquisition and conflict transformation.

## Unfreezing the conflict

Although war continues to serve useful political functions among non-nuclear rivals in the contemporary international system, not all types of war have equal utility. Therefore other ways of mitigating a conflict must be found. Other conflict de-escalation tools that are non-violent include compromise, agreements, third-party mediation, and leadership initiatives. To make use of any, some, or all of these tools the right atmosphere is required, but this is generally absent when the states in conflict have nuclear weapons. Therefore, although between nuclear states de-escalation of a conflict is dependent on compromise, agreements, third-party mediation, and leadership initiatives, these, in turn, are dependent on a conducive environment, one that is favorable, non-aggressive, and encouraging.

How is a conducive environment for conflict termination connected to the acquisition of nuclear weapons? Where low–medium-intensity crises become part of this medium intensification level, violence becomes part of the relationship, which is extremely unfavorable for conflict resolution. As Brecher puts it, "Frequent resort to violence accentuates the image of violence as a protracted conflict norm."[32] A proper environment for conflict de-escalation cannot be created. Aggressive behavior arises not so much from genuinely irreconcilable conflicts,

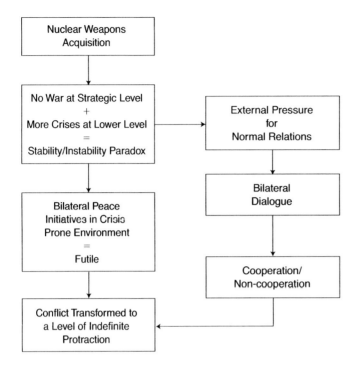

*Figure 3* Nuclear weapons and the actual flow of events

but more from mistrust, suspicion, and untrustworthy acts. The frequent eruption of crises creates a negative environment for conflict de-escalation through understandings and compromises between the parties or even through third-party mediation. Increased enmity tends to follow and the eruption of frequent crises "prolongs and perpetuates conflict, standing in the way of effective resolution."[33]

The protracted conflict could only change following a significant change in actor attributes, such as the emergence of an exceptional leaders and a sudden change of political/economic capability (regime change or economic collapse), or in situational attributes, for example if a third party makes a strong and sincere intervention with a view to terminating the conflict. If a leader in one of the states involved is strongly committed to changing the relationship and is also willing to face tremendous adversity, the situation could change dramatically. The leader's motivation may be a function of a state's economic and/or political decline or of his/her personal inclination to leave a positive mark on the country before retiring. If a state party to a conflict suffers from serious internal decline – economic, political, or military – it could have a substantial impact on the conflict. Poor economic performance might undermine a regime struggling for legitimacy.[34] In such situations, leaders may choose to initiate peace in the hope of improving the economy through new bilateral relations and trade and of gaining domestic support.

As mentioned before, this would also need a leadership initiative because economic hardship or political and military decline will not change the attitude of a state towards its rival. The leader has to take steps to change it. Thus actor attributes are extremely important. When states face economic or political decline domestic affairs require priority and the financial burden entailed may be enormous. At such a time, a state is unlikely to be able to concentrate on its conflict relations and keep up with arms races or even normal exchanges of threats and counterthreats. Improving relations with the rival state may help the declining state's economy if bilateral trade relations can be established. Sometimes leaders want their legacy to be positive even if their administration has been harsh. Thus a retiring leader may have personal reasons for making serious efforts to improve relations with states with which there has been conflict. This does not mean that every leader will try to do this towards the end of a term of office. If this was so, then conflicts would not be protracted because the leadership changes every five years in most countries and a conflict would not last longer than that. Obviously this is not what always happens. Finally, a strong but impartial and responsible outside power may change this relationship not only by managing the conflict but by creating an environment in which parties could settle their differences through meaningful dialogue. However, both sides must be willing to accept third-party intervention. This situational attribute therefore seems unlikely to terminate the conflict as it is improbable that both parties will consider conflict resolution at the same time. It is particularly improbable in an asymmetric conflict where the stronger power naturally declines the idea of conflict mitigation with the help of a global power even if that power is acting in the best interest of both states. Instead of a mediator, a facilitator may be more acceptable to the superior power in the conflict. Great power intervention should not amount to limited efforts to suppress or contain fighting in a crisis because that will have little effect on resolving the conflict. When a great power takes a strategic diplomatic initiative – meaning conflict management is essential for its regional strategy – it may impel parties toward agreement. However, one has to be careful about great power involvement. Under pressure from great powers, states in conflict may initiate dialogue in the midst of low-level violence and cooperate on non-controversial, positive-sum issues, such as trade, communications, or economic matters, which are expected to benefit both parties. Controversial, negative-sum issues such as territorial problems are not addressed because of the suspicion and hatred besetting them. Parties learn to live in this environment of cooperation and non-cooperation, and in the process the conflict is transformed completely.

The acquisition of nuclear weapons by the parties involved transforms a conflict, drawing it out indefinitely. Crises are embedded in each protracted conflict and their escalation to war depends on the nuclear status of the adversaries. Pre-nuclear states have a tendency to manage serious crisis through war, while nuclear adversaries tend to use violent clashes or low–medium-intensity conflict for crisis management. The deterrent effect of nuclear weapons creates a no-war situation, but heated crisis and low–medium-intensity violence remain part of the picture and often become more frequent as there is little probability of their escalating to war.

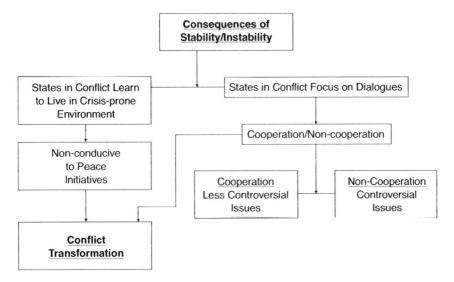

*Figure 4* Conflict transformed: indefinite protraction

The absence of war and presence of crisis create a situation where there is no proper security environment for conflict de-escalation and cessation.

Figure 4 demonstrates the linkage between the stability/instability paradox, a consequence of nuclear weapons acquisition, and conflict transformation through the indefinite prolongation of a protracted conflict.

## Summary

This chapter has presented a theoretical framework on the linkage between nuclear weapons acquisition and the life-cycle of a protracted conflict. It has argued that the nature of a protracted contract changes to one of indefinite protraction when states in conflict acquire nuclear weapons because the absence of wars and presence of more, and more intense, crises where hostility is intensified make it difficult to initiate and institutionalize a peace process. It further argues that dialogue initiated by the parties as a result of outside pressure is unlikely to resolve the root causes of the conflict and may simply produce cooperation on non-controversial issues where positive-sum gains are expected. The conflict is indefinitely protracted due to the futile peace initiatives and non-cooperation on zero-sum issues. The possession of nuclear weapons by India and Pakistan has changed the pattern of crisis, conflict, and war in South Asia. In the first three decades of the two countries' independence, crises escalated to war on three occasions. In the past two decades India and Pakistan have refrained from waging war. The events of 1986–7, 1990, 1999, and 2001 show that serious crisis may not escalate to all-out war. Similar crises were managed by war in pre-nuclear South Asia, for example the 1965 India–Pakistan War. However, these frequent crises also show that peace is unlikely to be achieved between these two countries, as was evident in the aftermath of the Lahore Declaration of 1999 and the Agra Summit of 2001. The following chapters use the main theoretical arguments of this study, taking the example of the India–Pakistan protracted conflict. The theoretical propositions of the study are tested against this case.

# Part II
# The India–Pakistan protracted conflict

# 4 Life-cycle of the protracted conflict

The India–Pakistan conflict in the South Asian region stands out as one of the world's most intractable conflicts of the twentieth and twenty-first centuries. The conflict, which began in 1947, survived the cold war and continues to be intractable. While most regional protracted conflicts of the cold war period are still alive – such as the India-China conflict, the Iran-Iraq conflict, the Arab-Israeli conflict, conflict in the Korean Peninsula, or the China-Taiwan conflict – and none of them are likely to be terminated soon, the intractability of the India–Pakistan conflict received tremendous attention from the international community as a result of the introduction of nuclear weapons into the conflict region in the 1970s and India's nuclear tests, followed by Pakistan's in 1998, making the conflict intense and dangerous (as discussed in the next chapter). This chapter aims to present the India–Pakistan conflict, highlight its attributes to demonstrate its intractability, lay out the primary and subsidiary issues in contention, and show the phases of the conflict with a view to portraying its present state and why it seems to be at the stage of indefinite protraction.

## Understanding the India–Pakistan conflict as protracted

The previous chapter has defined and illustrated the essential characteristics and attributes that must be present in a conflict for it to qualify as protracted. Typically, a protracted conflict is a high-conflict situation between two or more states, enduring for decades without termination, in which crises are embedded and where war remains a probability due to territorial aspects. The India–Pakistan conflict qualifies as protracted because it possesses all the necessary attributes. The conflict, between two parties, has already lasted sixty years and is yet to be terminated. Its history has entailed many inter-state crises – high, low–medium intensity, and low – and three wars, none of which was able to end the conflict. Outside powers have tried to mediate, but India, the big power in the bilateral relationship, has always had serious objections to the conflict being handled by anyone other than the contending states because the conflict by nature is bilateral. The parties have been involved in a conventional and nuclear arms race and the power struggle still continues.

Research has found that territorial disputes are likely to recur. This means that two states with territorial claims against each other are likely to become enduring rivals or protracted conflict states.[1] In the India–Pakistan case the single contentious territorial issue, Kashmir, has dominated the conflict since 1947 and disputes have recurred between the parties as a result, making them enduring rivals or protracted conflict states. John Vasquez contends that

> what makes territorial disputes so intractable is that concrete tangible territorial stakes, like pieces of land, that are in principle divisible, become infused with "symbolic" and even "transcendent" qualities that make them intangible, perceived in zero-sum terms, and hence difficult to divide.[2]

Thus, he believes that the territorial problems at the time of independence and the "fundamental territorial issues" underlying the India–Pakistan rivalry "should not be interpreted narrowly as the concrete stakes associated with the 'land' of Kashmir."[3] There is more to it. Kashmir is a symbolic and nationalistic issue for the contending states. Leaders have fought for this symbolic stake principally because they feared that failure to do so would encourage further attacks. India's former Foreign Secretary Muchkund Dubey, maintained, "For Pakistan, acquisition of Kashmir is the completion of its identity . . . so this dispute is of a difficult nature. India regards it as a symbol of the ethos of secularism."[4] Kashmir is a nationalistic issue for both Pakistan and India, in addition to being an ethnic/religious one. Protecting Kashmir has become part of the national psyche of both states. In Pakistan in particular, all government foreign policies pertaining to India revolve around this single issue, Kashmir. The government has, in fact, used this issue for nationalistic reasons to undertake aggressive foreign policies against India. Support from the people has been mostly spontaneous. Given these circumstances, Kashmir is a zero-sum game for India and Pakistan and neither party considers making concessions or compromises on the issue. This makes the conflict intractable. Research has concluded that states in protracted conflict over territorial issues are highly war prone and that crisis resulting from territorial issues can escalate to particularly intense levels of military confrontation.[5] This has been true for India and Pakistan. They have been war prone, as shown by the 1947–9, 1965, and 1971 wars. Additionally, of all the crises that have erupted between them, most have escalated to intense military confrontation. Even in the nuclear period, all four crises had the potential of escalation to very intense military confrontation. The Kargil crisis of 1999 was so intense that a number of scholars and policy-makers have called it the fourth war between India and Pakistan.

## The triggering issue: the conflict begins

The conflict between India, one of the largest democracies in the world, and Pakistan, a state ruled for most of its history by non-democratic military leaders, began in 1947 soon after British rule over the Indian subcontinent ended. Pakistan received its independence on August, 14 and India became independent on August 15. The primary mistake of the British government was to divide the Indian subcontinent into two nations. The principal objective was to create a Muslim Pakistan and a secular India with a Hindu majority. Partitioning India on religious grounds would not have been a bad strategy if Kashmir, a princely state with a Muslim majority and a Hindu Maharaja at the time of independence, had not decided to join India when the valley was stricken by crisis in October 1947 with the infiltration of Muslim tribesmen supported by Pakistan with the aim of seizing control of Kashmir. Afraid of losing Kashmir to Muslim Pakistan, the Maharaja signed a treaty of accession to India in October 1947. This triggered the first of the three India–Pakistan wars which lasted fourteen months. After the war, Kashmir was partitioned into Indian-held and Pakistani-held sections. Pakistan's section was further divided into Azad Kashmir, which had nominal autonomy, and the Northern Territories, which were under direct Pakistani control. India held three-quarters of the territory, and Pakistan the remaining quarter. Before the partition of Kashmir, "Kashmiris divided their support between pro-and anti-Pakistani parties. Partition caused the pro-Pakistani elites to flee to Azad Kashmir, leaving Sheikh Abdullah and his National Conference Party to pursue a relatively ambiguous pro-independence platform."[6] Sheikh Abdullah continued this policy until his death in 1982. His son, Farooq Abdullah, succeeded him, and failed to solve the conflict by negotiation. The Kashmiris grew discontented with their economic poverty and corruption in the territory. This triggered political mobilization and the creation of the Jammu and Kashmir Liberation Front (JKLF), espousing secessionist rather than irredentist aims.[7]

After independence, both India and Pakistan wanted full possession of Kashmir. This is still the most contentious issue between them and remains unresolved. Third parties, such as the United Nations, have infrequently tried to resolve this outstanding territorial issue between the South Asian neighbors and one of the first proposals was a UN resolution that a plebiscite should be held in the valley, (that is, Indian-held Kashmir.) The resolution became difficult to implement because India objected to the plebiscite, even though it had originally agreed to it. Its objection was a function of its insistence that Pakistan should withdraw from the valley before the plebiscite. Pakistan's position was that the plebiscite should be held and its results implemented. The partition of Kashmir described above was based on the Cease-Fire Line (CFL) recognized by both states when they accepted the UN's cease-fire proposal in 1949. The plebiscite was not carried out by the contending parties, although it could have been instrumental in resolving the conflict. In fact, if it had been implemented when it was first proposed, other issues would not have entered into the dynamics of the conflict, which might not then have been so long-lasting as it would not have been beset by the difficulty of resolving salient, multiple, and intertwined issues.

Since 1949 the Indian position, conditioned by its secular ideology,[8] has been that it cannot part with Kashmir for fear of triggering other secessionist drives in other Indian states, leading to the disintegration of the country. From this perspective, India considered Kashmir an issue of national consolidation. Additionally, the Indian Prime Minister Jawaharlal Nehru believed that the incorporation of Kashmir into India would strengthen the secular ideology of the nation when it was in its infancy and gaining the confidence of the people was important. It was also his belief that the Kashmiris wanted to stay as part of India.[9] From the Pakistani standpoint, although Kashmir was in part a territorial issue, it was predominantly a religious matter on which compromise was impossible. Kashmir had to be part of Pakistan for religious reasons.[10] On religious grounds, the Pakistanis have always believed that the Kashmiris want to be part of Muslim Pakistan rather than of India.[11] Thus, although Kashmir is a territorial issue, the religious aspect is intertwined in the dynamics of the conflict. Pakistan also regards Kashmir as its fifth province.[12] Consequently, the territory has been considered non-negotiable by all Pakistani leaders since 1947 and it has been at the center of foreign policy for all incumbent governments.[13]

Because Kashmir is India's only predominantly Muslim state and because of its uncertain legal/constitutional position, in 1950 the government granted the Indian part of Kashmir more autonomy than any other Indian state, "limiting India's jurisdiction in it to matters of federal interest, such as defense, foreign affairs, and communications."[14] The following year, UN Security Council Resolution 91 determined that the United Nations Military Observers Group for India and Pakistan (UNMOGIP), established in 1949, would continue to supervise the cease-fire between India and Pakistan.[15] Amidst tensions in the valley, in 1956 Nehru proposed that both parties should accept the de facto partition of Kashmir along the CFL,[16] but the proposals were vehemently opposed by Pakistan. Pakistan, for its part, sought UN mediation in the conflict, a proposal that was strongly rejected by India. Therefore Pakistan felt compelled to refashion its foreign policy and make strategic plans for occupying Kashmir by force. With this in view, Pakistan initiated the next India–Pakistan war 1965.

Before discussing the 1965 war and its aftermath, it is important to note that by the time the war started, a third actor – the Kashmiris – had become deeply involved in the conflict, although their participation was to increase after the war and particularly in the 1980s and 1990s. As Sumit Ganguly states, "both expatriate Kashmiris within Pakistan and the vast majority of the residents of the Kashmir valley are, to varying degrees, active participants in the conflict."[17] The Indian government had to deal with two actors simultaneously: Pakistan on the international front and the Kashmiris on the domestic front, the latter receiving financial, military, and moral support from the former, making matters much more complex for India. The Indian government's repeated use of force against Kashmiri insurgents was criticized by the international community and the Indians themselves. The insurgency in Kashmir, Ganguly asserts, is "the result of a fundamental paradox of Indian democracy: Kashmir represents both the mobilizational success and, simultaneously, the institutional failure of Indian democracy."[18] Along the same lines, Sumantra Bose regards the Kashmir problem as a function of India's political/democratic failure. Additionally, he discusses the negative implications of India's counterinsurgency strategies, describes Pakistan's intervention in Kashmir as counter-productive, and the Kashmiri separatist movement as non-communal in nature, and suggests that the solution lies in redefining Indian democracy and the "skilful renegotiation and complex redefinition of the concept and practice of state-sovereignty in South Asia."[19] The international community in general and Pakistan in particular have frequently pointed out this institutional failure of democracy in India. On the bilateral stage, while Pakistan has expressed its concern over the "widespread repression in Kashmir," India has accused Pakistan of assisting the insurgents.[20] Thus the debate continued.

## Other issues intertwined in the conflict

Beyond the bilateral territorial dynamics of the conflict, one must look at the ethno-religious composition of Kashmir. According to the conventional wisdom, the root cause of the India–Pakistan conflict is to be found in religious or ethno-cultural differences.[21] To Rober Wirsing, "it is concerned primarily with the role of religious identity in the dispute – with its role, on the one hand, in motivating the Kashmiri Muslim separatist movement and, on the other, in driving the state strategies of India and Pakistan toward Kashmir."[22] The role and salience of religion in the Kashmir dispute have been underscored by the former Vice Admiral of India K. K. Nayyar. He states, "There is no way that we are going to give away Kashmir. How will we manage the 130 million Muslims?"[23] Others feel that the political mobilization of Kashmiris took place on the basis of ethno-religious identities, not because these identities were in some predetermined way bound to collide both with one another and with Indian national identity[24] but because over the centuries, the Muslims in the valley had developed a different culture than the Muslims in the rest of India. Due to the geographic isolation of the valley Kashmir is predominantly divided into districts that produce religious divisions – the valley has a Muslim majority, Leh has Buddhist population, Kargil has Muslim population, and Jammu has Hindu majority; political mobilization is the only viable option when other channels to express discontent fail; seeing India's vulnerability in the state, Pakistan assisted the Kashmiri insurgents. In Pakistan, the Kashmir struggle was legitimized on the basis of the communalist discourse. Pakistan viewed Kashmir's identity as an extension of its own, not as the separate identity that the Kashmiris call *Kashmiriyat*.[25] Consequently, Islam was mobilized in Pakistan as a religious force to overcome the differences between "sons of the soil" and immigrants – Muslim immigrants from India – and between the provinces and the country's leadership. Islam therefore became the primary driving and legitimizing force in Pakistan's politics, underlying the viability of the federal unit.[26] Islam also increased Pakistan's regional power by opening up new foreign policies such as using activities in the name of *jihad* to deal with the problems in Kashmir and Afghanistan.[27] With these additional factors and with time, the India–Pakistan conflict has become much more complex to deal with.

Issues other than the territorial dimension of Kashmir may be less salient than the primary issue in dispute but they are nonetheless problems that make resolution of the conflict more difficult. Additionally, the Kashmir issue itself impacts negatively on those issues, making resolution even more difficult. As Stephen Saideman writes, while Kashmir is only one issue that divides the two countries, it is a very important one. Further, the dynamics that have exacerbated this specific dispute – ethnic politics in each country making moderation hard and rewarding extremism – also impact other contentious issues, challenging any effort to build bridges and reduce the rivalry.[28]

Apart from Kashmir, there are three other territorial disputes between India and Pakistan: these are over the Siachen Glacier, Sir Creek, and the Arabian Sea maritime boundary. A more recent quarrel involves India's construction of a barrage in the Jehlum river and a dam over the Chenab river, both of which Pakistan objected to because of the serious negative consequences it would suffer. It objects to the barrage because it might cause electricity shortages once water is withheld for an extended period and it objects to the dam because it would affect the Chenab's downstream flow into Pakistan. All these disputes have been extensively discussed by the parties but without positive results. Siachen Glacier is situated in the Karakoram Mountains, north of Kashmir. It has no economic or social importance because of its very high altitude. However, it is important for India because it is the dividing line between Azad Kashmir and Aksai Chin, Chinese-administered Kashmir. While the original CFL did not cover the area of the Glacier, under the 1972 Simla Agreement the CFL became the Line of Control (LoC) and was accepted by both sides. "Its depiction stopped south of the glaciers and was left blank in the north."[29] In the 1980s there were several violent India–Pakistan clashes over the Glacier which killed thousands of people in the area. In the early 1990s both sides wanted the Glacier to be demilitarized, but that proved impossible because of mutual suspicion. Thus, even though many efforts have been made to settle the dispute including the recent composite dialogue (see p. 134), the dispute remains unsettled.

Sir Creek is a 60-mile-long estuary situated in the marshes of the Rann of Kutch, which lies on the border between the states of Gujrat in India and Sind in Pakistan. After the 1965 war, Pakistan claimed title to half of the Rann, while India asserted that the boundary ran along the Rann's northern edge.[30] Although there has not been serious violence over this issue, reports of the presence of oil and natural gas in the area have raised the stakes for the parties.[31] These aspects complicate the dynamics of the India–Pakistan conflict.

## Escalation of the conflict

The India–Pakistan conflict thus had started with a brief period of crisis leading to a war in 1947 which ended in 1949. The two countries were "born feuding."[32] The beginning and escalation phases were blurred as the conflict escalated at the outset and remained in the high level of intensification stage for the next fourteen months. Although a cease-fire ended the actual war, the conflict was far from over. However, with the Indian and Pakistani acceptance of the cease-fire proposed by the United Nations, the crisis which had led to the war de-escalated and the conflict reached a low intensification level. The conflict is unique because instead of moving from a low level of violence to an intensification phase, it started off with the escalation phase and a high degree of intensification as war was introduced into the conflict soon after it began. More intriguingly, before the actors could exchange views and find they were incompatible, a war had started. This was primarily a result of the Hindu Maharaja's decision to annex Kashmir to India and Pakistan's quick decision to resort to force to oppose the decision. In fact, all the wars between the two parties have been initiated by Pakistan in an effort to settle the problem by force. As J. N. Dixit puts it, "Failing to acquire Kashmir by subversion and international pressure, Pakistan has fought three wars with India to meet this objective by military means," stressing that "Pakistan has been unsuccessful and continues to be unsuccessful in this adventurist endeavor."[33]

While many inter-state crises erupted between the two after the first war, each raising the conflict to the medium level of intensification, the war of 1965, fought over the disputed territory of Kashmir, raised the intensification level to high. A crisis for India was triggered when Pakistan sent about 5000 armed freedom fighters into the valley of Kashmir on August 5 to create a large-scale uprising against Indian control of the province. India dealt with them, but Pakistan continued to send more. When the Indian army crossed the cease-fire line on August 25, the crisis escalated into the 1965 war. Pakistan responded on September 1 by dispatching an "armored column across the cease-fire line in southern Kashmir and threatening the vital road linking the capital city of Srinagar with the plains of India,"[34] to which India responded by invading West Pakistan on September 5. The UN called for a cease-fire the following day.[35] As the war de-escalated, the conflict level dropped back to low intensification. The overall India–Pakistan conflict was still in the escalation phase with both sides building up their conventional arms to confront each other in a future war and continue their arms race. During the cold war Pakistan received most of its conventional weaponry from the US while India received supplies from the USSR and also focused on indigenous production. Pakistan's other arms supplier was China, a protracted conflict rival of India, complicating the situation further for the Indian side. The conflict was also characterized by sporadic inter-state crises. For the next six years, the conflict was in the low intensification period of the escalation phase.

The 1971 war, though fought not over Kashmir but for the liberation of Bangladesh, once again intensified the conflict. A problem between Pakistan's Eastern and Western wings developed into an India–Pakistan war. The day after the Pakistan army's crackdown on students of Dhaka University on March 25, the political leaders of East Pakistan declared independence as Bangladesh. This triggered a crisis for Pakistan, and intensified violence in East Pakistan. India became involved in the conflict as millions of East Pakistani refugees entered the country. It trained some of them to fight the Pakistani army. Minor clashes between the Indian and Pakistani armies in the fall of 1971 erupted into serious crisis. When India discovered that Pakistani troops had been concentrating on the Indian Punjab border since October 12 India crossed the border into West Pakistan, triggering a crisis for Pakistan, which responded on December 3 by attacking the Indian airfields in Kashmir. An India–Pakistan war started and continued for fourteen days, bringing the conflict to a high intensification level. The war ended on December 16 with Pakistan's surrender and the creation of Bangladesh as an independent state.[36]

The end of the war did not mean the end of the conflict, even though the level of intensification dropped from high to low. The war had a long-lasting negative impact on the conflict relations. India's victory, the creation of Bangladesh following the disintegration of Pakistan, and the power asymmetry thus created between the two countries humiliated Pakistan, whose hatred of India was consequently institutionalized. In the next sixteen years, India and Pakistan engaged in an arms race, but in addition to conventional weaponry, nuclear arms became the name of the game. Cold war dynamics were played out in the South Asian region. Pakistan took advantage of the Soviet invasion of Afghanistan and its military ties with the US strengthened from 1979 to 1989. Afghanistan led to a fundamental transformation of US-Pakistan relations,[37] enabling Pakistan not only to obtain modern and sophisticated conventional weapons from the US but also to develop its nuclear capability clandestinely. In the conventional realm, the Reagan administration granted Pakistan a five-year arms and economic assistance package which totaled $3.2 billion, including the F16 aircraft which would make the Pakistani air force qualitatively superior to its Indian counterpart. A new six-year package of $4.02 billion was offered to Pakistan in 1986, in spite of India's vehement objections.[38] Perceiving itself seriously threatened, India looked for Soviet assistance and the USSR provided substantial military hardware to India in the following years.[39] Indian efforts to acquire nuclear weapons and detonation of a peaceful nuclear device in 1974 sparked Pakistan's relentless drive to acquire a matching capability in the shortest possible time. As Pakistan's nuclear capability was factored into the equation by 1987, the conflict took off for an unknown destination. Its whole dynamics changed from this time on. It did not reach a high intensification level for the next twenty years even though it remained in the escalation phase throughout this period. It stayed at the medium intensification level, characterized by low–medium-intensity crises and violent military action short of full-scale war. Major General V. K. Srivastava contends, "When you talk of the spectrum of conflict, nuclear war is on one end and low-intensity conflict on the other end."[40] He further argues that the lower end of the spectrum involves proxy wars or cross-border terrorism, which represent low-cost options for the state initiating them.[41] This is why Pakistan prefers to use this strategy in the absence of the possibility of war in the nuclear period.

There were four crises during the nuclear period, and they were severe in terms of intensity. The last crisis was also protracted, lasting from 2001 to 2003. A protracted crisis of this nature never occurred during the pre-nuclear period of this conflict. The Brasstacks crisis of 1986–7, the Kashmir crisis of 1990, the Kargil crisis of 1999, and the Indian Parliament Attack crisis of 2001 were all severe in terms of intensity and potential for escalation. This is discussed in detail in chapter 7. Referring to the 1990, 1999, and 2001 crises, Savita Pande stated in 2002 that the, "last three attacks were the worst in the Indian history."[42] While that remains true, significantly, none of them escalated to the war level, even though they all had the potential to do so. During this period the India–Pakistan conflict experienced the stability/instability paradox. While there was stability in the sense of the absence of war after the two states acquired nuclear weapons, intense and frequent crises became more prominent. The role of nuclear weapons in the initiation of a crisis and the response of the defender is eloquently described by Sumit Ganguly and Devin Hagerty. With respect to the Kargil crisis, the worst of the four crises, they write that "absent nuclear weapons, Pakistan would probably not have undertaken the Kargil misadventure in the first place; but absent nuclear weapons, India would likely have punished Pakistan more severely for violating the LoC in such a blatant and duplicitous fashion."[43] An important point is that as the nuclear period started, India and Pakistan were not at peace because peace is a product of the absence of both war and crisis. In the India–Pakistan conflict even though there was no war, crises erupted during this period. Therefore, in terms of peace the pre-nuclear and the nuclear periods were the same. In neither period was there peace. What are the implications of these crises for the conflict? The answer to this question clarifies how and why the conflict has never been able to get past the escalation stage. Before probing this point it is important to discuss how Pakistan may gain by using low and low–medium-intensity violence in the conflict setting.

A dissatisfied and revisionist power in this asymmetric conflict,[44] Pakistan wanted to resolve the Kashmir issue by force in a situation where India did not want outside powers or even the United Nations to resolve it or act as mediators. Consequently, all three wars in the India–Pakistan conflict were initiated by Pakistan, even though it lost them all. At this juncture it is important to note that between 1947 and 2001[45] about 65 percent – meaning 28 out of 43 – of the inter-state disputes (those in which military force was threatened, displayed or used) were initiated by Pakistan. This is not surprising, given the power asymmetry between the two rivals in the regional theater. T. V. Paul calls the asymmetry between India and Pakistan, where "India is over seven times larger than Pakistan in population and size of national economy, and four times in territorial size," "truncated asymmetry."[46] Although Pakistan tried to address this disparity by procuring external military capabilities and alignments with extra-regional powers, it has not been able to match India's economic and military growth since the early 1990s. Consequently, it tried to use "asymmetric strategies such as supporting insurgency and proxy war to continue its struggle with India."[47] India was the preponderant power in the relationship. Pakistan has always been weaker than India, even though it may have gained some qualitative advantages in fighter aircraft at some point in the rivalry, and wanted to address its inferior capacity by developing nuclear weapons. India considers itself a status quo power and Pakistan a revisionist state. Given this and since Pakistan initiated disputes in the pre-nuclear era with its powerful neighbor when escalation was a possibility, it had more reason to initiate more crises – low or low–medium intensity – to annex Kashmir when escalation was less probable in the nuclear period. Pakistan has always had some advantages in the conflict. It "benefits from the terrain, the support of sympathetic segments among the Kashmiri population, and, during several phases of the conflict, qualitatively superior conventional weapons system."[48] Additionally, the terrain of

Kashmir allows limited "incursions and guerrilla operations"[49] which are not detected by India. An interesting and significant point to be noted here is that the overall power asymmetry does not matter much to Pakistan in the nuclear period and rather favors it for two reasons. First, at the nuclear level there is strategic parity and inter-state wars are unlikely to happen owing to the prospect of total devastation of both states in the event of escalation of a conventional war to the nuclear level. Therefore, full-scale conventional wars are unlikely. Second, India's preponderance of power only places it in an advantageous position if there is a full-scale long war. Knowing well that low–medium-intensity violence will not lead to full-scale war, Pakistan does not hesitate to initiate crises or launch attacks. According to Pervaiz Iqbal Cheema, "nuclear weapons have not solved the [India–Pakistan] problem, but it did prevent war in South Asia."[50] He further asserts that "no major war will give birth to more small wars and limited excursions or skirmishes."[51] In short and decisive low-intensity violence, Pakistan has the advantage over India. As Paul puts it, "Pakistan can checkmate India during the initial stages of a conflict, and this option has been an asset in the short war," which means it looks for opportunities to use its "superior strategies, tactics and resolve," which compensate for its overall military weakness.[52] The resulting crises do not bring positive outcomes for the initiator and the initiator does not even want them to. Paul Diehl, Gary Goertz, and Daniel Saeedi state, "For a rivalry to maintain itself under these conditions, the weaker side must leave the confrontations unsuccessful and unsatisfied, but still capable of mounting future challenges. . . . In the case of India–Pakistan, most disputes end in stalemate or indeterminate outcomes."[53] This is a key point because the overall conflict is left in a constant state of misunderstanding, suspicion, and hatred, which, in turn, negatively impact the relationship.

Two important points must be highlighted at this juncture. First, wars occur when policy goals cannot be attained by the normal means available.[54] This is relevant because Pakistan wanted UN or international mediation to resolve the conflict, while India was vehemently opposed to this proposal even though finding a bilateral settlement would be complicated and almost impossible. Therefore, war was the only option for the two sides to attain their perceived goals. Second, wars are generally counted among the very significant conflict behaviors for the termination of conflicts. As Brahma Chellaney notes, "there has never been peace between two rivals without a war. A decisive settlement is made through wars. Dismemberment is not enough."[55] The India–Pakistan case is no exception. Wars have been fought in order to bring a decisive settlement to the conflict. However, this salient and viable mechanism for terminating the conflict had to be ruled out after the acquisition of nuclear weapons by the adversaries from the 1970s. In Srivastava's words, "Any long-drawn, full-scale war is something of the past. World war or regional war is not on. A full-scale conventional war [between India and Pakistan] is a remote possibility since both states have nuclear weapons."[56]

Wars were avoided intentionally by the adversaries for fear of a nuclear exchange leading to total devastation. Instead, severe crises became part of the conflict setting. Thus P. Sahadevan contends that while nuclear weapons have maintained deterrence, they have done little for conflict resolution. In fact, they have increased the frequency of crisis situations since 1998.[57] He further states that these "crises emanate more from the Pakistani side,"[58] because it is obviously the weaker side in the bilateral relationship and needs to trigger them. But how does Pakistan gain from these crises or low-intensity conflicts? From the viewpoint of India, Air Commodore Jasjit Singh explained what a state can achieve with the strategy of low–medium-intensity violence. He stated that by just "operating below the nuclear level, in ten years India can have Kashmir. Half of the frontier posts will be taken every now and then. Military can be put up-front."[59] If this can be said about India, then Pakistan, by using the same strategy, could gain at least parts of Indian-held Kashmir in the same time span.

It is also important to consider the political institution in Pakistan that helps it to maintain low- or low–medium-intensity violence in the India–Pakistan conflict theater. Pakistan has been ruled by the military for most of its history and that says much about why the country has frequently initiated violent military confrontations with India, especially when there was a nuclear shield allowing lower-level crises to occur. The military has always been eager to resolve the Kashmir dispute by force. In the absence of a civilian government for most of its history, Pakistan has opted to use force to address its conflict with India. Instead of taking advantage of a no-war situation in the presence of nuclear weapons to resolve the conflict, it has made efforts to create continuous violence. Thus, for the Pakistani side, the advantage of knowing that a crisis will not escalate owing to the presence of nuclear weapons cannot be overemphasized. However, this factor alone might not have made the frequent initiation of crises possible if the military had had a lesser role in decision-making. Trying to trace the connection between conflict resolution and political institutions, the former Indian Prime Minister I. K. Gujral stated that the India–Pakistan problem is connected to the Pakistan "army's mind-set. As long as 50–60 percent of the money is spent on the armed forces, this problem will continue."[60] He further argued in the context of Pakistan that "excursions into democracy were very brief. Whenever there were democracies, we [India] tried to cooperate, even in Nawaz Sharif's period."[61] Thus, unless secularism and democracy are practiced and institutionalized in Pakistan, crises will occur and the possibilities of a resolution will be slim.

The four crises in the nuclear period – the Brasstacks crisis, the Kashmir crisis, the Kargil crisis, and Indian Parliament Attack crisis – were all severe in terms of escalation potential. Most significantly, in seventeen years the two countries had four crises (the last in 2001). In contrast, in the pre-nuclear period, there were seven crises in thirty-nine years, of which three led to war. These occurred in the 1940s, 1950s, 1960s, and 1970s, whereas the four crises in the nuclear period erupted during 1987–2001. Since 2002 and the de-escalation of the last crisis between India and Pakistan the conflict has not witnessed a serious inter-state crisis even though low-intensity violence continues to jeopardize normal relations between the nuclear rivals. Constant low-intensity crises or violence negatively impact a conflict, as stated in chapter 3. New non-traditional dynamics of wars and violence make the relationship more complex. Bhabani Sen Gupta states that if nuclear weapons are considered to be deterrents and rule out war, then that "is a contribution to the uneasy and unstable no peace, no war situation between India and Pakistan."[62] The acquisition of nuclear weapons has not stopped the insurgency in Kashmir even though it may prevent a full-scale war. When the two countries come to settle their conflict they will have to begin at the level of insurgency, move on to terrorism then the political level, and finally reach the nuclear level.[63] Additionally, during the nuclear period, both India and Pakistan have tried to increase their nuclear capabilities and there is an ongoing missile race, factors which only aggravate the conflict. All these attributes of the protracted conflict have contributed to freezing the India–Pakistan conflict at the escalation phase, in which the contending states experience low-to-medium intensification of violence short of war.

## No de-escalation and indefinite protraction of the conflict

The de-escalation phase of the conflict, which is a function of compromise, settlement, agreement, leadership initiatives, or third-party mediation, cannot be reached in a crisis-prone environment. Each effort to settle the differences is important, but the subsequent implementation or follow-up needed requires understanding between the two parties. This is impossible when violence or crisis remains the order of the day, as is the case with the India–Pakistan conflict. As mentioned before, from the late 1980s till 2002 there were four severe crises, which had negative impacts on the conflict. However, as the crises developed and the situation thawed, efforts were made to make peace. But before a peace initiative could be taken, another crisis erupted. The Lahore Declaration and its aftermath provide a case in point. The Lahore Declaration was a path-breaking agreement between the two states in 1999, just a year after India and Pakistan tested their nuclear weapons. It set the stage for possible conflict resolution, not only through discussion of many important confidence-building measures but also through the Indian Prime Minister's visit to Lahore for the purpose, one of the most important goodwill gestures made by any Indian leader in the hope of resolving the enduring conflict. But, "while the Lahore ink was getting dry, preparations were going on for Kargil,"[64] one of the worst non-war crises in the India–Pakistan conflict's history. While totally unacceptable to the Indians, to the Pakistanis even the initiation of the Kargil crisis has a good explanation. As Niaz Naik puts it, "Our people thought that the bunkers are open; let us go and occupy them. They tried to send a few patrols and that triggered Kargil."[65] On the reasoning behind Kargil, he states, "The idea was to put pressure on India to come to the negotiating table."[66] He explains why India needed to come to the negotiating table even though in Lahore concrete negotiations had been conducted between the two countries. In the months before Kargil secret negotiations were going on between India and Pakistan and, according to Naik, the two leaders almost agreed on a resolution of the conflict. In Lahore it was also decided by the prime ministers A. B. Vajpayee and Nawaz Sharif that one representative from each country would hold talks on a comprehensive solution. Niaz Naik was chosen by Nawaz Sharif as Pakistan's representative, while K. Misra was the Indian spokesperson. According to Naik, the talks, which were held in secret, were progressing very well, but the whole process was jeopardized when Vajpayee, under the influence of some of the Bharatiya Janata Party's (BJP) hawkish politicians, threatened Pakistan. That is what triggered Kargil from the Pakistani perspective.[67] The Indians and others do not see things through the same lens, however. Ashley J. Tellis *et al.* argue that when Pakistan acquired its nuclear capabilities in 1998 and this was made known to the public, the leaders saw a new window of opportunity and "more robust forms of immunity." In the light of this situation, the country continued "its objective of 'strategic diversion,' that is, enervating India through the mechanism of LIC [Low Intensity Conflict] even as it pursued more positive goals such as attempting to secure Kashmir."[68] Whatever the motive for provoking such a serious crisis and continuing the policy long after Kargil was over, Pakistan created a crisis-prone environment in the nuclear age, aggravating conflict relations and obstructing paths to peace.

From the late 1980s a new dimension of threat appeared in the conflict. While "bombings, strikes, and demonstrations became virtually endemic,"[69] and the Indian government blamed Pakistan for fomenting violence in Kashmir, cross-border terrorism became embedded in the conflict. This continued in the 1990s and in 2000. The 2001 attack on the Indian Parliament, which coincided with the 9/11 attacks on the United States, forced the New Delhi government to make future peace efforts conditional. India demanded a complete halt to cross-border terrorism before any efforts to resolve the outstanding issues between India and Pakistan. This still remains a central obstacle in the peace process between Islamabad and New Delhi, as terrorism continues to haunt the Indians. All peace efforts have been jeopardized by the eruption of crises (discussed in chapter 8) and so there has never been a de-escalation of the conflict.

The India–Pakistan conflict has not been able to move forward to reach the de-escalation and cessation phases. This means that it became frozen as the parties became nuclear states and for the stability/instability paradox dynamics. By not allowing the conflict to move forward to the escalation phase, and then reach the de-escalation and cessation phases, the acquisition of nuclear weapons has in fact extended the protracted conflict between the two countries. Diehl et .al. maintain that "the India–Pakistan rivalry is ongoing and shows no signs of abating,"[70] at a time when dialogue is in progress between the two nuclear neighbors. This is because even dialogue cannot produce the desired results as the environment is non-conductive to the cooperative behavior which could lead to conflict termination. Additionally, while the dialogue may produce positive results on non-controversial issues such as trade, culture, and communications, it cannot resolve the controversial territorial issues.

While this remains the general situation in the India–Pakistan protracted conflict, there is optimism for conflict resolution in a nuclear South Asia. Some in Pakistan believe that nuclear weapons acquisition can contribute to conflict resolution. It has been argued that because there has been more violence in the conflict setting in the nuclear period, it receives more attention from the international community, especially the US, which makes the two belligerents cautious about escalation. Because there is the potential for escalation, and nuclear exchange may result, there is pressure from the international community to settle the conflict. As Shireen Mazari states, "The international pressure is more now that there are nuclear weapons [in the hands of India and Pakistan]. Pressure to settle the problem is there."[71] Nasim Zehra expressed a similar view, adding in the dynamics of the 9/11 attacks. Focusing on the role of external powers in the conflict, she stated that "the international environment does play a role [in conflict resolution]."[72] Zehra cites the example of the US which changed its policies in the nuclear period: "the US went from a policy of ignoring, to containing, and now solving Kashmir."[73] In the context of the Kargil episode, Tellis et. al. note that a number of senior Pakistani military officers who were associated with orchestrating the Kargil operation believe that nuclear weapons "prevented a wider conflict and more intense war even as they served to catalyze US diplomatic interest in bringing the conflict to a conclusion."[74] Whether Pakistan was happy with how the crisis was concluded is another story, but it is a fact that the US became interested in the conflict because of the dynamics of the nuclear capabilities in India and Pakistan. This is perhaps the greatest advantage of nuclear weapons proliferation in South Asia. However, not everyone believes that the US intends to terminate the India–Pakistan conflict by putting pressure on the parties to end the violence. Cheema believes that the "US wants to minimize the tension between India and Pakistan – not to solve the problem."[75] He further asserts that the US simply wants to reduce the problem and the Indians are fully aware of it.[76] Ganguly and Hagerty agree with this line of reasoning, arguing that the US role in these crises of the nuclear period was to act as a "facilitator of peace, providing both sides with the political cover they needed to stand down while still saving face."[77] Whether the US intends to resolve the conflict is unclear, but the fact remains that these crises between India and Pakistan have focused the attention of the international community, especially the United States.

It is uncertain whether Pakistan creates crises because it wants to attract international attention to help resolve the conflict or whether international attention is a consequence of violence in the nuclear age in South Asia. In other words, is Pakistan creating more crises in the nuclear period in order to attract international pressure to resolve the Kashmir issue given that it cannot be resolved bilaterally, or is international attention simply a consequence of the uneasy and violent environment in South Asia? It is also unclear whether this is a conscious strategy adopted by Pakistan to address the issue or in order to grab Kashmir bit by bit, as Jasjit Singh claims. Whatever the cause of the crises, if international pressure helps to resolve the conflict then there is less reason to worry about a nuclear India and Pakistan.

A protracted conflict that is frozen at the escalation phase can only move beyond this stage and reach the goal of termination with the help of mediation, leadership initiative, or domestic factors. The latter two are generally interconnected because leaders are usually motivated to take a special interest in conflict resolution by some sort of domestic pressure such as extreme economic hardship or political unrest. Of course leaders must be willing to take the initiative themselves, which means they must be flexible in their attitude. In the India–Pakistan case, although

A. B. Vajpayee seemed eager to go the extra mile to create an atmosphere for conflict resolution and President Pervez Musharraf also seemed inclined to seek accommodation, Pakistan's domestic political compulsions made it difficult to pursue the strategy of reciprocity at the right time, as is discussed in chapter 8. This shows that even leaders are unable to do much in terms of conflict resolution if a proper peaceful environment is absent.

## Summary

This chapter has presented an overview of the India–Pakistan conflict from its beginning in 1947 over the salient territorial issue, Kashmir, to which other issues have become attached, all combining to make the problem difficult to resolve. It showed that the conflict has been protracted indefinitely because it could not move beyond the escalation phase and then reach the de-escalation and cessation phases owing to the introduction of nuclear weapons which has created a situation of no war and constant crises, in a non-peaceful environment unsuitable for the resolution of the conflict.

# 5   Introduction of nuclear weapons into the conflict

South Asia was the first region to experience the politics of nuclear dynamics in the intractable conflict between India and Pakistan. By 1964 the nuclear club was complete and a decision not to allow new states to join was taken by the nuclear states in the late 1960s. The Nuclear Non-Proliferation Treaty (NPT) made this policy official. When India refused to join the Treaty when it opened for signature in 1970, and Pakistan followed its rival's lead, the value of nuclear weapons to these belligerents, which had then been engaged in a bilateral protracted conflict for twenty-three years, was manifest. Although theoretical at that stage, the value of nuclear weapons to India became known to the world when it tested its peaceful nuclear device in 1974, to the alarm of the international community, especially the five nuclear states, whose ideal of non-proliferation was shattered. Pakistan saw this as a serious security threat, given that India had been instrumental in the secession of East Pakistan in 1971, and a power asymmetry was already pronounced in the conflict. Since then, South Asia has been known as a region with nuclear interests and Pakistan's India-centric nuclear policy in the aftermath of its rival's nuclear tests corroborated this line of argument. From this period on India and Pakistan became serious proliferation concerns. The purpose of this chapter is to present when, how, why, and under what circumstances nuclear weapons were introduced into the India–Pakistan protracted conflict with a view to demonstrating the connection between the cause and effects of this example of proliferation. Because a nuclear deterrent capability was the primary goal for both states, deterrent stability was desired and achieved at the war level, making room for instability at the lower levels of conflict – a consequence, which was not considered when the strategic calculations and decisions were made – and creating a crisis-prone environment non-conducive to conflict resolution. The introduction of nuclear weapons into the India–Pakistan conflict had the unintended consequence of making the protracted conflict intractable.

## The conflict embraces nuclear weapons

When India started its nuclear program in the 1950s it was geared to civilian needs. However, in the early 1960s, Homi Bhabha, the founder of India's atomic program, asserted that if the Indian government so desired, his scientists would be capable of making a bomb within eighteen months.[1] It is often stated that Bhabha started the program with peaceful civilian intentions but became an advocate of nuclear weapons after China tested its nuclear device in 1964,[2] two years after the Sino-Indian war in which India was roundly defeated. His advocacy did not have much importance in some Indian policy-making circles at the time primarily because the government was more inclined to probe other ways to secure India's position vis-à-vis China, namely through security guarantees and alliances. India's Prime Minister Lal Bahadur Shastri went to the west to discuss India's security situation, and all his interlocutors, including the British Prime Minister, advised him to take the non-proliferation route to security. But unconvinced, India opted for a nuclear weapons program to address its security needs in the extra-regional sphere, vis-à-vis China, and also to elevate its international status. Sumit Ganguly writes that "the political fallout in India over the Chinese nuclear explosion cannot be underestimated. Prime Minister Lal Bahadur Shastri, who had inherited Nehru's mantle, faced extraordinary pressures to abandon India's commitment not to develop nuclear weapons."[3] India launched its nuclear weapons program after China conducted its first nuclear test in 1964, "in part to meet the Chinese threat and in part to promote its national status as an actor-to-be-reckoned-with on the world stage."[4] However, India made efforts to reach out to nuclear states such as the US, the UK, and the Soviet Union to obtain nuclear guarantees even when Indira Gandhi became the Prime Minister. As she failed to obtain the guarantee that she had hoped for, domestic pressure mounted for a reassessment of India's nuclear posture. As expected, the 1974 peaceful nuclear test had some negative consequences. Canada suspended its nuclear cooperation, believing that India had converted nuclear fuel from the research reactor it had supplied. A new non-proliferation security regime was created, known as the London Suppliers Group, to monitor and control supplies of dual-use technology. India's refusal to sign the NPT and Pakistan's defeat in the 1971 war had triggered Pakistani interest in developing a nuclear capability. Its interest became more intense following India's nuclear test of 1974, making the India–Pakistan conflict proliferation prone.

In the following decades, both countries expanded their nuclear programs, developing short-range and medium-range ballistic missiles capable of carrying nuclear warheads.[5] In 1983 India started a comprehensive missile development program known as the Integrated Guided Missile Development Program, which incorporated an intermediate-range (2500 km) missile, a battlefield support (150 km) missile, surface-to-air missiles, and an anti-tank missile. The Prithvi, a Pakistan-specific short-range missile, was first tested in 1988 and then in 2000. Several variants of this missile ranging from 150 km to 350 km were developed. The Agni, an intermediate-range ballistic missile, was designed to reach China. Agni I, with a range of 1000 km, was first test-fired in 1989 and Agni II, with a range of 2000–2500 km, was first tested in 1999. The Indian government then tested Agni II several more times.[6] Pakistan also had an active missile program by the 1980s. In addition to its indigenous missile production, which includes short-range and intermediate-range missiles such as the Hatf series and Shaheen series respectively, Islamabad is known to have received M-11 missiles with a range of

300 km from China in the early 1990s. The Shaheen series' design is based on the Chinese-supplied M-11 missiles, while the Ghauri series is based on the North Korean Nodong missile design. Ghauri I has a 1000 km range and Ghauri II is believed to have a range of 2300 km. Thus, Pakistan's missiles are also reasonably developed compared to India's. With the introduction of the Ghauri missiles Pakistan showed India that it had developed a credible response to Indian missile capabilities.[7]

Nuclear opacity was maintained by both India and Pakistan till 1998. For both states, overt proliferation was not an option for many years because of pressure from the international community. However, overt proliferation was important for India in the context of the Sino-Indian protracted conflict. China was a declared nuclear state and at some point India had to test its nuclear weapons and come out of the closet if it was to establish a credible relationship of deterrence with its adversary. Since India and Pakistan maintained the status of covert proliferators in the 1980s and 1990s (until 1998), scholars and policy-makers worried about their ability to use the strategy of nuclear deterrence. In May 1998, India and Pakistan both came out of the closet and declared their nuclear status to the world by conducting underground nuclear tests. In April 1998 Pakistan tested its medium-range ballistic missile Ghauri, and within a month, on May 11 and 13, India conducted five underground nuclear tests, which were followed by Pakistan's nuclear tests on May 28 and 30,[8] even though the international community, especially the United States, urged it not to follow suit. It is believed that Pakistan's Ghauri test triggered the Indian nuclear tests because "the BJP's [Bharatiya Janata Party] historic toughness on national security would have seemed hollow if the government did not respond decisively to the new Pakistani threat."[9] The former Indian Prime Minister I. K. Gujral's views about nuclear weapons tests corroborate this belief. He was asked by many state leaders why India did not test nuclear weapons while he was in power. He stated, "Why did I not test [nuclear weapons]? I didn't see any benefit in it. Five leaders were there [before me], why did they not test?"[10] This indicates how Pakistan changed the situation by the Ghauri missile test, making it pertinent for India to take a tough stance and test nuclear weapons. He discusses the accountability of leaders in a democratic country, saying that people must know whether they are secure from external threats and that it is the responsibility of a democratic leader to ensure that they are. Along the same lines, he stated,

> I was not signing the CTBT [Comprehensive Test Ban Treaty]. Chirac asked me, "Why don't you sign?" I said "Let me ask you a counter question: Will you stop testing?" He said, "Yes." Our difficulty is very different. Clinton in 1997 asked me the same question. I said "I am within your [US] shooting range. Pakistan had tested a weapon from China. If you were the Prime Minister of India, what would you do?" As the Prime Minister, whenever we go home one billion people ask me, "Are we safe?"[11]

Some doubt this line of reasoning because they believe that the "tests were authorized earlier."[12] Whatever the reason, it is undeniable that the Indian tests shocked the world, but Pakistan's response brought a new and serious proliferation problem to the forefront of security studies. The world condemned these tests, which undermined the NPT and made the universe proliferation prone, and there were fears that other regional states facing security threats would follow India and Pakistan, increasing the possibility of nuclear accidents. Economic sanctions were consequently imposed on both states, but this in no way prevented them from pursuing the nuclear path, working on their respective nuclear doctrines, and depending on the strategy of nuclear deterrence for war avoidance purposes. The sanctions were lifted in the wake of the attacks on the United States of September 11, 2001, primarily because Pakistan's assistance was required by the US in its war on terror. India and Pakistan got away with their nuclear tests due to the changed global environment.

It is relevant to understand how the cold war dynamics were played out in South Asia, especially in the nuclear realm. The regional rivals received financial and military assistance from the superpowers and other countries during the cold war, as both India and Pakistan are strategically located. Of the two, Pakistan was most favored because the US considered it a front-line state against Soviet communism. This enabled Pakistan to receive financial aid and military assistance worth millions of dollars from the United States, and relieved it of serious US pressure to give up the nuclear option. The US considered it in its security interest to assist Pakistan, a country bordering Afghanistan which was invaded by the Soviet Union in 1979, rather than to persuade Islamabad to give up its nuclear ambition and sign the NPT. China has also assisted several facets of Pakistan's nuclear program. India was much closer to the Soviet Union, but received less support from Moscow than Pakistan did from Washington. Nevertheless, India, too, was not much pressured by the superpowers during the cold war period to renounce its nuclear ambitions or to join the NPT. This lack of superpower attention on the nuclear issue in South Asia during the cold war made it easier for both India and Pakistan to advance their nuclear plans. In this protracted conflict into which crisis and war are embedded, there is no reason to believe that the propensity to proliferation would have been any less if the cold war political dynamics had been different and the superpowers had put more pressure on the two states to roll back their nuclear programs. Systematic analysis indicates that 45 percent of militarized disputes take place within the context of enduring rivalries and that war is almost eight times more likely in the case of the most serious and enduring rivalries than between pairs of states in an isolated conflict.[13] Given that the India–Pakistan conflict is one of the most serious in the contemporary world, war was expected to remain a central crisis management mechanism.[14] The risk of small incidents igniting wider problems remains a reality in the conflict. Thus, nuclear weapons were perceived as essential deterrents to war by New Delhi and Islamabad in the cold war and the post-cold war periods.

India's primary security concern was China, a major extra-regional power. India has been in an asymmetric protracted conflict with China since 1953 over territorial claims, and it saw the acquisition of nuclear weapons as a way of addressing the power asymmetry and deterring China from making any further attack and territorial gains. India believed that with a nuclear capability it could establish a long-term strategic deterrent relationship with China, while strengthening New Delhi's bargaining position vis-à-vis Beijing should there be a Sino-Indian confrontation in the future.[15] China did not ratify the NPT till 1992, raised serious objections during the CTBT negotiations in 1996, and had conducted forty-three nuclear tests – twenty-three in the atmosphere and twenty underground – by that date. Pakistan was India's other protracted conflict rival, although India was the preponderant power in this territorial asymmetric conflict. All three wars between these two parties were launched and lost by the weaker power, Pakistan, making New Delhi believe that Islamabad would not miss any opportunity to seize Kashmir by war in the absence of a deterrent capability. Interestingly, India's two rivals, China and Pakistan, have been strategic allies since the 1960s and formed an "anti-status-quo alliance" against India in 1962.[16] This created an uncomfortable situation for India, making its proliferation drive more valid and essential. In the India–Pakistan conflict, the latter had military support from both the US and China, provided to counter balance India in the region. In the 1965 war, Pakistani forces had equipment worth more than $700 million provided by US military assistance.[17] An interesting statement was made by the former Prime Minister Gujral in which he explained how important it was for India to address the Chinese and Pakistani nuclear threats. He said, "One doesn't proliferate for the fun of it."[18] Given India's twin protracted conflicts and the strategic alliance between its rivals, the acquisition of nuclear weapons seemed rational and essential in the light of regional and extra-regional security considerations. Thus the Indian decision to aquire nuclear weapons was made in the context of China, but the weaponization programme was accelerated in the context of Pakistan.[19]

India's and Pakistan's nuclear programs had quite different rationales. For India, the real concern was China, as discussed above; Pakistan only became a concern once it started its own nuclear weapons program. It was always believed by Indian strategic thinkers that if China could be taken care of, they would inevitably be able to deal with Pakistan, a weaker state in the conflict. Therefore, India moved ahead with its nuclear program with China in mind, although this does not mean it was unconcerned about the threats that emanated from Pakistan. It simply means that India had more reason than Pakistan for developing nuclear weapons.

Pakistan's only security concern was India and its quest for nuclear weapons was a product of this security problem. While the Indian nuclear test of 1974 gave a strong "impetus to the Pakistani program," it is believed that Pakistan did not initiate its nuclear program after the Indian test but had already started it after its defeat at the hands of the Indian forces in 1971.[20] Ashok Kapur argues that Z. A. Bhutto's term of office as prime minister was unique not because he was successful in developing the bomb, but because the pattern of nuclear activities which occurred during the 1972–7 period had a clear anti-India direction.[21] Due to the Pakistani military's inability to face India's significant conventional superiority, the Pakistani decision-makers chose to invest in a nuclear weapons program.[22] It is argued that Pakistan compensated for its conventional military imbalance by developing nuclear weapons.[23] Interestingly, although Pakistan initiated all three wars in the India–Pakistan conflict theater, as it was the loser each time it realized that it cannot risk losing territory in a future regional crisis or war. To preclude that possibility, Pakistan decided to acquire a deterrent capability to protect itself from superior conventional attack by India, while enabling it to engage in low-intensity violence to achieve its goal of unification with Kashmir. Kashmir has always been the main subject of contention and possible cause of war between India and Pakistan. This territorial problem was central to the conflict and the consequent hostility and rivalry had to be stabilized, and this could be achieved by the possession of a deterrent capability. Pakistan had such an overwhelming need for a deterrent capability vis-à-vis India that some Pakistanis have argued that they would have needed nuclear weapons even if India had not acquired them.[24] When Pakistan realized that nuclear deterrence was important, it sought external nuclear guarantees from its allies. Like India, Pakistan failed to obtain anything positive. Although the general view is that Pakistan obtains military assistance from China, Aga Shahi claims that when Pakistan sought protection under the Chinese nuclear umbrella after the Indian nuclear test of 1974, it was bluntly rejected; the US likewise refused to provide protection at this sensitive time.[25] In consequence Pakistan embarked energetically on a clandestine nuclear weapons program, and "successfully imported technologies that have allowed it to achieve a degree of nuclear parity with India"[26]within a decade.

## Positive goal of proliferation attained

The acquisition of nuclear weapons by India and Pakistan was a function of their protracted conflict, although for India, China was a salient consideration. A major ramification of the India–Pakistan conflict has been the acquisition of nuclear weapons by both countries. While this has been seen by some scholars as a positive contribution in the realm of conflict stability, others believe that instability could result owing to many factors including war by accident, the role of the military, and organizational reasons.[27] Others have argued that stability could breed instability in this particular context. But surrounded by these negative responses, India and Pakistan proved to the world that they had achieved the positive goals for which they had developed nuclear weapons. To them, these are deterrent weapons; they were acquired in order to deter war recurring in the conflict, and this object has been achieved.

In the first two decades after the introduction of nuclear weapons into the conflict, there were increasing doubts in the international community about whether deterrence works if states' nuclear status is opaque. Since India and Pakistan maintained opacity in the 1970s and 1980s, it became a cause of international security concern. South Asia did not aspire to cold war-style nuclear deterrence although the word "deterrence" was commonly used by the contending states. Instead of transparent communication, the two rivals used tacit communication of capability, intentions, and resolve for war avoidance. There was some uncertainty as to the value of such deterrence. While many doubted whether deterrence could work under conditions of opacity, India and Pakistan were confident of their ability to deter future war with the possession of undeclared nuclear weapons.[28] The facts show that South Asia enjoyed peace in terms of absence of war during the period of undeclared nuclear weapons possession by India and Pakistan. While accidents could have happened and the military regimes in Pakistan could have decided to use nuclear weapons for organizational reasons, they did not. The no-war situation during the period proves these assumptions, predictions, and hypotheses false.

The last war between India and Pakistan occurred in 1971, after which the parties made efforts to acquire nuclear weapons. From 1971 till 1998, when the two states detonated their nuclear weapons and declared themselves nuclear states, the overall conflict was in the escalation phase, as shown by several crises in the conflict setting and the engagement of both parties in conventional and nuclear arms races. They could also be seen to be building strategic alliances and developing ballistic missiles during this period. While the eruption of each crisis raised the intensification phase from low to low–medium, subsequent de-escalation lowered it, as stated in the previous chapter. Yet the overall conflict remained at the escalation phase. During this escalation phase of the conflict, especially after both states had acquired a nuclear capability which they regarded as being a deterrent, there were serious apprehensions about their ability to maintain a stable deterrent relationship with weapons that were "non-weaponized." The Indians and Pakistanis, however, were both of the opinion that non-weaponized deterrence suited their situation at the time and was working well. To assure the international community that deterrence works and to show how it works, General Sundarji argued in 1996 that

> both India and Pakistan have indeed weaponized and are deployed in as good a state of readiness as they would need for minimum deterrence to be effective against each other. "Weaponization" need not mean that the nuclear warhead has already been married to the bomb-casing or placed in the missile's warhead compartment. Likewise, "deployment" need not mean that the completely assembled missile has to be in or very near its launch pad.[29]

Additionally, to maintain such deterrence, matching capability was not important. Equality in terms of numbers did not matter; equal security was important. Rejecting the idea and importance of matching numbers, General Aslam Beg argued that destruction can be caused by just a few weapons and it is ultimately the fear of retaliation that decreases the likelihood of a full-fledged war between India and Pakistan.[30] In the realm of communication, an essential aspect if deterrence is to work, they developed informal and indirect means to communicate under conditions of opacity – leaders' statements and interviews, media news, western publications, CIA reports and assessments – that both sides understood.[31] The no-war situation and non-escalation of crises prove that deterrence of some sort did work in the India–Pakistan conflict during the period in question.

An interesting point in the context of crisis escalation and non-weaponized deterrence was raised by Sumit Ganguly and Devin Hagerty. They examine the India–Pakistan nuclear crisis of 1984, triggered by India's discovery of Pakistan's development of nuclear weapons, which impelled it to plan a strategy to destroy the program in its infancy.[32] India contemplated a preventive air strike against

Pakistan like the one by which Israel destroyed Iraq's nuclear program in Osirak in 1981. While this proposal was discussed within the policy-making circle and the Indian military leadership, Prime Minister Indira Gandhi believed that such an attack would be met by counterattacks against India's nuclear installations,[33] spreading radiation in the country.[34] Although India considered the option of taking out Pakistan's nuclear facilities, it finally decided not to do so. According to Ganguly and Hagerty, this was because of something they call "boosted conventional deterrence"[35] in the bilateral relationship. They argue that during the transition period when both India's and Pakistan's nuclear weapons status was changing, there was no actual nuclear deterrence because nuclear weapons were only at the development stage, but during this period pure conventional deterrence was not the only form of deterrence either. They argue that "the prospect that conventional assets can be used to kill far beyond their basic potential when targeted against nuclear installations" deterred India from launching a preventive attack against Pakistani nuclear facilities.[36] This conclusion is extremely important because it proves that even when both India and Pakistan were on the verge of developing nuclear weapons and when each was unsure of the other's development level, they were deterred from launching a conventional attack for fear of escalation. Some form of nuclear deterrence was in evidence even during this period and the conflict benefited from some degree of stability due to this unknown nuclear weapons status.

The violence of 1989 and 1990 between India and Pakistan could have escalated to war in the absence of nuclear weapons. India's and Pakistan's nuclear weapons capability maintained stability through deterrence under steadily deteriorating conditions during this period. Pakistan was constantly accused by India of supporting the pro-independence uprising on Indian Kashmiri territory that flared up in 1989. While Pakistan always denied the charges, it sympathized with the Kashmiris and believed itself entitled to ownership of the entire state. Two important and serious crises erupted during this time frame, namely the Brasstacks crisis of 1986–7 and the Kashmir crisis of 1990.[37] Although both had the potential of escalating, neither did, which begs the question: What stopped these crises from escalating? The answer was clear in the minds of the Indians and Pakistanis. There would be no war between the belligerents in the nuclear age, as demonstrated by these two crises. Two other important crises erupted during the nuclear period, the Kargil crisis of 1999, and the Indian Parliament Attack crisis of 2001–3. Although there was less doubt as to whether deterrence could work given the transparent form of communication established after the nuclear tests, both these crises had a serious potential of escalation. As mentioned earlier, the Kargil crisis is often called the fourth war between India and Pakistan due to its intensity and the use of India's airpower for the first time since 1971. According to Brahma Chellaney, Kargil was a full-fledged war – but a localized war.[38] The Parliament Attack crisis was the longest in the two states' history and involved the largest troop mobilization on both sides. K. K. Nayyar asserts, "The attack on the Parliament is the beginning of a new era, just like the September 11 attack on the US."[39] This statement alone shows how seriously the attack was taken by the Indians. Nevertheless, both these crises de-escalated without war, demonstrating deterrence stability in the conflict. Some argue that "there are two stabilizing factors in South Asia – the US, as the manager, and nuclear weapons in India and Pakistan."[40] This is important because the two factors are, in reality, interconnected. Even though nuclear weapons deter wars when regional rivals are in possession of them, the US makes serious efforts to manage violence and crises in a conflict when nuclear weapons exist. Nuclear weapons were developed with the aim of attaining deterrence and they brought with them the stability both India and Pakistan were looking for in the conflict. This positive goal of nuclear weapons acquisition was achieved by India and Pakistan and made their conflict stable on one level.

## The negative outcome of proliferation

Stability means different things to different scholars and policy-makers. If absence of war means stability, then South Asia witnessed stability both during the period of opacity and after India and Pakistan openly declared their nuclear weapons. If absence of war is not sufficient to create stability, as some tend to believe, then the India–Pakistan conflict has not been stable in the nuclear period. This is primarily based on the notion that stability is a function of both absence of war and absence of crisis. If peace is a function of stability, and stability in turn is a product of absence of both war and crisis, then the India–Pakistan conflict has not had stability or peace, as stated in chapter 3 above. This demonstrates the negative implications of the acquisition of nuclear weapons for stability and peace, and ultimately for the conflict.

The two crises during the period of opacity and the two others after 1998 show that serious crises were part of the conflict setting after the two states acquired nuclear weapons, whether undeclared or declared. Uday Bhaskar eloquently expresses the phases of the conflict in terms of the importance of Kashmir and within the context of the nuclear dynamics. He sees the conflict as divided into three phases. (1) In 1947–71, there was certain trajectory to the Indo-Pakistani relationship. Pakistan was very much affected by the global and regional dynamics. (2) In the post-1971 period, every other problem in the region affected Pakistan. In 1971–86 (or the end of the Zia-ul-Haq period), a pattern can be seen. (3) After 1987–8, India and Pakistan's relationship entered a period of turbulence. Low-intensity conflict became more common. Intelligence agencies became more important. Bhaskar further states that in the "1947–71 period, Kashmir was not a big item between India and Pakistan. In post-1971 too Kashmir wasn't that important. Post-1988 Kashmir acquires a certain centrality. Non-state actors get some kind of empowerment."[41] Why Pakistan empowered these irregulars is another question, but the fact remains that new and non-traditional means were used to foment violence in Kashmir in the nuclear period more than previously. Placing the Kargil crisis in the nuclear context P. R. Chari states,

> This was surely an unintended consequence of the tests, which were meant to heighten Indian and Pakistani security by deterring nuclear and conventional

aggression. The availability of the nuclear deterrent to Pakistan encouraged its undertaking the Kargil intrusions, while increasing its cross-border terrorism and proxy war in Kashmir. In fact, the presence of the nuclear deterrent now seems to inform Pakistan's chimerical policy to incorporate Kashmir into its body politic.[42]

Whether or not this was part of the strategy when the development of nuclear weapons was discussed by the strategists and decision-makers of both states remains unclear, but serious crises seem to have erupted more frequently in the nuclear age than previously. This is discussed in detail in chapter 7.

Crisis events in South Asia during this period brought the India–Pakistan conflict into the international limelight. The changing pattern of crisis, conflict, and war renewed interest in regional security studies. While crises between two states in conflict are common, escalation into serious violence or low–medium-intensity conflict cannot be explained by reference to regime type or leadership role. Nuclear weapons seem to have changed the general pattern of the relationship in the India–Pakistan protracted conflict. The weapons have contributed to the prevention of a full-scale war but not of low–medium-intensity violence in the subcontinent. Some even believe that the period of opacity was better than the period when nuclear weapons were declared. Chari maintains that nuclear weapons have achieved very little in terms of making the parties secure and that there was greater advantage in keeping the option open. "They have not fully weaponized. Conflict has become more dangerous. It hasn't made them [India and Pakistan] more secure."[43] There are grounds for thinking that the parties are less secure in the nuclear period – whether non-declared or declared. Nuclear weapons therefore have brought with them a permanent non-peaceful environment in which low–medium-intensity violence erupts frequently in an otherwise non-war context. Crisis appears to offer the best strategy that a weaker power can use against its stronger counterpart to make territorial gains, whether by grabbing portions of territory during a crisis or by calling on the international community to use pressure to settle the outstanding differences. Jasjit Singh argues that Pakistan wanted to show that the India–Pakistan conflict theater was "a nuclear flashpoint."[44] Indian policy-makers did not identify or analyze these negative effects of proliferation prior to making the decision to acquire nuclear weapons.

The negative effects of nuclear weapons acquisition are real and have impacted the conflict. There are no extended peaceful periods due to the frequent eruption of violence short of actual war.

## Nuclear weapons entrench the conflict

Instead of bringing peace, the introduction of nuclear weapons to the India–Pakistan conflict has created a long-lasting non-peaceful environment. This in turn hampers the exploration of conflict resolution possibilities. Violence breeds hatred between the two parties and where violence remains embedded, peace is compromised. In the midst of violence, any efforts to seek peace that might be made by a bold leadership are doomed to failure in the absence of the trust that is essential for them to succeed. If an overturn peace towards is followed by a serious crisis, as was the case after the Lahore Peace Process and the Agra Summit, it becomes hard for any leadership – whether democratic or non-democratic – to trust its adversary and start the process again. As Chari states, "Dialogue between leaders requires trust. How do you have dialogue if you have mutual suspicion?"[45] Chari further discusses the ideas that formal state-to-state dialogue may be jeopardized by unruly elements who do not want peace, and that even secret diplomacy cannot work without trust and confidence. He states, "Secret diplomacy doesn't work too well. In 1998 Niaz Naik from Pakistan engaged in secret diplomacy, but the Indian High Commission in Islamabad blew the secret mission. It was a counter reaction of the same in the Pakistan High Commission in Delhi."[46] Although India believes that Pakistan cannot be trusted and that it is Pakistan that jeopardizes the peace initiatives in the bilateral relationship, Pakistan takes the opposite view. Pervaiz Iqbal Cheema cites the example of the Lahore Summit claiming that it was agreed that all outstanding issues should be resolved during the summit, including Kashmir. However, when Vajpayee went home and his national media asked him whether he had agreed to resolve the Kashmir issue, he said, "I only meant Azad Kashmir."[47] Using this as an example, Cheema observes, "This is the kind of attitude that creates doubts."[48] Discussing the ongoing dialogue, he maintains, "I am doubtful if the Indians mean it honestly when they talk about dialogue": he feels that the Americans pressure the Indians and they want to give the impression that they want peace. "It is a tactical ploy."[49] Where there is lack of trust, which is a function of the eruption of violence in the conflict setting after every peace initiative, each statement by a rival is scrutinized through the lens of suspicion.

Indians and Pakistanis have made different interpretations of the connection between nuclear weapons acquisition and conflict resolution. Raj Chengappa asserts, "Development of nuclear weapons was thrust upon India."[50] India had no option but to proceed with the nuclear weapons program due to Pakistan's unrelenting drive to develop bombs in the post-1987 period. Chengappa further states that for the Indians, the "rationale for developing [nuclear weapons] was not conflict resolution,"[51] a view shared by others. Savita Pande states that "nuclear weapons acquisition was not supposed to help in initiating negotiation between India and Pakistan."[52] It should not surprise the Indians or the Pakistanis if these weapons have not done much to resolve the conflict because they were not developed with that purpose in mind. Pakistanis see the situation differently. Cheema asserts that "the Indians made the Pakistanis nuclear" and "they are responsible for creating doubts."[53] He continues to argue that the Indians were responsible for the "strength of our [Pakistan's] armed forces and they contributed to the situation India–Pakistan has been in since the introduction of nuclear weapons.[54] Pakistan wanted to address its power asymmetry and feel secure with its giant neighbor which won all the wars the Pakistani government initiated. In addition to these goals, Pakistan, the weaker power, wanted to internationalize the conflict. This would only be possible if the region could be seen as a nuclear flashpoint. Although Pakistan may not always have been in control of the violence fomented in the valley of Kashmir, its support for the elements carrying out the violence made it a party to the creation of the atmosphere of dangerous instability. Its intention to attract the attention of the international community counterbalances its role in provoking violence. The value of nuclear weapons cannot be over-estimated. Mushahid Hussein states that it was Pakistan's nuclear test that made Vajpayee visit the country which had caught up with India in the arms race.[55] This means that the two countries' acquisition of nuclear weapons opened the door to peace. Pakistanis see nuclear weapons as a tool for conflict resolution. This may have been a consequence of the nuclear tests, but nuclear weapons were not built to attain this goal. India acquired nuclear weapons to address the Chinese nuclear threat; with time, the threat from Pakistan also had to be addressed, especially when it developed its nuclear weapons capability. If the reason for acquiring nuclear weapons was simply security, though even security was not attained on all levels, conflict resolution or overall conflict stability should not have been expected to follow.

If the conflict between the two nuclear states is resolved, it will essentially be as a result of new thinking or a new strategy on the part of policy-makers in the light of the changed circumstances of a nuclear environment. In the absence of a change in thinking, the effect of nuclear weapons will only be to protract the conflict. Policy-makers must understand that nuclear weapons will not auto-matically resolve the problem and dependence on them will only generate more crises in the conflict. Only when this is understood will new thinking emerge. However, some observers think it unlikely that the line of strategic thinking will change. Chari argues that India and Pakistan have "a mutual interest in conflict continuance. This is a function of the political elites' strategic enclave."[56] If this is correct, then the conflict is unlikely to change in the future.

If conventional wars have become a thing of the past, then subconventional wars will also have to disappear from the conflict setting if a peace process is to be launched. Some degree of peace is required to re-establish trust, an important element in the initiation of conflict resolution. Peace is a product of the avoidance of both conventional war and non-conventional conflict. In the absence of either condition, a conflict cannot change in the desired direction. As Amitabh Mattoo states, "I don't think it [nuclear weapons] is gradually transforming the conflict due to the absence of full-scale war. Subconventional wars will also be obsolete. This will demonstrate then that they [India and Pakistan] are destined to coexist and more inclined to negotiate."[57] The words "subconventional wars" and "cross-border terrorism" are often used interchangeably. To Pakistan, cross-border terrorism can be discussed only once dialogue has been established. Cheema comments, "You can move these baskets with dialogue," but "conditional dialogue is not acceptable"[58] to Pakistan. This was a key point of contention between India and Pakistan in the aftermath of the 2001 Parliament Attack. While both sides believed in the significance of dialogue, the Indians made dialogue conditional on Pakistan stopping cross-border terrorism first. This was unacceptable to the Pakistanis. Cheema further believes that the "Indians did not cooperate on Kashmir; if they did it would be easier for Pakistan to control the *jihadis*"[59] and then cross-border terrorism could possibly be contained. However, subconventional wars are unlikely to disappear from the conflict theater. In K. Subrahmanyam's words, "How will the conflict be resolved? The conflict is about Kashmir for Pakistan. For us [India] it is the Two Nation Theory. It is about the clash of civilization. Terrorism is only a strategy." Subrahmanyam continues,

> Today the war is not against terrorism. It is against those who use it as a strategy, who use extremist views, [who] have mono-culturalism and no tolerance. It is a war against democracy and non-democracy. It is a clash between multi-culturalism and mono-culturalism, between democracy and intolerance."[60]

Terrorism is one of the most important points of contention in the India–Pakistan conflict resolution process. Nothing can work if violence is the order of the day and nothing can be implemented unless terror attacks stop. This will only happen in conditions of tolerance and respect for human beings, and these are products of democracy. This all points to the conclusion that Pakistan must change its political institutions if any peace process is to work because without tolerance and understanding, violence will only breed more violence and the parties in conflict will be unlikely to implement any resolutions made during negotiations owing to mutual suspicion, resulting in the intractability of the protracted conflict.

## Summary

This chapter has studied the introduction of nuclear weapons into the India–Pakistan conflict. Nuclear weapons acquisition by both India and Pakistan was a result of their security problem. Both required a deterrent capability to avoid war in the conflict theater, though for India the need for deterrence was more compelling on account of the Sino-Indian conflict. The positive and negative results of nuclear weapons acquisition were discussed. It was shown that the conflict which motivated the two states to acquire nuclear weapons has been protracted in consequence.

# 6  Crises and wars in the pre-nuclear period

The intractable conflict between India and Pakistan has undergone a number of crises and wars, these being major characteristics of every other such conflict. What makes this regional conflict different from others is the way it divides into two periods – the pre-nuclear and the nuclear, the latter subdividing into the undeclared and the declared phases. The nuclear dimension brings a new element to the eruption, process, and characteristics of crises and wars. Those in the pre-nuclear period differed from those in the nuclear period. This chapter discusses the various crises and three wars that occurred between the parties to the conflict in the pre-nuclear period, demonstrating their propensity to escalate crises. It shows how easily the conflict reached a high degree of intensification on three occasions. It also demonstrates the connection between escalation and non-possession of nuclear weapons.

## Crises and escalation from 1947 to 1986

The rivalry between India and Pakistan has resulted in a total of eleven inter-state crises[1] between 1947 and the present. Seven of these occurred in the pre-nuclear period, 1947–86. Four of the seven occurred in the first fifteen years, 1947–62, three in the next fifteen years, 1963–78, and none, in the last seven years, 1979–86. These statistics show that the first few decades of a conflict are more intense in terms of crisis eruption than those that follow. A comparative analysis of the periods shows a crisis hierarchy between them, with a gradual decline in each successive period, which could be caused by a number of factors. However, no decline is apparent in the number of times a crisis was escalated in the periods under consideration. For example, the first period saw four crises, of which one, that is 25 percent, erupted into war. This propensity to escalate increased in the second period, with three crises, of which two, that is two-thirds, escalated to war. The third period, with no crisis or war, is unique.

The first decade witnessed the largest number of inter-state crises, as is normal in the initial phase of an intractable conflict. Of the three crises of the 1940s, Junagadh (1947–8), Kashmir I (1947–9), and Hydrabad (1948), only the second escalated to war, the first war between India and Pakistan. In the 1950s, the Punjab War Scare I was the only crisis which did not escalate to war. Before discussing these crises and wars, it is pertinent to comprehend that a war over Kashmir was inevitable from the start. Junagadh, Hydrabad, and the Punjab crises did not have the potential to escalate, being over less significant issues than Kashmir on which, compromise was possible. Kashmir I had quite different political dynamics from the other three crises in consequence of the significance of the territory and the two parties' unwillingness to negotiate over it. This is proved by the fact that the conflict over this issue has continued ever since. It is, thus, no surprise that the crisis over Kashmir escalated to war.

The second period saw three crises: Rann of Kutch (1965), Kashmir II (1965–6), and the Bangladesh crisis (1971). Both the last two led to full-scale wars, while the first remained a medium-intensity crisis. The Bangladesh crisis scarcely affected India per se, being initially an intra-state civil war between Pakistan's Eastern Western wings. It turned into an international war with Indian involvement in the crisis, following a huge influx of refugees from East Pakistan to India. This full-scale war was initiated by Pakistan and won by India. Given the atypical nature of India's involvement in the Bangladesh crisis, two points can be underscored: all wars between India and Pakistan had Kashmir as their primary cause during the pre-nuclear period and crises over Kashmir always triggered wars.

The third period of no crisis or war was a marked improvement over the earlier pattern. The two important features of the non-nuclear period are: the decrease in the number of crises as the conflict extended, with a fourteen-year gap between the fourth and the fifth crises, showing the two parties felt the need to trigger a crisis less often; and the fact that every crisis over Kashmir during the period escalated to war. These features point to the significance of nuclear weapons in controlling escalation, which will be discussed in the next chapter. By 1979–86 the parties appear to have become war-weary and crisis-weary and ready to maintain a low profile. However, the real reason for this restraint may have more to do with the transition to nuclear status, as during this period as well as being engaged in a conventional arms race, the two states were making efforts to develop nuclear weapons. Thus the third period was markedly different both from the first two periods when India and Pakistan definitely did not have nuclear weapons and from the nuclear period when each had knowledge of the other's nuclear capabilities. In consequence, during this period the states could not risk triggering a crisis for fear of escalation.

## The first India–Pakistan crisis: Junagadh, 1947–8

The Junagadh crisis, the first of the many crises that have occurred between India and Pakistan, started on August 17, 1947 and lasted till February 24, 1948. For India, the crisis erupted when it heard of Junagadh's decision to become part of Pakistan on August 17, 1947. It responded by approving a plan to occupy Junagadh's subject states, Mangrol and Babariawad, with civil personnel accompanied by a nominal military force. This meant a crisis for Pakistan. After the departure of the pro-Pakistani Nawab from Junagadh, the state government requested India to assist in its administration. India gave instructions for the occupation of Junagadh on November 9. On November 11, Pakistani Prime Minister Liaquat Ali Khan responded to an Indian request for talks on Junagadh by saying that since Junagadh had acceded to Pakistan, there were no grounds for discussion, and India had violated Pakistani territory. But because Junagadh is not contiguous with it, Pakistan could not defend it and on February 24 a plebiscite decided by a large majority that India should hold the territory.[2] This ended the crisis.

## The Kashmir I crisis and war, 1947–9

The first fifteen years of the India–Pakistan conflict witnessed violence of different intensities. Even before institutionalizing their independence, India and Pakistan were locked in a crisis which led to their first war, from 1947 to 1949. Pakistan showed no hesitation in starting the war and India reciprocated in kind. Though inconclusive, the war has left a permanent mark on the India–Pakistan conflict.

On October 24, 1947 Pakistan invaded Kashmir, sending in armed forces and Pakistan-backed Muslim tribesmen from the North West Frontier province. In a predominantly Muslim Kashmir, the Hindu Maharaja appealed to India for help.

> India responded on the 26th, only after receiving Kashmir's formal accession, by ordering an airlift of troops, equipment, and supplies into the area.[3] The Indians pursued both diplomatic and military tracks in battling Pakistan over Kashmir, lodging a complaint against Pakistani aggression with the UN Security Council on January 1, 1948, while simultaneously engaging the Pakistanis in periods of intense ground combat.[4]

On February 6, 1948 rebel forces launched an attack on Naushara. Pakistani officers realized that the Azad Kashmir forces could not hold back the Indian army. They decided to keep the Pakistani Seventh Division in position behind the front. Pakistan launched an unsuccessful attack on Poonch which resulted in an Indian spring offensive. Fierce fighting continued for fourteen months. The crisis over Kashmir ended for both India and Pakistan with a UN-mandated cease-fire on January 1, 1949.[5]

In this crisis and war Pakistan launched an offensive against India without much consideration for the consequences. It knew that it was weaker than India at the time of partition when, Sumit Ganguly states, "all movable military infrastructure had been divided on a 30:70 ratio between Pakistan and India" and Pakistan's army was "desperately short of officers."[6] This makes it hard to understand why Pakistan initiated the war. The easiest answer is that escalation to war was not going to hurt Pakistan more than non-escalation. The crisis was a typical one for territorial control immediately after independence and war is also a typical crisis management technique. Additionally, it is important to note that neither India nor Pakistan had any intention of taking each other's territory in this or any other war. The war revolved around Kashmir and even though Pakistan was the revisionist state, "it did not seek to unravel the Indian state and did not harbor visions of wider territorial conquest."[7] As P. R. Chari puts it, "India has never taken the wars beyond its borders with the exception of the Bangladesh War."[8] Since the aims were limited, escalation was possible. The important question is whether or not such escalation would be contemplated in the nuclear period.

## Crisis over Hydrabad during the Kashmir crisis, 1948

The Hydrabad crisis is interesting because it was triggered during an ongoing crisis and war between India and Pakistan over the disputed territory of Kashmir. Hydrabad is purely Indian territory and Pakistan had no claim over it. However, when internal disturbances occurred then, Pakistan lost no chance to aggravate the matter, creating a crisis with India. The second largest princely state after Jammu and Kashmir, Hydrabad had great importance for India. It had a majority Hindu population, but was ruled by a Muslim Nizam and most of its political decision-makers were Muslim. However, instead of wanting to be part of either Pakistan or India at the time of independence, the people wanted to create an independent Hydrabad. Tension mounted throughout 1947 and 1948. On August 21, 1948, the state proclaimed independence and requested the UN to discuss India's economic blockade and the violence in the state. This triggered a serious intra-state crisis for India. It tried to restore law and order by sending in troops. With the installation of a military administration and the appointment of a military governor in Hydrabad, the crisis ended on September 18, 1948.[9]

Pakistan should never have been involved in this crisis. However, on September 23 when the Nizam of Hydrabad requested the UN Security Council to withdraw the case it had put forward against India,[10] Pakistan protested and continued to press for discussion. Hydrabad's complaint was included in the Security Council provisional agenda, although it was later dropped. India protested on the grounds that this was a totally internal Indian affair, and Hydrabad was not an independent state entitled to request UN interference. The crisis ended without any inter-state violence.

## The Punjab War Scare I crisis of 1951

The crisis of 1951 also had its roots in a protest made by India to the UN Security Council. Following Pakistani violations of the Kashmir cease-fire agreement of January 1, 1949, India launched a protest against Pakistan to the UN in June 1951. It stated that India was gravely concerned about the situation and the "financial war propaganda" which was growing every day, giving it grounds for suspicion of a forthcoming outbreak of hostilities. Pakistan did not feel the situation had changed. However, on July 7, 1951, Pakistan moved a brigade within 15 miles of the Kashmiri district of Poonch. These military movements and talk about *jihad* there made India feel there was a crisis, to which it responded by placing its troops along the Punjab border and in Jammu and Kashmir. This triggered a crisis for Pakistan.[11]

The crisis did not escalate to war, not because Pakistan did not consider war but because its Chief of Staff General Ayub Khan stated that it was unprepared for war,[12] so the crisis was managed by diplomatic channels. It wound down in August with the withdrawal of both armies. As mentioned before, during this pre-nuclear period, war remained the primary crisis management technique and when it did not happen, it was due to lack of military preparedness on the part of the states involved.

## The Rann of Kutch crisis of 1965

The fourteen-year gap between the Punjab War Scare I crisis and the Rann of Kutch crisis shows that the contending parties did not resort to crisis as lightly as in the nuclear period. Since escalation was always a possibility in the pre-nuclear period, initiation of a crisis was carefully planned. The party that initiated the crisis knew that it might mean having to fight a war. Military preparedness had to be considered in case a crisis escalated.

The Rann of Kutch, a princely state, acceded to the Indian Union in 1947. However, Pakistan claimed the northern part of the territory, resulting in minor incidents in 1956. In 1965, Pakistani forces started patrolling areas that were claimed by India. In January 1965, several border skirmishes occurred in the Rann, "a largely trackless waste" which "had a poorly demarcated border."[13] On April 8, India and Pakistan attacked each other's police posts in the Rann of Kutch. After six days both parties agreed to stop fighting, but severe military hostilities resumed in the last week of April. The UK called for a cease-fire on May 11, 1965, proposing that the two sides should return to their positions of January 1, 1965. The crisis finally ended on June 30, 1965 when both India and Pakistan agreed to the terms of the cease-fire.[14]

## The Kashmir II crisis and the 1965 war

The 1965 war between India and Pakistan shows how readily war was resorted to in the pre-nuclear age. The military government of Pakistan saw an opportunity it could exploit when anti-India rioting took place in Kashmir.[15] The Kashmiris, however, were unwilling to show violent opposition to Indian control of the territory in spite of Pakistani encouragement. Rather, they turned the Pakistani "intruders over to the Indian authorities."[16] In September 1965, the Pakistan army infiltrated across the cease-fire line in Kashmir, and so provoked the Indians to cross the international border. For India, the crisis began when Pakistanis infiltrated into Kashmir to create a massive uprising against Indian control of the state of Kashmir. The guerrillas at first successfully occupied several positions in the area, but India regained the lost posts in August and, in early September, fought off an attack in the Chhamb sector of southwest Kashmir. Prime Minister Lal Bahadur Shastri took the unexpected decision of authorizing the Indian armed forces to expand the scope of the war beyond Jammu and Kashmir, across the international border with Pakistan. Thus, India launched a counteroffensive, invading Pakistan through the frontier in the Punjab area, between Lahore and Sialkot.[17] India's sending several thousand troops across the 1949 cease-fire line triggered a crisis for Pakistan. J. N. Dixit writes, "It was now Pakistan's turn to be surprised. They had not anticipated India expanding the area of conflict to cover the important province of Pakistan –

Punjab, threatening its capital, Lahore."[18] The armies of India and Pakistan confronted each other across the Punjab border, occupied each other's territory, and violated the cease-fire agreement, triggering an all-out war which lasted four months until January 1966 when a UN-ordered cease-fire was accepted by the two parties. In the same mouth, with dedicated mediation by the Soviet Union, the two states finally signed a permanent cease-fire agreement, the Tashkent Declaration.[19] But although the Soviet Union was able to promote a general peace treaty at Tashkent, it could not prevent war between India and Pakistan in 1971 over Bangladesh.[20]

The 1965 crisis and war underscore how little restraint both India and Pakistan showed in crossing the cease-fire line of 1949 and in using war as a crisis management technique. This was a result of the absence of nuclear weapons from the conflict at the time.[21] This crisis management technique was abandoned soon after India and Pakistan acquired nuclear capabilities. But in the absence of nuclear weapons, India did not hesitate to respond with counteroffensive mechanisms. For example, India's objectives were "to thwart any kind of Pakistani territorial acquisition" and "to resort to multiple options to make the military resistance to Pakistan successful."[22] With this objective, India decided not to limit the area of conflict, but to expand its military operations till Pakistan was compelled to move out of Jammu and Kashmir.[23] Comparing the 1965 crisis to the medium-intensity crises of the 1990s, K. Subrahmanyam observes that in 1965 when Pakistan sent 5000 armed forces across the cease-fire line, India responded by an immediate escalation, crossing the line itself, which triggered the 1965 war. However, when Pakistan acted in a similar manner in the 1990s, when both countries had nuclear capabilities, India refrained from crossing the cease-fire line. He contends that this new strategic decision was a result of Pakistan's nuclear capability.[24] India adopted prudent crisis non-escalation strategies to address Pakistan's threats. Two points must be clarified, one about the methodology of comparison and the second about crisis initiation. First, out of the three wars that the parties fought, the 1965 war is the only one with features comparable with the medium-intensity conflicts of the 1990s or after 2000. For example, the Bangladesh war was unique in the conflict, as stated earlier, so using it in comparisons would result in methodological error. The 1947 war was also different in that, although it was a war over Kashmir, there was no cease-fire line until 1949, so when Pakistan triggered the crisis leading to the first bilateral war India could not complain about the line being violated. The war was a scramble for territory that each claimed at the time of independence. By the time of the 1965 war and the crises thereafter, if Pakistan or India had crossed the cease-fire line, later the line of control (LoC), it would be liable for violating the territorial integrity and sovereignty of the other. Second, if nuclear weapons made India cautious in its responses to Pakistani aggression, why was Pakistan not deterred from provoking crises which were unlikely to produce positive results? The answer is straightforward. As stated in the previous chapters, the nuclear capabilities of both states provided a safety shield for Pakistan, the weaker power in the conflict, enabling it to initiate crises without fearing escalation.

Explaining how the Kashmir II crisis started and led on to the 1965 war, Ganguly states that Pakistan saw a "window of opportunity" in the early 1960s which it felt bound to exploit. He argues that by that time Pakistan thought the major powers had lost interest in Kashmir, that neither multilateral nor bilateral arrangements would be able to settle the India–Pakistan problem, and that India's decision to integrate Kashmir fully into the Indian federation of states granting special rights and status to Kashmiris, would tend to favour the Indian side. Furthermore, India's attempt to "revamp its military infrastructure," after its defeat in the war with China in 1962, would increase its military potential and "foreclose the possibilities of meaningful military action" by Pakistan.[25] On the last factor, Gabriella Blum states,

> In October–November 1962, India suffered a disastrous defeat in its war with China, along the Himalayan frontiers. While it was making efforts to recover its heavy damaged military infrastructure, Pakistan, who was keeping a wary eye on India's growing armament, saw an opportunity to fulfill its aspiration of seizing all of Kashmir.[26]

In addition to these factors, Timothy Hoyt argues that Pakistan believed that its military technology had a decisive edge, that its troops were superior, and that the Indian political leadership was weak.[27] All these caused Pakistan to explore the existing "window of opportunity" and foreclose the future "window of vulnerability." In essence, Pakistan's military planners were planning a preventive war[28] in the light of India's military build-up plans after the 1962 Sino-Indian war. By 1965, Indian armed personnel included 870,000 in sixteen divisions, two of which were deployed in Kashmir, eight along the western and eastern borders with Pakistan, and six along the Sino-Indian border. Pakistan had only seven divisions deployed against India in West Pakistan and one division in East Pakistan. In terms of arms and aircraft, there was a big gap in India's favor: India possessed 700 aircraft, against Pakistan's 280.[29] Pakistan's military government under Ayub Khan launched a preventive war on India, anticipating that India would soon complete its military build-up and then Pakistan would have no chance of conquering Kashmir. Unfortunately, "Pakistan's strategic efforts suffered from overoptimistic planning, poor intelligence and analysis, and a serious underestimation of the political will and military capacity of its Indian adversary."[30]

"Operation Gibraltar," the codename of Pakistan's plan to infiltrate the Kashmir valley and foment a local uprising there, was motivated by a few more considerations than those mentioned above. These factors influenced the decision-makers in Pakistan. Aware of its serious power asymmetry with India, Pakistan planned its strategy in the belief that India would not give active resistance to Pakistan's new mission. This belief was based on factors including a "limited probe" Pakistan had initiated in the disputed area of the Rann of Kutch that year: India's response had been fairly passive and the problem had been referred to the international arbitration commission. Pakistan interpreted this response to mean that India was demoralized after its defeat by China and did not want to face another battle so soon. The other factor was that the Pakistanis expected strong Kashmiri support for their plan and, additionally, Chinese support in the event of war.[31] In reality, Pakistan turned out to have underestimated the Indian response and Kashmiri support for India; there was no formal agreement between Pakistan and China about military assistance in war. Instead of supporting the Pakistanis, the local Kashmiris handed the infiltrators over to the Indian authorities. In politico-strategic terms and policy objectives, Pakistan was defeated in the 1965 war,[32] even though at its conclusion India controlled 720 square miles of Pakistani territory in Punjab and Pakistan controlled 220 square miles of Indian territory in Rajasthan.[33]

## The Bangladesh crisis and India–Pakistan war of 1971

As stated earlier in the chapter, unlike the previous two wars, the Bangladesh war was not waged over Kashmir – although the war generated military action along the other Indo-Pakistani border, including Kashmir – or for any direct India–Pakistan territorial gains. It was a civil war which turned into an inter-state war and became an integral part of the India–Pakistan conflict for a number of reasons, including India's role in the liberation struggle of Bangladesh, the disintegration of Pakistan and the subsequent power asymmetry between India and Pakistan, and the consequences of the war in the realm of conventional and nuclear arms levels. The war and Pakistan's disintegration also undermined the Pakistan religion-based claim to Kashmir since it had been unable to keep its Eastern wing from separating on the basis of religion. Finally, the war was significant for its conclusion by the Simla Agreement of 1972, signed by both India and Pakistan, according to which the India–Pakistan conflict was to be resolved bilaterally, as India had intended from the start. Bhabani Sen Gupta rightly states, "I think it would be correct to say that the separation of Bangladesh from Pakistan added an edge to the Kashmir conflict."[34]

The roots of the Bangladesh crisis were connected to the Pakistan's protests against India's interfering in its internal affairs by granting the liberation fighters shelter, training, and military equipment and providing them with moral and diplomatic support. India ignored Pakistan's allegations throughout the nine months from March 25, 1971 to December 3, 1971. In consequence, Pakistan launched an air attack on India's northwestern military and air bases on December 3, 1971. India retaliated with its air force on December 4, starting the bilateral war which ended on December 17, 1971. Although operations in Kashmir concentrated on three key points, Poonch, Chhamb, and Kargil, India's objectives in the western sector were limited. It held its position along the cease-fire line, seized tactical territorial advantages, and inflicted the maximum possible damage on Pakistan's military assets, especially its armor and heavy weaponry.[35] A detailed description of the crisis, the actors involved, and the war is necessary at this point.

The crisis over Bangladesh had three actors: East Pakistan/Bangladesh/liberation fighters, Pakistan, and India. This makes the crisis unique in the India–Pakistan conflict relations. On March 25, 1971, East Pakistan faced crisis when the Pakistan army attacked the student dormitories of Dhaka University. The East Pakistani political leaders declared the independence of Bangladesh the following day. Pakistan responded to this crisis by banning political activities and violence in the Eastern wing of the country. Extreme violence and severe fighting started immediately and continued in the spring and summer of the year. Millions of people fled to India for refuge and many of them were trained by the Indian army to fight the West Pakistani army. Thus India provided not only shelter, food, and clothing to the refugees, but also financial, military, and moral support to the liberation fighters, making them highly capable of fighting the Pakistan army. While India got involved in the intra-state conflict through its assistance to the liberation struggle, throughout fall 1971 it was engaged in minor clashes with Pakistan. The situation reached its peak on October 12 when Pakistani troops were found near the Indian Punjab border. India responded on November 21, when it crossed into West Pakistan. On December 3, Pakistan retaliated with an air attack on Indian airfields in Kashmir, which was met by Indian counterattacks.[36] India's response included air, sea, and land operations. Michael Brecher and Jonathan Wilkenfeld state, "Indian forces poised on the East Pakistan border overwhelmed the Pakistani troops in the seceding territory within a fortnight."[37] Pakistan's surrender to the Indian forces ended the war on December 17, and a new sovereign country, Bangladesh, was created in South Asia.

While this crisis was not exactly bilateral, facts prove that on the bilateral level India and Pakistan did not hesitate to resort to military force and attack each other's airfields when the situation demanded. For Pakistan, it was a matter of desperation and urgency to stop Indian support for the liberation fighters. As the situation worsened, by the end of fall Pakistan could foresee its own dismemberment. However, it initiated and escalated the crisis with little hesitation. India obviously felt a strong response was required when Pakistani troops were along the Indian Punjab border. However, as long as Pakistan did not take the step of crossing into Indian territory, India could restrain itself from crossing into West Pakistan. Again, India showed little hesitation in making the next move, though well aware that it could start an international war. The events of 1971 belong to the non-nuclear era of the India–Pakistan protracted conflict. Escalation was determined solely by whether the parties felt militarily prepared to fight a war. Both India and Pakistan then did.

## Non-crisis, 1979–86

After several crises and wars, the conflict between India and Pakistan entered a period of calm. From 1979 to 1986 there was no crisis between them. Although this was a non-nuclear phase, Pakistan did not try to initiate a crisis even though it was extremely dissatisfied with the division of Kashmir following the Bangladesh war. What explains this? First, Pakistan realized that the 1971 war had had a direct negative impact on its ability to fight another war with New Delhi. The country was devastated on the military, diplomatic, political, and psychological levels. In the next few years Pakistan was fully focused on rebuilding its conventional military capabilities and infrastructure. It tried to develop alliances and obtain military hardware from its partners, especially the US. The last two crises had also influenced Pakistan's decision not to start another one. The country could not be confident of non-escalation. In addition, escalation could not be contemplated during this period because both India and Pakistan were developing nuclear weapons, and the nuclear status of each was unknown. On May 18, 1974, India conducted an underground nuclear explosion of what it called a peaceful nuclear device, and became "the sixth nation in the world to have demonstrated the capability to do so."[38] Pakistan then began a relentless quest to develop nuclear weapons, although there are reports that it wanted to do so immediately after its defeat in the 1971 war. Stephen P. Cohen states,

> The linkage between the shock of 1971 and the nuclear option is even tighter in Pakistan, and for Zulfiqar Ali Bhutto a nuclear weapon had the added attraction of enabling him to reduce the power of the army. Ironically, Pakistan has wound up with both a nuclear program and a politically powerful army.[39]

On the Indian side, the reasons for peace were different. India was satisfied with the division of Kashmir in the wake of the 1971 Bangladesh war and wanted to maintain the territorial status quo. Consequently, the government of India tried to consolidate its position in Kashmir in the next several years.[40]

As stated in the previous chapter, India did not dare to launch a preventive attack against Pakistan's nuclear installations, fearing retaliation against its own nuclear facilities. If these were devastated India would be disadvantaged in its conflict with China.[41] The government of Prime Minister Indira Gandhi was advised by India's senior military to launch a preventive attack against Pakistan's Kahuta nuclear facility in 1984.[42] Gandhi considered but rejected the plan for fear of retaliation and, possibly, for fear of escalation to nuclear war. Some believe that the argument is weak because India knew through its own and US intelligence reports and leakage that "Pakistan had not yet achieved the nuclear capability to assemble and deliver nuclear weapons."[43] India's fear was rather that Pakistan would retaliate by striking Indian nuclear targets, killing thousands of Indians and destroying the expensive nuclear program in one blow.[44] This argument could be partly correct because although Pakistan was still working on indigenous missile production in the 1980s it had already acquired F16s which could carry nuclear weapons. It had started working on its nuclear program after 1971 and in more than a decade had acquired a nuclear weapons capability.[45] Pakistan was said to be able to conduct computer-simulated tests by 1987–8.[46] If it was so advanced by 1987 in the nuclear realm, was it that less advanced just three years previously? It might have been less advanced, but who could say for certain and how credible were the reports that came out of the intelligence community? Could India depend on such information and launch an attack without being fully sure of the implications? It is likely that the Indian government was unsure about the nuclear status of Pakistan when it contemplated an attack on its rival's nuclear facility and this lack of certainty restrained it from implementing the plan for a preventive attack. This uncertainty constitutes "some form of deterrence," whether "hybrid" or not, and is valuable during the transition to nuclear weapons status.

Nor did Pakistan, generally the instigator of any crisis in the India–Pakistan conflict, initiate any crisis during this period. Other regional issues made Kashmir seem less important to Islamabad. The 1974 Indian nuclear test, Pakistan's covert nuclear weapons program, and the Soviet invasion of Afghanistan in December 1979 – all influenced Pakistan's decision. Since Kashmir was always the trigger for crises, that it was given less significance during this period meant there were no crises. While this argument has some value, the change in strategic behavior owes much to the transition to nuclear weapons. Such a period tends to be peaceful because the adversaries are unsure of each other's nuclear capabilities and retaliation mechanisms, and cannot risk starting a crisis for fear of escalation. A weak power can trigger a crisis easily in a non-nuclear period because any predictable or unpredictable escalation would mean simply fighting a conventional war. Similarly, in the nuclear period, crisis can be launched with less hesitation because there is clear deterrence between the parties in conflict and possibilities of escalation are almost non-existent. In between these two extremes lies the "transition to nuclear status" period, where escalation may not mean simply fighting a conventional war owing to the lack of transparency in the nuclear weapons field. Therefore, even triggering a crisis could be dangerous for the initiator, inhibiting it from doing so.

Kashmir turned violent again in the late 1980s when armed insurgency against Indian rule resurfaced in Jammu and Kashmir, killing large numbers of people and challenging Indian dominance of the region. Some observers argue that the Indian government was responsible for the Kashmiris' political mobilization because its regional development efforts made them aware of their political rights.[47] Pakistan aggravated India's intra-state troubles by foregrounding religious identity. President Zia-ul-Haq's policies revolved around Islamization and the Pakistan army was restructured; Islamic teachings were given a place in military education. This Islamic ideology had a spillover effect in other sectors of society. Zia strongly believed that Islam could save Pakistan from external and internal threats. The Afghan war further complicated regional politics. The Soviet withdrawal and the victory of the *mujahidin* proved that *jihad* can succeed, triggering a new Pakistani strategy of low-intensity violence designed to extort Kashmir from India. This involved some serious crises and low–medium-intensity violence, which are discussed in the next chapter.

## Summary

This chapter's primary aim was to depict the escalation of crises in the India–Pakistan conflict during the pre-nuclear period. Of the seven crises that occurred during this period, three escalated to war, a remarkable number compared to the nuclear period when crises never escalated to war. The non-crisis period from 1979 to 1986 was the transition to nuclear weapons phase when the rivals were unsure of each other's nuclear capabilities and could not risk provoking a crisis. This phase is technically the most peaceful of the India–Pakistan protracted conflict since there was no war or crisis, unlike the pre-nuclear period – which witnessed crises and wars – and the nuclear period – which experienced serious and more frequent crises, as discussed in the following chapter.

# 7 Crises and non-escalation in the nuclear period

The India–Pakistan conflict survived seven inter-state crises and three wars in the pre-nuclear period, as discussed in the previous chapter, and faced four serious crises in the nuclear period, none of which escalated to full-scale war, although each had the potential to do so. In addition to these four crises, the conflict has witnessed continuous low–medium-intensity violence ever since the belligerents acquired nuclear weapons capability. The purpose of this chapter is to analyze the causal connection between nuclear weapons acquisition and the eruption of crises and continuation of violence in the conflict. This illustrates the disadvantages of possessing nuclear weapons. It also demonstrates the significance of the stability/instability paradox in the realm of conflict between nuclear states.

Crises in the nuclear period include the Brasstacks crisis of 1986–7, the Kashmir crisis of 1990, the Kargil crisis of 1999, and the Parliament Attack crisis of 2001–3. The intensity of these crises was medium since there was no-full scale war in any of them although they featured terrorism, proxy wars and low–medium-intensity violence strategies. Why the intensity of violence and the strategies of India and Pakistan in the nuclear period were different from those in the pre-nuclear period is an important question. Two important factors from the domestic and individual level of analysis, often used to understand strategy and foreign policy changes, are regime type and leadership change respectively. Although other domestic variables such as economic factors, cultural attributes, public opinion, domestic political needs, or bureaucratic reasons could all contribute to explaining the frequency of these crises, they cannot fully explain it for the simple reason that crises seem to be constant in the nuclear period. Economic necessity may compel a state to initiate a crisis to settle a long-term conflict, but economic needs are not constants, while crises seem to have been continuous. Economic problems may be the cause of a crisis but cannot explain the frequency or continuation of crises. According to the cultural explanation, borne out by empirical cross-cultural research, some cultures are more aggressive than others, so more likely to initiate crisis. For example, Americans are more prone to physical aggression than the Japanese.[1] Pakistanis may be more prone to aggression than Indians, but this explanation is inapplicable since it cannot explain why people from the same culture were not as aggression-prone in the pre-nuclear period. While public opinion can impose pressure on the government to solve bilateral issues through crises and violence, it is unclear why public opinion would be different in a pre-nuclear situation. And did Pakistan's non-democratic political elites ever care about public opinion?

Governments may want to divert people's attention from domestic troubles to international affairs, and wars are often used for this purpose. While this may explain the initiation of one specific crisis or one war, it is incapable of explaining the violence and proxy wars that became integral parts of the India–Pakistan protracted conflict. Nor can it explain the frequency of crises because the domestic situation changes all the time. The governments of Nawaz Sharif and General Pervez Musharraf faced different domestic problems. Bureaucratic factors could help to explain some of the crises, but do not shed light on why the Kargil crisis, one of the worst in the history of India–Pakistan, took place under a democratic Pakistani government when the military's role should have been less prominent. An additional point that should be mentioned is that the military would rather to wage war than live in a crisis-prone environment which does not demonstrate its superiority in technology and fighting skills. Although the regime type seems to be an important factor that may well explain Pakistan's initiation of crises, the important and serious Kargil crisis took place in the nuclear period between democratic states.

Leaders have a significant role in foreign policy-making and the Indian Prime Minister A. B. Vajpayee proved what a leadership change can mean when he decided to take the bus trip to Lahore in 1999 to reassure his country's arch-rival Pakistan, which had just tested its nuclear weapons in 1998 as a retaliatory measure against Indian nuclear tests. However, a study of the India–Pakistan crises reveals that leadership changes have made no difference to policy changes pertaining to crises. Pakistan's tendency to provoke crises has not changed with changes of ruler; nor have India's policies on reacting to these crises changed with changes of democratic leaders.

Thus, power/capability changes, a systemic attribute, must be considered for the light they shed on policy changes on crises and war in the nuclear period. The acquisition of nuclear weapons indicates a power change in the conflict which, in turn, is connected to policy changes by the two countries toward crisis initiation and crisis management techniques. The four serious crises and continuous low–medium-intensity violence during the nuclear period support the notion that crises in this period have changed in terms of frequency, continuity, protraction, intensity, and the strategies employed to address them. A detailed discussion of these crises and the general crisis-prone and violent environment is required.

## The Brasstacks crisis of 1986–7

In 1986, the Indian army under the leadership of General Sundarji conducted a massive military exercise codenamed "Brasstacks" in the Rajasthan desert. This was perceived as a crisis by Pakistan. Although it is believed that the operation was primarily "intended to test the readiness of the Indian army and its conventional deterrence strategy,"[2] and to convey a message to Pakistan to cease its support for the Sikh insurgency in Punjab,[3] as part of its action-reaction policy Pakistan deployed its armed forces. India responded by occupying defensive positions, turning the situation into an international crisis known as the Brasstacks crisis of 1986–7.[4] It is stated that "the size and the formation of the exercise were unprecedented."[5] In terms of manpower, equipment, the display of force, and the placing of additional ammunition close to the exercise area near the Pakistan border, this marked an intense crisis in the rivalry. The size and the location of the exercise alarmed Pakistan, which decided to boost its own routine military exercises, "Saf-e-Shikan" and "Flying Horse."[6] The problem did not end there. After the completion of their scheduled exercises the Pakistani forces did not return to their peacetime stations, but moved toward border positions in Punjab and Kashmir. This continued deployment of the Pakistani armored forces brought new anxiety for the Indians. They were concerned that

> first, the Pakistani forces were so arrayed that they could, in a pincer movement, cut off their Indian counterparts in strategic areas; second, a demonstration of force by Pakistan along sensitive border areas in Punjab could embolden the Khalistani terrorists, who might think they were to receive overt military support; and third, access to Kashmir could be interdicted by the Pakistani forces.[7]

Consequently, India, in response, also occupied forward positions in Punjab and Kashmir. By January 1987, the adversaries were facing each other in confrontational mode. Nonetheless, the leaders of the two countries managed "to deescalate without violence."[8] In fact, they used their diplomatic representatives, the High Commissioners, to convey their concerns and agreed in a telephone conversation to scale down the deployments and defuse tensions.[9]

The termination of the crisis without escalation was not easy. Rajiv Gandhi, the Indian Prime Minister, sent tough messages to Pakistan via its High Commissioner that India would take the required steps if Pakistani troops were not withdrawn promptly. This triggered a dialogue between General Sundarji of India and the Vice Chief of Army Staff of Pakistan. Additionally, the American Ambassador to India was contacted by the Indian Minister of State for Defense to inform him about India's concerns pertaining to Pakistani troop deployment, a message that was passed on to the Pakistanis. The American Ambassador also suggested to the Pakistanis that they start an open dialogue with the Indians to decrease the tension. Pakistan likewise conveyed its concerns about Indian troop deployment through the Indian High Commissioner S. K. Singh. All this led to several talks and meetings, and proposals were exchanged on how to defuse the crisis and design confidence and security-building measures with a view to avoiding such crises in the future.[10] This de-escalation process demonstrates prudence on the part of the leaders of the two states and seems too good to be true in context of the India–Pakistan conflict relations. Given how easily crises had escalated in the pre-nuclear period, de-escalation without even violence when war seemed imminent would probably have been impossible in the absence of nuclear weapons.

The nuclear dimension to the crisis explains a lot more than any other factor.

Some people have argued that there was some power asymmetry in conventional weapons in favor of Pakistan at the time of the Brasstacks crisis, which dissuaded India from escalating it. Although the overall military balance was in India's favor, Pakistan had some qualitative advantages because of its newly acquired aircraft and other military equipment given by the US for assistance in the Afghanistan war, and this inhibited India from making war plans.[11] While this may be true to some extent, it is difficult to prove that Pakistani military advantage was the driving force behind Indian restraint. Had there been no nuclear dimension, this argument would have received a great deal of prominence because after all a war is waged with capabilities and military strength and the balance of capability is the first calculation a state makes before making a war plan. Given the existence of nuclear weapons in the conflict, the argument of conventional asymmetry carries less conviction. Nor did the US play a major role in defusing the crisis. It primarily tried to "dampen the development of a conflict spiral based upon incomplete information, misperception, and mutual distrust ... the American role was salutary."[12] Given the inadequacies of these factors in explaining the de-escalation of the crisis, the role of nuclear weapons must be considered.

An analysis of the nuclear dimension of the crisis does not deny the fact that the diplomatic path was explored by prudent policy-makers, but underscores the question of why diplomatic means were used to defuse a crisis that had so much potential for escalation. As stated in the previous chapter, India and Pakistan were on the verge of developing nuclear weapons in 1986, and the period 1979–86 witnessed a "transition to nuclear weapons status." By 1987, Pakistan's possession of nuclear capability was not unknown to the Indians. However, to rule out any confusion, Pakistan, at the height of the Brasstacks crisis, sent clear information to India that it had acquired nuclear weapons through an interview its chief nuclear scientist, Abdul Qader Khan, gave to a prominent Indian journalist, Kuldip Nayar, organized by Mushahid Hussain, the editor of the Pakistani newspaper the *Muslim*. In the interview Khan stated, "Nobody can undo Pakistan or take us for granted. We are here to stay and let it be clear that we shall use the bomb if our existence is threatened."[13] That was the first time any Pakistani scientist or leader had mentioned the existence of a nuclear bomb and it was a clear signal from Pakistan to India on the use of nuclear weapons if conventional deterrence failed. Khan primarily confirmed that "the US Central Intelligence Agency's assessment that Pakistan possessed nuclear weapons capability was correct."[14] After the crisis, Hussain claimed that A. Q. Khan's message was "directed against those detractors of the Islamic bomb. To the Indians, it was a 'hands-off' message at a time when New Delhi has been carrying out massive warlike exercises all along our eastern border."[15]

Some doubt has been cast on the importance of the nuclear dimension in defusing the crisis on the grounds that tension was about to end when the interview was held.[16] However, a few points must be noted. First, the Indian armed forces were placed on operational alert on January 23 and the interview was on January 28,[17] just a few days after the Pakistanis realized that the crisis could escalate to war. Then Pakistan's Foreign Secretary, Abdul Sattar, arrived in New Delhi on

January 30, two days after the interview, for five days of discussions on de-escalating the crisis, and the first troop withdrawal took place on February 11–19, 1987.[18] So the timing of the interview does seem relevant to the de-escalation. Of course the interview was not published until March 1, 1987,[19] but the publication was less important than the interview itself. It was given in order to break the news to Indian policy-makers rather than to the general public who would be informed by the media. Second, even if the interview was simply Pakistan's last chance to send a tough signal, India already knew that some form of deterrence had been operating between the two states since they each became aware of the other's nuclear capabilities.[20] J. N. Dixit argues that although India had known about Pakistan's possession of nuclear weapons since 1983–4, the publication of Nayar's interview in the Indian, Pakistani, and foreign media made it a "sensational revelation."[21] In a world where nuclear weapons acquisition was shrouded in secrecy, statements of this nature were used to inform adversaries of the possession of nuclear capabilities and the intent to use them if necessary.[22] Dixit argues that Pakistan had already tried to use Indian journalists "to generate dissension in Indian policies and where possible to scare or frighten India."[23] He continues, "It is now generally acknowledged that the interview was an orchestrated attempt at coercive diplomacy by Zia,"[24] who was confident that the declaration would not have serious negative consequences at a time when the US needed Pakistan's assistance in the war in Afghanistan against the Soviets. A few years later, the Indian report on the Kargil crisis observed that the Pakistani government believed that "[Pakistan's] nuclear capability would forestall any major Indian move, particularly across the international border, involving use of India's larger conventional capabilities. [Pakistan] appears to have persuaded itself that nuclear deterrence had worked in its favor from the mid-1980s."[25] In sum, the de-escalation of the 1986–7 Brasstacks crisis was primarily a function of the nuclear dynamics that had worked in the conflict since the mid-1980s.

## The Kashmir crisis of 1990

Just two years after the de-escalation of the Brasstacks crisis, the India–Pakistan conflict was beset by low–medium-intensity violence owing to renewed insurgency in Kashmir (discussed on p. 73). During the violence, a new crisis erupted in 1990 when "an indigenous insurrection in the Kashmir valley, quickly backed by Pakistan, threatened to provoke a war between India and Pakistan."[26] As the conflict escalated, Pakistan's Prime Minister Benazir Bhutto proclaimed the Kashmiris' right to self-determination and some high-level politicians threatened *jihad* and suggested using nuclear bombs if India waged war on Pakistan.[27] According to some reports, at this point India and Pakistan were on the verge of nuclear war[28] in what is sometimes called their "Nuclear Crisis."[29]

According to Seymour Hersh, quoting a reliable intelligence report to Washington, Pakistan's chief of armed forces General Aslam Beg had authorized technicians at the Kahuta Research Laboratories to assemble nuclear weapons and use them at the proper time; as the crisis intensified with the build-up of Indian conventional forces in Kashmir and Rajasthan, Pakistan "openly deployed its armored tank units along the Indian border and, secretly, placed its nuclear weapons arsenal on alert."[30] General Beg has strongly refuted this allegation, denying that Pakistan mobilized its aircraft or nuclear capabilities during the crisis. He claims that in the 1990 crisis Pakistan was not in a desperate situation in which it would have to use nuclear weapons. He says the crisis started when the Kashmiris revolted against the Indian government, creating tension and confrontation along the line of control, with increasing outbreaks of gunfire. The Indians accused Pakistan of instigating the events and so tension built up between them, but neither side had mobilized its troops. Under the circumstances Pakistan had no need to ready its nuclear weapons, which it would only do "in a desperate situation where capitulation is a possibility or defeat is expected,"[31] neither of which pertained in 1990. In fact, this crisis demonstrates the functioning of non-traditional nuclear deterrence between India and Pakistan at a time when their nuclear status was undeclared and when communication of intentions was not transparent.[32] Pakistan had already acquired its nuclear capability by then and India had been made fully aware of it through various sources, including the media and intelligence community reports. Devin Hagerty states that whereas in 1987 Indian leaders considered Pakistan to be "an aspiring nuclear weapon state," in 1990 they perceived it as "an actual nuclear weapon state."[33] According to George Perkovich, by 1988–90 Pakistan had acquired the capability to assemble nuclear weapons,[34] and this was confirmed by Pakistan's President Zia-ul-Haq in an interview to *Time* in 1987 in which he stated that "Pakistan can build a bomb whenever it wishes," because it had acquired the technology to do so.[35] India had also reached an advanced stage of nuclear capability. Perkovich comments, "devices were made that could be turned into weapons if India was attacked."[36] All this was understood. The then Indian Army Chief General Sundarji stated, "Any sensible planner sitting on this side of the border is going to assume Pakistan does indeed have nuclear weapons capability. And by the same token, I rather suspect the view from the other side is going to look very similar."[37] Although there was "a significant possibility of war between India and Pakistan in 1990 . . . no decision-maker in New Delhi, Islamabad, or Washington could entirely rule out the possibility that such a war might escalate to a nuclear exchange,"[38] a fact that inhibited India and Pakistan from escalating the crisis to war. Sumit Ganguly and Devin Hagerty argue that in the absence of the possibility of escalation to nuclear war, "India would have been much more likely to punish Pakistan for its transgression in Kashmir."[39] Agreeing with this reasoning, K. Subrahmanyam observed:

> In 1965, Pakistanis sent 5000 armed intruders into Kashmir. We dealt with them and they continued to send . . . more. The Indian army crossed the cease-fire line and hit the areas . . . that escalated into the 1965 war. Now . . . for seven years, India has not crossed the cease-fire line. Therefore, [it shows] the chances of war occurring between India and Pakistan are low . . . compared to what happened in 1965 and 1971. This is because of Pakistan's nuclear weapons capability. It is quite obvious that there is not likely to be any war

between India and Pakistan now, unless one or the other is going to cross the line of control at the frontier.[40]

Simply put, the crisis de-escalated without war because the two sides had nuclear weapons.

The de-escalation could be attributed to the Gates mission, sent by the United States to defuse the potentially nuclear India–Pakistan crisis. Whereas Robert Gates, the US Deputy National Security Council Advisor, could not have stopped India and Pakistan from fighting a conventional war had they decided to do so, in fact they treated the "Gates mission as a face-saving mechanism to pull back from a brink over which they had already decided not to go."[41] In a nuclear-free conflict, India would have used its conventional military capability to launch a punishing attack on Pakistan. Ganguly and Hagerty believe that the Gates mission would probably not have been sent if the belligerents had not acquired nuclear weapons capabilities.[42] In 1990 the cold war had just ended and the US had little interest in regional matters when it had to consider important systemic changes with serious policy implications. Ganguly and Hagerty's point is important for two reasons. First, they show that whereas the Gates mission may have been the secondary cause of peace, the primary one was nuclear weapons. Second, one of Pakistan's motives for provoking crises in its conflict with India in the nuclear era has been to draw international, especially US, attention (as stated in chapter 6). This substantiates the theoretical propositions of this study. The acquisition of nuclear weapons by the two states has created deterrence, forced the US to become involved in de-escalating potentially serious nuclear crises, and provided Pakistan with the opportunity to create crises in which it may make small territorial gains, and, more importantly, to internationalize the Kashmir issue against Indian wishes.

## The Kargil crisis of 1999

From 1990 to 1999 the India–Pakistan conflict witnessed low–medium intensity violence in Kashmir and mutual hostility increased, not surprisingly given Pakistan's constant assistance to the insurgents and India's constant accusations that Pakistan was supporting cross-border terrorism and orchestrating proxy wars and violence in the valley. According to Russell Leng, sporadic low-level hostilities began in 1984 and continued into the late 1990s.[43] However, there was no major crisis during this nine-year period, primarily because after the 1990 crisis when Pakistan's nuclear capability was made known to the Americans, who no longer needed Pakistan's assistance following the end of the Afghanistan war, the US cut off its security and military assistance to Pakistan, creating a conventional power asymmetry between India and Pakistan. However, in May 1998, as India tested its nuclear weapons and Pakistan followed suit, the India–Pakistan conflict changed in remarkable ways. After the shock felt by each side at the other's nuclear tests, the situation between the belligerents calmed down although there was world condemnation and sanctions were imposed on the two countries. The relationship even appeared amicable from late 1998, with the Indian Prime Minister's visit to

Lahore and the signing of the Lahore Declaration, which provided for confidence-building measures. It was felt that the India–Pakistan conflict was on the road to some kind of peace, if not full resolution. Unfortunately, between early May and mid-July India and Pakistan resumed hostilities in what is known as the "Kargil crisis," which, as stated earlier, is often called the fourth war between India and Pakistan due to the intensity of the fighting.[44] In the words of Jasjit Singh, "Kargil was an armed conflict between two military forces. It was a war from that perspective. Two militaries fought in a localized region."[45] He continues, "a limited war is possible – it has happened before – and will happen again."[46] Kargil caused more than 1000 battle-related deaths.[47] However, to the Pakistanis, it was a "major military skirmish."[48] Nasim Zehra states that "the scale, engagement, the level of deployment" all prove that Kargil was not a fourth war between India and Pakistan,[49] and alleges that India needed to project it as a fourth war and indeed the level of the Indian response made it look like one.[50] In reality, this was also just another crisis in the nuclear era, where both sides used limited-aims strategy, even though India used air power for the first time since 1971. That the crisis wound down without a full-scale inter-state war requires explanation.

Just one year after the nuclear tests, Pakistan triggered the crisis by intruding into the heights of Kargil in the spring of 1999, conducting a medium-intensity operation, a new strategy. While Islamabad hoped to capture the heights without a fight and present New Delhi and the international community with a *fait accompli*, it was ready for a medium-intensity operation. In the Kargil episode, Pakistan's professional military acted as *mujahidin*, moving into Indian territory. This intrusion and seizure of the Kargil heights on the Indian side of the line of control (LOC) in Kashmir caused the most serious fighting between Indian and Pakistani armed forces since the last war in 1971. It is believed that Pakistan carried out nuclear tests before provoking this serious crisis in the India–Pakistan conflict theater.[51] India became aware of the crisis when its intelligence services discovered Pakistani regular forces lodged in mountain redoubts on the Indian side of the line of control.[52] For Pakistan, the crisis began when, against its expectations, India responded with full military vigor. For the next two months intense fighting continued between the two armed forces. The Indian armed units attacked the Pakistani forces and Indian air force jets bombed their bases high in the Himalayan peaks. However, the Indian forces stayed on their side of the line of control.[53] Three important questions must be answered. First, why did Kargil start when the India–Pakistan conflict was in a state of detente with the beginning of the Lahore Peace Process? Second, what strategies were used by both states to make it a unique and intense crisis short of war in the nuclear era? Third, why did the crisis de-escalate without a full-scale war? The answers to these questions will underscore the significance of the stability/instability paradox in the nuclear era, in consequence of which Pakistan initiated the crisis.

Many observers see Kargil as the result of a combination of factors including fragmented decision-making, changes in the military leadership, strategic opportunity, and the prospect of losing out in Kashmir.[54] Pakistan had reacted with anxiety to India's efforts prior to the crisis to convince the international community that it had addressed human rights issues in Kashmir, held fair elections there, and was ready to restore law and order, consolidating its own position.[55] Pakistan's decision-makers concluded that they had to revive insurgency if they were to have any future role in the problems of Kashmir. While the decision-makers were split on these points, the military saw strategic advantages in the incursions into Kargil which, they thought, could compensate for their setbacks in Kashmir. The importance of the change in military leadership cannot be overestimated. Kargil was the "brain-child" of General Pervez Musharraf, then the army chief of Pakistan. It is believed that Musharraf withheld a lot of his strategic plans from Pakistan's democratically elected Prime Minister Nawaz Sharif. Scott Sagan writes, "Although Prime Minister Nawaz Sharif apparently approved the plan to move forces across the line of control, it is not clear that he was fully briefed on the nature, scope, or potential consequences of the operation."[56] The question is: Would Musharraf have undertaken this endeavor in the absence of nuclear weapons? It is argued that the Pakistani military planned the Kargil operation in late 1998 and focused on "the tactical effects of a surprise military maneuver," but this belief was based on "the logic of what has been called the 'stability/instability paradox' – that a 'stable nuclear balance' between India and Pakistan permitted more offensive actions to take place with impunity in Kashmir."[57] After the Indian and Pakistani nuclear tests, the military on both sides believed that full-scale conventional war could not happen in the conflict.[58] The Pakistani perspective was that nuclear tests had "reduced the risk that limited military hostilities would escalate to a general war."[59] According to Daniel Geller, empirical evidence supports the view that nuclear crises escalate to higher levels short of war than conventional ones.[60] If this is so, limited conventional wars can occur when there is a nuclear shield.

The nuclear factor was the primary driving force behind the initiation of the crisis. To understand the reasons for Kargil, Russell Leng states that "the new environment created by the nuclear tests in 1998 encouraged Pakistan to launch the Kargil operation on the assumption that India would not respond by attacking across the LoC at a strategically more favorable location."[61] The Pakistanis believed that fear of a full-scale conventional war escalating to the nuclear level would inhibit India from expanding the limited war. Kargil was primarily a typical attempt by the weaker state in a conflict to address the issue in dispute by making a limited probe to demonstrate its will and commitment to fight and defend its territory.[62] Limited territorial gains represented the central goal of the Pakistanis in this crisis. This is typical of the strategy whereby the weaker party in a conflict provokes crises in a nuclear environment in which full-scale war is unlikely. The nuclear weapons tests gave Pakistan enough confidence to embark on this endeavor. Samina Ahmed argues that "nuclear weapons played a major role in shaping Pakistan's military strategy toward India in the planning of the Kargil episode and during the onset of the crisis."[63]

With respect to the strategies used by both sides, Kargil is a unique crisis in the India–Pakistan relationship. At the tactical level, Kargil was a typical limited probe involving a small, carefully controlled incursion along the LoC, in which Pakistan thought it would be able to reverse course if it met firm Indian resistance.[64] After

Pakistan started the incursions, when it met no opposition from the Indian side, it expanded the scope of the probe. This meant India now had to respond with vigor and strong resolve. Expanding the scope of the incursion was Pakistan's greatest mistake. "As the fighting in Kargil escalated, Pakistani military planners remained firm in their belief that India would be deterred by Pakistan's nuclear weapons."[65] In the escalation phase, the Indian air force used combat air power in the high mountain ranges above 15,000 feet in altitude. Pakistan, for its part, deployed large numbers of surface-to-air missiles and air defense weaponry in the battlefield across the LoC on the Indian side. Subrahmanyam states, "In Kargil, Pakistan thought they were being smart. They thought they had advantages. They, however, didn't have the infrastructure. Once India started escalation, they found that the Pakistanis lacked the infrastructure."[66] Thus, the Indians could have used their advantage and escalated further, but they did not. The Indian army did not cross the LoC, it is believed, for fear of the conflict escalating to the nuclear level.[67] Subrahmanyam gives the Indian version of Kargil: "Nuclear deterrence operated [in Kargil] and the Pakistanis say that. We don't think that it was a major factor, but a factor anyway."[68] Both India and Pakistan concentrated on waging a limited conventional war, focused on the Kargil area, rather than spreading it to areas along the LoC where India had the advantage, making the crisis unique in the India–Pakistan conflict. According to the Indian government's Kargil Review Committee Report, the Pakistani operation was "a typical case of salami slicing," a cold war term for attempts to make small territorial gains that are unlikely to prompt the other side to risk military escalation leading to full-scale war, perhaps even nuclear.[69]

The de-escalation of the Kargil crisis, after it had reached an intensity to escalate to full-scale war, needs to be explained. A salient factor which can be backed up with evidence is the intervention of the US. It is undeniable that the Clinton administration was worried about a nuclear confrontation between the new nuclear states, India and Pakistan, over the Kargil crisis. Prior to the episode, there had been widespread speculation that the nuclear tests by the states in conflict made South Asia a "nuclear flashpoint." The Pakistanis expected US intervention, but of a different kind. They thought the US would pressure India not to escalate the crisis, given the nuclear environment, if it looked likely to do so.[70] This expectation was largely based on the overt nuclearization of the region, which made any disputes there the object of special concern for the international community. In fact The US pressured the government of Nawaz Sharif to de-escalate as fast as possible. The possibility of a nuclear war made the Americans persuade India and Pakistan to end Kargil. Some believe that

> Pakistan flashed its signal of nuclear preparedness during Kargil. India signaled as well. Part of the reason why this de-escalated fast was because of the nuclear weapons. After everybody expected that the war would go on till September, it stopped abruptly. Sharif agreed to it. Ground reasons were also there. All-out war was a possibility, but nuclear weapons deterred it. General S. Padmanabhan indicated that Pakistan was in a state of nuclear readiness. There was a nuclear element in that war.[71]

The warring parties refrained from escalating the crisis even before US pressure to de-escalate. The Indians understood that a full-scale war would be disastrous for both states and de-escalated the crisis without a war.

The primary lesson India took from Kargil was that it had to be prepared to confront Pakistan over such limited probes in the future. Kenneth Waltz believes that Kargil proved that "deterrence does not firmly protect disputed areas but does limit the extent of the violence."[72] In a similar vein, Indian Rear Admiral Raja Menon stated, "The Kargil crisis demonstrated that the subcontinental nuclear threshold probably lies territorially in the heartland of both countries, and not on the Kashmir cease-fire line."[73] Major General Srivastava states that in

> Kargil, for example, both were nuclear states – we with bigger army, tanks, etc. said [to Pakistan] that you attacked and now we will take you on. If you enlarge it we will. But the war was in Kargil only. It did not even spread into the valley – Jammu and Kashmir. That was the last nail in the coffin.[74]

However, the Indians have started to realize that limited wars may not only be fought but also won. S. D. Muni argues that "limited war is still a possibility between India and Pakistan and can be won."[75] Thus, nuclear weapons are "deterrents with constraints."[76] This belief that the use of the military force must be limited in the India–Pakistan conflict theater made India realize that new strategies must be developed to face the new kind of medium-intensity conflicts with Pakistan, based on conventional war remaining limited in terms of escalation. Ganguly states, "One such strategy would involve attacking in a wide band along the international border without making deep incursions into Pakistani territory," triggering a similar Pakistani response, with the aim of capturing as much territory as possible along border areas and using them "as bargaining chips for Pakistani concessions in Kashmir."[77] What strategy will be used by India in a future crisis like Kargil remains to be seen. For now it is believed that full-scale war is a thing of the past and stability prevails in the conflict realm.

After the Kargil crisis wound down in July 1999, the next two years saw India–Pakistan relations flare up over Kashmir every once in a while. But exactly two years after the crisis a new peace initiative was taken by the Pakistani President Pervez Musharraf, the same man who orchestrated Kargil. General Musharraf visited India in July 2001 with a view to establishing more confidence-building measures although this was unsuccessful. However, the pattern of crises in the nuclear India–Pakistan conflict continued even after this peace overture. A new crisis was triggered in December 2001, illustrating the notion that stability at the war level breeds instability at the crisis level,[78] generating and maintaining hostility in the conflict.

## The Indian Parliament Attack crisis of 2001

With the international community focused on the terrorist attacks on the United States of September 2001 and the threat of terrorism mounting, a new crisis faced

India when terrorists attacked the Indian Parliament – a symbol of democracy – on December 13, 2001. Six terrorists believed to be part of the Lashkar-e-Taiba group attacked the Indian Parliament building in the capital, New Delhi, and a gun battle started between the security forces and the attackers. It ended with death of all six attackers along with eight members of the Indian security forces. The attack was unacceptable to the Indian government and the general public and reminded them of the attack on the Jammu and Kashmir State Legislature on October 1, 2001, in which at least twenty-six people were killed,[79] which was orchestrated by this and other terrorist groups. On December 14, 2001, the Indian government made a connection between the attack and Lashkar-e-Taiba, and claimed that the group had acted on behalf of Pakistan.[80] It made three specific demands to Pakistan: ban the two terrorist groups – Lashka-e-Taiba and Jaish-e-Mohammed – because they were responsible for two major attacks on India – on the Jammu and Kashmir Legislature and on the Indian Parliament; extradite twenty individuals, who, according to India, had been involved in terrorist activities on Indian soil; stop cross-border terrorism and infiltration of insurgents into Kashmir.[81] India also began significant troop mobilization, triggering a crisis for Pakistan which began its own troop mobilization. India deployed about 800,000 troops along the border, while Pakistan responded by similar deployments. The resulting intense hostility between them lasted for more than eighteen months. This was the longest crisis the conflict has ever witnessed. South Asia was considered a nuclear flashpoint because the belligerents were unwilling to budge from their respective positions for any length of time. India reiterated that it would only pull its troops out on one condition – Pakistan must stop supporting the terrorists. Pakistan proclaimed its innocence but seemed prepared for an eventual military confrontation. However, even this protracted crisis de-escalated without major war.

Responding to the demand that it should stop cross-border terrorism, Islamabad claimed, first, that India's accusation was false. But what does cross-border terrorism mean? In Mushahid Hussain's words, "It is not terrorism, it is a freedom uprising. One could say it is a cross the LoC. It happened due to Indian brutality. We should support them as it is a genuine cause."[82] He further states that the insurgency began as a "popular, spontaneous, indigenous and widespread movement."[83] Second, there was the question of who should decide whether or not Pakistan was supporting cross-border terrorism. Pervaiz Iqbal Cheema asked, "If we stop cross-border terrorism, who determines that? Why not have a third-party monitor [it]? Ask the South Asian Association for Regional Cooperation (SAARC) to do that."[84] India had always refused to allow any third party to be part of this bilateral conflict, so the question of monitoring by a third party was never discussed by the two states. Third, Pakistan wanted a simultaneous discussion on cross-border terrorism and Kashmir.[85] A year after the crisis de-escalated, Aga Shahi stated,

Vajpayee says he wants talks with us. At the same time he makes it conditional on ending cross-border terrorism. We have done our best. India tries to dictate us. We cannot give up our stand on Kashmir. We do not support cross-border terrorism, but we are incapable of stopping it.[86]

This raises the important question of what Pakistan can and should do to manage the terrorists. Pakistan felt that these were genuine points and concerns, which India was unwilling to discuss.

Many people felt that the situation in December 2001 could have led to all-out war, had nuclear weapons not existed. Indian and Pakistani troops remained in Kashmir for more than a year, but the situation did not escalate. This proves that nuclear weapons had created deterrence.[87] Hussain stated in 2002, "We came closer to a war last year than Kargil."[88] He further states that the Kargil incursion was limited to within 70 kilometers of the line of control and did not go across the international border.[89] Another typical comment is "If it was pre-1980, this would have been a war. There is resistance and disinterest to wage a war today due to nuclear weapons."[90] Singh stated, "The responses can't be like 1965 now on the part of India. They have put a ceiling on the level of escalation. There is no further level beyond that."[91] Amitabh Mattoo concurs: "Nuclear weapons reveal to them [the two states] that they can't fight a war. Once it happens, you have to think about everything short of war."[92]

Others have argued, however, that war was a real possibility. Diplomatic and economic means had been used to deter war as long ago as 1971, but not in 1999 because there was no time one "morning India woke up to see that the Pakistanis are in Kashmir."[93] Thus nuclear weapons had not created a special situation in which avenues other than war were first explored to resolve the crisis. However, the de-escalation was the result of a cautious decision taken by Indian policy-makers. The Indian Prime Minister told the Indian Parliament as early as December 19, 2001, when the crisis had just become heated, "There can be no hasty decision in choosing between war and peace. We must be patient and take a comprehensive view of all options."[94] Similarly, the former army chief stated, "There is a limit to which counterterrorist operations can be intensified. The government will have to understand that this could lead to horizontal escalation and a full-blown conventional conflict."[95] The question then arises: Why did India mobilize 800,000 troops during the crisis? Subrahmanyam argues that India had to mobilize troops in such a crisis, but realized its threshold. He stated, "Military moves would be counterproductive. To put pressure on Pakistan was the reason for Indian troop mobilization."[96]

Just two weeks after the Parliament Attack, Vice Admiral K. K. Nayyar stated, "Pakistan must roll back its terrorist position or we will raise the cost for them."[97] He meant costs of three types: (1) diplomatic – recalling the High Commissioner; (2) economic – banning flights and a range of economic measures to wreck exports of cotton and rice markets; and (3) military – indulging in hot pursuit. Military force was seen as an option,[98] but placed lowest in the hierarchy of steps. In fact, India took two major non-military steps: recalling its High Commissioner from Pakistan and stopping transportation links between the two states. Muchkund Dubey described the Indian government's position as the following: "Let Pakistan feel that its action of facilitating infiltration has heavy costs, but non-military initiatives have to be taken on account of nuclear weapons."[99] In S. K. Singh's view, military measures would be used only if consistent diplomatic and economic pressure did not work. More importantly, they would be taken to induce China and the US to put pressure on to Pakistan to retreat and give up its terrorist activities.[100] The Parliament Attack was a significant crisis which gave India the opportunity to put pressure on Pakistan to eliminate terrorism.[101] Thus whereas it had been Pakistan which had always wanted US intervention in the conflict, now India realized that the US might help it control Pakistan's support for terrorism in Kashmir. While India may never have initiated a crisis to engage the US in the India–Pakistan conflict, in a changed world environment where the US had also been a victim of terrorism, India realized that the US would sympathize with its endeavours to uproot terrorism. The former Indian Prime Minister I. K. Gujral commented, in the context of possible US involvement in the crisis, "I don't see war among us [between India and Pakistan]."[102] He continued, "With the end of the cold war, war will take place only where America permits it."[103] This may be so, but why should the US be more concerned to stop India and Pakistan from escalating their crises now than it was in the 1970s and early 1980s? Primarily because the west now considers South Asia to be a zone where nuclear war could be waged between democratic India and non-democratic Pakistan. As Rasheed Khalid states,

> Because of nuclear weapons the situation is alarming to the international community. The sole superpower doesn't sit back and relax. It puts pressure on us. That is what nuclear weapons did in South Asia. Americans come into action as soon as a crisis starts.[104]

This should not come as a surprise to the Pakistanis. As stated earlier, Pakistan has initiated crises in order to internationalize the conflict and attract the attention of the US, and has done so successfully. Ahmed argues that Pakistan has often used "nuclear weapons as an instrument of diplomatic bargaining, persuading influential external actors such as the United States to intervene."[105] The reason behind this strategy is simple. According to the Kargil Report, Pakistan did not interpret the Simla Agreement in the same way as India, and never accepted the aspect of "bilateralism." Therefore, "it is no surprise that Pakistan subsequently stepped up its efforts to internationalize the Kashmir issue and seek third-party intervention, projecting the LoC as a temporary arrangement."[106]

The west has long feared that the continuing: crisis between India and Pakistan could make South Asia a nuclear flashpoint. However, the Indians never believed nuclear weapons would be used to end the crisis. As K. Santhanam put it in early 2002, "Everyone is talking about a nuclear flash-point. . . . We are not two crazy countries who would embark on nuclear war just like that."[107] Bhabani Sen Gupta gave a good reason why nuclear weapons would not be used in a limited war such as India and Pakistan waged in Kargil: "If there is a war between India and Pakistan and it is confined within Kashmir and it doesn't become an international war, the use of nuclear weapons becomes even more suicidal."[108] Several steps have to be crossed to reach the nuclear threshold. As Jasjit Singh puts it, "Conflict has to erupt into a conventional war. Vital territory must be lost or major military force must be lost for it to reach the nuclear war level."[109] Territorial conquest is no longer the aim of war as it used to be in the past, so war in Kashmir would be confined to Kashmir, in which case nuclear weapons would have no use other than for political bargaining. Asked under what conditions Pakistan would use its nuclear weapons, Cheema answered, "Whenever our survival is at stake we will not hesitate to use everything – including nuclear weapons."[110] Pakistan's survival was not at stake in the Parliament Attack crisis, so the use of nuclear weapons was not in question.

The four crises of the nuclear period show that a universally accepted definition of crisis needs to be changed. When states have nuclear weapons, wars do not happen, so crisis can no longer be defined as meaning a "heightened probability of war." "Heightened probability of war" should be replaced by "heightened probability of low–medium-intensity violence short of actual war" in the case of nuclear weapons states.

In addition to these four crises, the India–Pakistan conflict was afflected by low-intensity violence from the late 1980s. Studies suggest that the insurgency in Kashmir had its origin in Pakistan. Lawrence Saez maintains,

> It is undeniable that several radical pan-Islamic insurgent groups operating in Kashmir have their operational roots in Pakistan. These radical fundamentalist organizations are broadly split between those that seek to liberate Kashmir from India and then either remain independent or annex it to Pakistan and those that have more ambitious goals of spreading a jihad.[111]

The goal of an insurgency operation

> was to annex the state of J&K [Jammu and Kashmir] through a proxy war by infiltrating militants to foment trouble in the state under the garb of a jihad, take militancy to uncontrollable levels, and at an opportune time, strike with regulars, if necessary, to finally integrate J&K with Pakistan.[112]

The goal has remained unchanged for a protracted period, even though it may never be achieved.

## Summary

This chapter has demonstrated the connection between four major crises of the nuclear period and the possession of nuclear weapons by India and Pakistan. The continuous low-intensity violence in the conflict theater in this period was also a result of the two states' acquisition of nuclear weapons. All four crises were shown to have been initiated by Pakistan once escalation had ceased to be a possibility. India became reluctant to escalate for fear of a conventional full-scale war turning nuclear. The weaker side initiated crises mainly so as to make small territorial gains and draw the international community, especially the United States, into conflict resolution. As expected, The US intervened owing to fear of nuclear escalation, but limited its role to defusing crises and pressuring the parties to start dialogue.

# 8 Futile peace initiatives in the midst of violence

Nuclear weapons in the hands of India and Pakistan have delivered stability in terms of war and instability in terms of crisis, as shown in the previous two chapters. The frequent eruption of crises and at times continuing lower levels of violence have made it difficult to initiate a peace process or consolidate one that has been initiated. This chapter aims to demonstrate the negative impact of crises on peace initiatives, a consequence of nuclear weapons acquisition. The period of study is from 1998 to 2007–8, the declared nuclear period. Two important peace initiatives are discussed and analyzed with a view to highlighting the good intentions of the initiators and their ultimate failure owing to the eruption of a new crisis in the conflict setting.

The consequences of this stability/instability paradox are grave for the conflict relationship. War is the ultimate instrument used by states to end conflicts. As war is no longer available for this purpose where there are nuclear weapons, other means must be employed. However, other means, especially dialogue and diplomatic negotiations, can be used only if the conflict relationship is not in crisis (as discussed on p. 86). Instability in the relationship draws out the conflict. In other words, if crises erupt frequently because war does not occur, as seems to be the case in South Asia, then the conflict experiences instability, which is not conducive to settlement. Thus conflict is unlikely to be resolved if crisis is a constant factor. Eqbal Ahmed states that "since war is not an option, Pakistan's policy is reduced to bleeding India; and India's to bleeding the Kashmiris, and to hit out at Pakistan whenever a wound can be inflicted."[1] Additionally, if crises erupt frequently, then the two parties are constantly engaged in some form of violence and are never "free from the psychological legacy of an ongoing conflict."[2] Their mutual hatred is reflected in official statements and policies, which disturbs the relationship further.

The India–Pakistan protracted conflict is in the escalation phase and most often experiences a medium degree of intensification due to frequent low–medium-intensity crises. However, the degree of intensification also fluctuates, sometimes dropping to low intensity when a crisis ends. However, policy-makers cannot seize the opportunity to start a negotiating process because of the adverse legacy of the prior crisis. Then another crisis erupts before a peace process can start. For example, the Kargil crisis jeopardized the Lahore Peace Process, initiated by the Indian Prime Minister A. B. Vajpayee in February 1999, which had resulted in one of the strongest confidence-building measures between the parties in conflict. Just three months after the signing of the Lahore Declaration, some of the most serious fighting since 1971 took place in Kargil. However, although the general feeling in South Asia was that the leaders would not take another initiative to settle their differences, in 2001 the Indian Prime Minister invited the Pakistani President Pervez Musharraf to a summit meeting in Agra. While the results were not satisfactory,[3] both parties expressed their interest in continuing the dialogue. But within just five months, the Indian Parliament was attacked by terrorists and India immediately accused Pakistan of having involvement. The two countries then deployed their forces along the line of control (LoC) and almost severed diplomatic ties (see pp. 111–12). India and Pakistan cancelled their airline connections and recalled their diplomats. The world feared a nuclear war between them since the situation deteriorated day by day. While prudent policies not to escalate the crisis to war were taken, it was more than a year before the two countries finally decided to move their heavy forces away from the borders. Although the crisis de-escalated, the conflict cannot start to de-escalate in such a crisis-prone environment. Many in India are dissatisfied not only with the Pakistani government but also with their own government for its patience with Pakistan.[4] Public opinion in India since the Parliament Attack has been very negative towards Pakistan, making it impossible for a democratic Indian government to initiate a new round of negotiations. Similarly, Pakistanis were unhappy because their country was blamed for every internal crisis in India. Thus even if peace initiatives are taken with good intentions, they are jeopardized by a new crisis. Rivals go back to their war-prone mentalities, hatred resurfaces, and the conflict is further protracted. A discussion of the efforts to make peace in the crisis-prone India–Pakistan of the nuclear period shows why they are doomed to failure.

## The Lahore Peace Process and after

Hostility between India and Pakistan increased after the May 1998 nuclear tests because a new round of the nuclear arms race had begun. The international community condemned both countries for conducting the tests and imposed economic sanctions on them. Although India and Pakistan believed that the tests had in fact reduced the likelihood of war between them, the international community was not willing to accept this logic, given their conflict-prone history. Some in the west believed that there was an increased risk of a nuclear war between them.[5] Nevertheless, the prime ministers of India and Pakistan met in Colombo, Sri Lanka, that July and again in New York in September 1998 with a view to resuming bilateral peace talks. This was followed by the first round of a composite dialogue in October 1998 when the foreign secretaries met in Islamabad and peace and security, confidence-building measures, cooperation, and Jammu and Kashmir were discussed. Sumit Ganguly attributes the leaders' decision to initiate this dialogue to world condemnation and sanctions.[6] This seems quite plausible, given the fragile nature of the dialogue leading to the peace process. If dialogues are initiated by the contending parties of their own free will, perhaps a new and more intense crisis would not always erupt a few months later, and the peace process would not be jeopardized. At the October 1998 meeting it was agreed to start a bus service between Delhi and Lahore from February 1999. In December 1998, when Pakistan's Prime Minister Nawaz Sharif visited the United States and asked America to intervene in the Kashmir problem, President Clinton explained that the US would only become involved with the agreements of both parties. Clinton stated, "The US can be effective . . . only if both parties wanted us to do so. . . . There is no place we have injected ourselves in a dispute in the absence of an agreement on both sides. Otherwise, it does not work."[7] Pakistan realized that at this stage a peace initiative would help to stabilize the situation. Unexpectedly, the Indian Prime Minister A. B. Vajpayee took the bold initiative of traveling to Pakistan to inaugurate the bus service and meet the Pakistani Prime Minister. He believed that the time was ripe for conflict resolution and stated that peace was their only option.[8] This statement is significant because it demonstrates the positive attributes of nuclear weapons acquisition. In other words, after the acquisition of nuclear weapons there was no point in keeping the conflict alive as war, formerly one of the options for conflict resolution for states engaged in protracted conflicts, becomes unlikely. Vajpayee felt that having a meeting in Lahore would help to create a propitious political atmosphere, as "the nuclear weapons program of India and Pakistan had created a more critical strategic and security environment in the subcontinent."[9] He hoped that a nuclear Pakistan would be willing to "engage in a substantive dialogue with greater self-confidence and an equally greater awareness of the dangers of a nuclear confrontation."[10] His bus trip from Delhi to Lahore was a confidence-building measure to thaw the India–Pakistan conflict. Pakistan's democratic Prime Minister Nawaz Sharif reciprocated the Indian move. On February 20, 1999, the day after Vajpayee's arrival, the leaders of the two states signed the Lahore Declaration.

Remarkable progress was made with the Lahore Declaration. The two parties agreed to take steps to reduce the risk of accidental or unauthorized use of nuclear weapons – something western scholars and policy-makers have been worried about – and to undertake a total moratorium on nuclear tests, and made a commitment to give each other advance notice of ballistic missile tests.[11] These agreements represented confidence-building measures necessary for achieving a durable peace in South Asia. The declaration's preamble stated that the parties were "convinced that durable peace and development of harmonious relations and friendly cooperation will serve the vital interests of the peoples of the two countries, enabling them to devote their energies for a better future."[12] Ganguly maintains that the Indian government placed a lot of hope in the peace process and believed that Nawaz Sharif was genuinely interested in starting "a new era in the Indo-Pakistan relations."[13] People on both sides of the border were extremely happy with the visit of Vajpayee, the reciprocity shown by Nawaz Sharif, and the subsequent initiation of the peace process.[14] Diplomatic negotiations seemed to be successful with the establishment of rules and procedures to regulate bilateral relations on certain levels, inspiring optimism for the termination of the conflict on both sides of the border.

Gabriella Blum comments on Vajpayee's bus trip and the initiation of the peace process: "It all seemed like the beginning of a beautiful friendship. It was not."[15] Less than two months later India test-fired an Agni II missile, giving notice to the Pakistanis in accordance with the norms of the Lahore Declaration. The news was "greeted with surprise, suspicion, and heightened guardedness"[16] in Pakistan. The Kargil crisis that followed surprised not only the Indians but also the international community. J. N. Dixit writes, "The [peace] effort proved to be abortive, with Pakistan's incursions into the Kargil area and the resulting conflict occurring within three months of this imaginative move on the part of India."[17] Whether or not the crisis was triggered to counter the Indian missile test is unclear, but it is certain that the peace process, so carefully crafted and inspiring so much enthusiasm and optimism on both sides, was reduced to ruins. Some observers have even argued that Pakistan initiated the Kargil crisis because the US showed no interest in mediating the Kashmir problem which needed international attention.[18]

As stated in the previous chapter, Kargil, one of the worst crises of the nuclear period between India and Pakistan, erupted primarily because the two countries possessed nuclear weapons. Ashley J. Tellis *et al.* assert that "Pakistan's possession of nuclear weapons functioned as the critical permissive condition that made contemplating Kargil possible."[19] The peace process was just a prelude to the Kargil crisis. The one drew the belligerents a step closer to peace and the other pushed them many steps away. Pakistan's incursion into Kargil a few months after the peace process began destroyed the temporary cordial relationship. Trust between the rivals did not have time to be institutionalized during the three months' peace between the signing of the peace process and the beginning of the Kargil crisis. On the contrary, Kargil made the Indians suspect the Pakistanis of playing a double game    making peace and planning war simultaneously. They became angry and frustrated.[20] The Indian government now doubted Pakistan's ability and intention to make peace with India. New Delhi not only changed its strategies for dealing with Islamabad, but came to a new understanding of its rival's thinking. New Delhi realized that it "really cannot do business with Islamabad because it is an essentially untrustworthy partner."[21] The crisis intensified the hatred between India and Pakistan. Blum writes, "The revelation that an invasion of Kargil was planned even as the Lahore Declaration was being signed was fatal to the peace process initiated the previous year and extinguished any trust hitherto existing between the two people and governments."[22] Pakistan took advantage of the Graduated Reduction in International Tension (GRIT) strategy Vajpayee adopted in February 1999. Since Pakistan had not changed its domestic or foreign policies, it could not play a new game in an old context. The old context was very much predominant and the old pattern of crisis and conflict continued. For Pakistan, though, "Kargil was about many elements – about lack of trust and dialogue which went off track."[23] Although the Clinton administration pressured Pakistan to draw back when the crisis was at its peak, and India appreciated this US diplomacy, Kargil's primary effect was to reinforce the Indian "convictions that the international community cannot be allowed to railroad India into consummating some kind of a 'peace process' with Pakistan, given the past failures of both Simla and Lahore."[24] After Kargil, Pakistan did not change its overall policies toward militancy and proxy wars. Consequently, nor did India change its image of Pakistan. If anything, it changed for the worse because India realized that under no circumstances would Pakistan ever fail to use a window of opportunity for an attack on India. The Pakistani policy of winning Kashmir through militancy, proxy wars, and force remained the same.

India-Pakistan relations deteriorated yet further on account of the change in Pakistan's domestic political institutions. One of the consequences of the crisis was the coup d'etat by which Pakistan's army chief, General Musharraf, took over the country, ousting the elected Prime Minister Nawaz Sharif in October 1999. India's response was negative for two reasons: first, it considered there was a better chance of good relations with a democratic Pakistan, as evidenced by Nawaz Sharif's gesture toward India; and second, Musharraf was "the architect of what Indians considered the betrayal of the Lahore process at Kargil."[25] To make matters worse, General Musharraf, in an interview to the *Hindu*, described the discussions between Nawaz Sharif and Vajpayee as a "farce," and said he would have to investigate whether the Lahore Declaration and the Memorandum of Understanding made any sense any more. He also stated that he would continue to support the militants in Kashmir. He believed that profound suspicion and mistrust would continue to characterize the India-Pakistan relationship.[26] India's response was extremely negative. It refused to deal with the army chief or have any dialogue with a non-democratic Pakistan unless it stopped cross-border terrorism. It refused to attend South Asian Association for Regional Cooperation (SAARC) meetings and made efforts to isolate Musharraf's government in the Non-Aligned Movement, Commonwealth conferences, and the UN.[27] All these intensified mutual antagonisms till mid-2000.

Low-intensity violence continued between India and Pakistan after the crisis ended with the retreat of Pakistani troops from the Kargil region. Pakistan's reliance on violence to change the Kashmir situation continued despite the de-escalation of the crisis. In December 1999, an Indian Airlines aircraft was hijacked to Kandahar shortly after taking off from Katmandu. The hijackers, who were Pakistani nationals with links to Inter-Services Intelligence (ISI), demanded the release of thirty-five jailed terrorists including Mohammad Masood Azhar (the religious leader who supports Muslim separatists in Indian-administered Kashmir and who founded Jaish-e-Mohammed in early 2000). Seven days after the Indian government released three terrorists, the hijackers released the passengers.[28] This episode had a strong negative impact on the relationship between the two countries. Tellis *et al.* assert, the "Kargil fiasco does not appear to have extinguished Pakistan's belief that violence, especially as expressed through support for the Kashmir insurgency, remains the best – if not the only effective – policy choice for pressuring India on Kashmir and other outstanding disputes."[29] This belief is all the more predominant in the minds of the military in Pakistan. Moreover, the Pakistan army was displeased with the outcome of the crisis and their forced withdrawal from Kargil under foreign pressure.[30] With the military in power, cross-border firing, infiltration, and support for the Kashmiri militants increased.

Relations between the two states sank to their lowest level in decades. Powerful individuals on opposite sides of the Kashmir border have their own agenda and fighting may continue even without the consent of the two governments. For example, in 2000 when India announced a unilateral cease-fire and Pakistan reciprocated, insurgent groups such as Lashkar-e-Taiba and Hizbul-Mujahideen did not accept it and the levels of violence in Kashmir did not decline.[31] This raises new problems in the conflict setting. Although Pakistan may not always be part of the low–medium-intensity violence that plagues the conflict, India accuses it of involvement, exacerbating tension amongst the parties. Perhaps Pakistan is involved in the continuing violence in Kashmir, but maintains a denial strategy. The truth is difficult to gauge. The resulting situation of hostility and animosity between the parties makes progress toward peace very difficult. Pressure from external powers and bold leadership may break the deadlock, as was the case after Kargil with serious US pressure to de-escalate and then negotiate.

Leaders have made peace initiatives during periods of calm, showing that if there was total stability in the conflict – a function of absence of war and crises – they could have found ways to settle their differences. At least the peace process would have time to be institutionalized, building trust and understanding, and favoring compromise by both sides on outstanding issues. A new peace overture in 2001 highlights the connection between periods of calm and moves for peace. Such moves have not been a monopoly of the Indians. Pakistan has also made efforts for peace. The next peace process was planned by India, but the trigger was Pakistan's declared intention to offer the hand of friendship to India once again with a view to dialogue.

## The Agra Summit and its aftermath

Throughout 2000, Pakistan made many efforts toward a resumption of negotiations and finally offered a no-war pact. All these offers were rejected by India for one reason – it wanted Pakistan to stop supporting the insurgents in Kashmir before any new peace measure was undertaken.[32] While Pakistan's efforts were genuine, it could not overcome India's concerns about Pakistani assistance to the insurgents. Whether or not Pakistan does assist them is uncertain, but India has learned from past experience that Pakistan may say one thing and do another, undermining trust between the two countries. Additionally, if militants' actions and statements show that Pakistan is involved in the insurgency, then it is difficult to blame India for suspecting Pakistan. For example, in July 2000 the head of Lashkar-e-Taiba, Mohammed Saeed, stated that the *jihad* against India would continue until Kashmir becomes part of Pakistan.[33] Whether the insurgents support Pakistan or Pakistan supports them, India does not want Pakistan to be engaged in its internal affairs. After India unilaterally declared a cease-fire in December 2000 and Pakistan reciprocated by offering a truce along the line of control (LoC) and troop withdrawal was completed, the border areas became significantly calmer. The Indian Prime Minister Vajpayee invited General Musharraf to a summit in Agra, and was accepted. There had been no new crises in the conflict theater. Two years had passed since the Kargil crisis, allowing a new environment conducive to peace to emerge. While the summit did not produce satisfactory results, both parties expressed their desire to continue the dialogue. Musharraf's visit to India and willingness to rule out a military solution to the Kashmir problem demonstrate that military regimes may also be interested in peacemaking in a propitious environment.

At the three-day summit in Agra, the two parties exchanged drafts on their positions on various bilateral issues, notably Kashmir and the nuclear issue. But despite the prevailing optimism, agreement could not even be reached on a joint declaration at the end of the summit. Pakistan's insistence that the Kashmiri All Party Hurriyat Conference (APHC) should be recognized as a legitimate participant in the dialogue, and India's refusal, created deadlock. Later, Prime Minister Vajpayee told the National Executive of the Bharatiya Janata Party (BJP) that General Musharraf was not serious about peace. He stated,

> An inescapable conclusion to be drawn is that there is not even a tentative meeting ground on the substance of political issues under discussion between India and Pakistan . . . Pakistan is not willing to accept the objective realities of its supporting the secessionists against India . . . Pakistan has decided to continue its undeclared war against India not only in Jammu and Kashmir but in other parts of the country.[34]

Thus, the summit amounted to little more than a visit by a military dictator.

It could be argued that neither Vajpayee nor Musharraf was ready for a summit so soon after a serious crisis and while sporadic violence in the conflict was a salient issue. Vajpayee wanted to have contacts with Pakistan "on the margins of the SAARC [South Asian Association for Regional Cooperation] summit and the UN General Assembly session,"[35] but some of the leading BJP elites and advisors, notably L. K. Advani who thought the creation of a bilateral framework could make a breakthrough in the conflict, encouraged him to invite Musharraf to India. Similarly, Musharraf's statements prior to the summit show he was not ready for constructive talks with Vajpayee. In interviews with the *Times of India* and *Asian Age* he said that any discussions with India would be dependent on resolving the Kashmir issue. He added that although terrorism and violence were not acceptable in Kashmir, he did not regard the secessionists as terrorists. He further believed that *jihad* was justified, being a violent struggle for self-determination. Thus Pakistan supported the freedom struggle politically, morally, and diplomatically, but was not involved in the violence in Kashmir.[36] Given their views, why did the two leaders come face to face? Vajpayee wanted to project India as a country committed to peace, and Musharraf saw the summit as a way of legitimizing his position as head of state. The US was also putting heavy political and diplomatic pressure on Pakistan to compromise. But however little the Agra Summit achieved, it showed that both India and Pakistan wanted some kind of continuing dialogue and saw this as a way of resolving their conflict. However, recurrent crises undermined any potential for a thaw in the relationship.

In October 2001, the Kashmiri Legislative Assembly in Srinagar, capital of Indian-administered Kashmir, was attacked by Kashmiri militants. In the post-9/11 climate, the US became extremely concerned about the situation in Kashmir which could potentially trigger nuclear confrontation in South Asia. Anxious to obtain assistance from Pakistan in its war on terror, the US advised India not to retaliate against Pakistan for the attacks in the State Assembly in Jammu and Kashmir. It condemned the attacks, but did not acknowledge Jaish-e-Mohammed to be an organization sponsored by Pakistan.[37] India decided to take the US advice, hoping that America's new-found concern with terrorism might make it address India's longstanding complaints against Pakistan. Although Indian policy-makers were prudent in this instance in the absence of proper evidence of Pakistan's involvement, it could not continue this policy when the Indian Parliament was attacked in December 2001 by militants who it believed were acting at the behest of the Pakistanis. The intense troop mobilization along the Kashmiri border and the subsequent tough stance were indicative of India's firm response to this attack. All high-level ties were cut and a number of cooperative arrangements were suspended. As stated in the previous chapter, even though the crisis de-escalated without a war, it had serious potential for escalation and was one of the longest crises in the conflict's history. The crisis remained at high intensity throughout, causing extreme anxiety in the international community about possible nuclear escalation. The US realized that terrorism would have to be eradicated from the region, and for this, the Kashmir problem would have to be settled. Although India has not been able to trust Pakistan since Kargil, and the Agra Summit only reinforced this position, it was reassured by the fact that the US, for the first time in the history of the India–Pakistan conflict, had been discussing terrorism and Pakistan's part in it. The role of the US is not to mediate but to see that Pakistan refrains from supporting the militants in Kashmir. For India, this would represent progress toward dialogue on outstanding issues.

The role of the US after 9/11 in changing Pakistan's policies on terrorism must be recognized although Pakistan's President publicly denies that its conciliatory moves were made under US pressure. He stated, "No one can put pressure from outside but there can be some suggestion for this purpose."[38] These are significant statements from a military leader who faces criticism from extremists and fundamentalists in his own country. Strong US pressure must have motivated General Musharraf's address to the people of Pakistan in January 2002, in which he pledged that Pakistan would not allow terrorists to operate from within its territory. His statement was followed by actions: around 2000 militants were arrested and several Islamic organizations involved in militancy and sectarian violence were banned. However, shortly after, a number of the militants were released and the banned organizations started operating under new names.[39] Only a few months later, in May 2002, militants attacked an Indian army residential complex near Jammu, killing more than thirty people.[40] Pakistan's denial of any connection with the attack was disbelieved by India and both countries intensified their troops along the LoC and clashes resulted. India expelled the Pakistani High Commissioner, and diplomatic relations were broken off.

A year or so later a new round of bilateral discussions and negotiations started. In April 2003, Vajpayee announced that he wanted Pakistan to resume bilateral talks with India. He took measures to restore diplomatic relations, declared a cease-fire along the LoC and Siachen Glacier, and resumed the transportation links which had been halted after the attack on the Parliament. On January 6, 2004 the leaders of India and Pakistan met at the Twelfth SAARC Summit in Islamabad, and agreed to restart their dialogue and resolve all outstanding issues including Kashmir in a cooperative manner. The foreign secretaries met the following month and made commitments to composite dialogue on all bilateral issues, including peace and security, Kashmir, Siachen Glacier, Wullar Barrage, Sir Creek, terrorism, drug-trafficking, and other issues of bilateral concern. The change of power in India in 2004, when Manmohan Singh took office as Prime Minister, did not apparently upset the dialogue initiated by Vajpayee. Amid fresh peace overtures by India and Pakistan, President Musharraf said that his country would only work for a no-war pact with India followed by joint reduction of troops and de-nuclearization of South Asia if the Kashmir issue had been resolved.[41] Such statements upset the continuity of any overtures for peace. However, in the absence of inter-state crisis, dialogue is still continuing though making slow progress, and, since 2004, liable to constant disruption by continuous low-intensity violence. As Gabriella Blum puts it, "Times of crisis push them apart; relative calm, peaceful gestures, and third-party intervention draw them closer together."[42]

The possession of nuclear weapons has created a de facto no-war zone, particularly with regard to Kashmir. Tellis et al. use the term "ugly stability" to describe the "no peace, no war" code of conduct observed in the conflict, especially in the context of the Kargil episode.[43] Other commentators are skeptical as to whether the two countries have learned the art of nuclear-induced restraint. Robert Wirsing argues that nuclear weapons may have de-escalated the crisis in 1999, but did not deter Islamabad from initiating a military operation against New Delhi in the first place, so the Kargil crisis cannot be used to predict escalation possibilities in any future crisis.[44] While this is true, the facts so far show that crisis has not resulted in escalation. Thus the acquisition of nuclear weapons has been conducive to, rather than subversive of, stability at the war level in the India-Pakistan conflict. The facts also show that the acquisition of nuclear weapons has created more, sometimes severe, crises and continuous violence in the India–Pakistan conflict setting, given that escalation has been ruled out, mostly due to Pakistan's belief that violence can resolve its strategic problems with India. It is believed that "owing to the presence of nuclear weapons, India and especially Pakistan would be particularly enticed to engage in various types of sub-conventional conflicts at the lower end of the conflict spectrum."[45] A Kargil-type event remains a possibility as long as subconventional violence is regarded as a valuable strategy. The evidence suggests that these frequent inter-state crises do not create an environment conducive to initiating peacemaking or continuing an existing peace process. Kargil and Agra both prove this point. Jasjit Singh commented on the consequences of Kargil, Agra, and the Parliament Attack as follows: "After Kargil people in India were angry and frustrated. Hijacking took place. Agra didn't work. Then the

Parliament [Attack happened]. Terrorists are trained in Pakistan. Who are these people? Where are they coming from?"[46] Indians started to ask these questions and expressed anger and frustration at Pakistan's repeated provocation of serious crises, damaging the peace process. Even Prime Minister Vajpayee, had to face serious domestic opposition for the lenient attitude he showed when he invitated Musharraf to the Agra Summit after the serious crisis in Kargil. Savita Pande asserts, "Indians have the right to know why the Prime Minister invited Musharraf to Agra after Kargil."[47] Thus, not only the decision-makers were unhappy with Pakistan's role in recurring crises, even the ordinary people in India started questioning why the government should offer friendship to a nation that cannot be trusted.

The continuation of low–medium-intensity violence has a tremendously negative impact on the overall relationship, precluding trust, which is essential for peace-making, and institutionalizing hatred between the peoples of the two countries. Although India is thought to be more affected by the negative impact of these crises, Pakistan is not immune to the effects of the "crisis and peace pattern" in the conflict. Khalid Mahmud stated in 2003, "The BJP government is in the habit of making contradictory statements. Just a couple of days ago it talked about a pre-emptive strike against Pakistan. Then Vajpayee came up with the peace plan. Why have the Indians offered this peace plan now?"[48] It is hard for Pakistan to trust the Indians who show no consistency in their words and deeds. Illustrating this point, Mahmud said,

> Vajpayee's trip to Lahore was an instance. He didn't talk to Nawaz Sharif in the Colombo Summit and after that the Indians went to New York and suddenly something changed. The same thing happened in the Agra Summit. Indians said no talks can happen, but then there was the invitation to Agra.[49]

Although these policy changes could have been a function of US pressure, the point is that it is difficult to trust India's words. Indians have no choice but to take a harsh stance when they are faced with an unexpected crisis initiated by Pakistan, but they want to make peace during the brief periods of calm, perhaps because they realize that in the absence of war peace has to be attained by other means, or perhaps under pressure from the US. Whatever the reason, these contradictory statements are the result of crises triggered by Pakistan. But they are difficult for Pakistan to understand and accept. No matter who pressures the two sides to hold talks and no matter what results from the talks, as Stephen P. Cohen states, "In times of crisis, most [cooperative endeavors] simply ceased to function, and whatever 'lessons' about cooperation have been learned seem to have evaporated."[50] This is the pattern of India–Pakistan cooperation and crises.

The two sides also have some preconceived notions about each other which intensify in times of crisis and violence. For example, the Pakistanis feel that the core issue is not Kashmir but India's attitude toward smaller states. "Kashmir is an embodiment of that attitude."[51] In addition, Mushahid Hussain maintains, "Indians see Pakistanis as mad people, driven by Jihadis" because it suits them to castigate Pakistanis and Muslims for domestic political reasons.[52] Pakistanis find this unacceptable. According to Shireen Mazari, the "Indian mindset must change. It cannot use force to attain its objectives and it must stop trying to emulate the US."[53] Likewise, Indians think Pakistan cannot be trusted and will take every opportunity to plunge India into crisis.

Making a connection between hatred and protraction of a conflict, Raj Chengappa states, "After a big hit [crisis], hatred is more. If you continue to promote hatred, you will continue conflicts."[54] Constant violence and crises generate extreme hatred between the belligerents and this becomes entrenched in the minds of the people, even if the leaders may be able to change their attitudes. S. K. Singh argues, "Pakistanis generate the capacity to hate among the Pakistanis. The Pakistani mind knows how to hate. Unless this changes, conflict resolution is unlikely."[55] P. Sahadevan states, "Transformation – setting the process for conflict resolution – is, therefore, not there. The mood is not there. Thus, there is no de-escalation of the India–Pakistan conflict."[56] Furthermore, if peacemaking is constantly jeopardized by new crises and this becomes a pattern, not only are more suspicion and more hatred generated, but the patience of the party on whom crisis is inflicted becomes stretched. After the Indian Parliament Attack K. Santhanam stated that there had been a "loss of patience" in the India–Pakistan conflict and that India's "patience is exhausted." [57] The former Indian Prime Minister I. K. Gujral asked: "What is democracy? [In] every social structure, there is some system. In a democratic India, Parliament is a symbol of sovereignty."[58] Therefore, terrorist attacks, which are underhand techniques, cannot be tolerated by India.[59] Asked for evidence of whether Pakistan was connected to the Parliament Attack, he stated, "This is not a Court case where evidence must be given."[60] In similar vein, K. Subrahmanyam argued, "We don't have to produce any evidence. This is not a criminal Court. Pakistan must recognize that terrorism is a disease. They should join the fight against terrorism."[61] When important decision-makers say there is no need for evidence of the rival's responsibility for violence and crises, it is clear how little they trust the rival state. However, Pakistan has often spoken about holding dialogue, since the Parliament Attack, perhaps under US pressure, but the Indians did not believe that their intentions were genuine. The India–Pakistan conflict was beset by suspicion, a result of all these crises coming from the Pakistani side. Pande asked, "Dialogue for what . . . dialogue with the deaf?"[62] She also maintained that if Pakistan was serious about dialogue with its counterpart, then it would make serious efforts to stop terrorism because "at the moment the main crisis is [Pakistan-sponsored] terrorism that has to stop."[63] However, the Pakistanis took the opposite view. As Mazari puts it, "India is not prepared to have dialogue."[64] Mahmud stated, "You can't have dialogue in a vacuum. The first step would be to de-escalate the confrontation."[65] He added that the real test would be if the Indians were willing to move toward normalization of relations, reinstating air and bus services between India and Pakistan, which they had unilaterally cancelled. These would not be big concessions, but could help to facilitate talks.[66] These sentiments make it difficult for the conflict to pass through the escalation phase even though "dialogue" and "dialogue to have dialogue" have continued in the India–Pakistan conflict.

Both India and Pakistan understand that if they do not make peace South Asia cannot compete with the other regions of the world, and progress in all spheres is compromised. Some Indians believe that because there is ultimately no choice for Pakistan but to make peace with India, it will eventually come to the negotiating table with proper intentions, motivated by concern for its own survival. K. K. Nayyar states, "Disparity between the two entities is already such that there is no choice [for Pakistan] but to have peace with India. In ten years Pakistan will fall behind. So they will make peace."[67] But it remains difficult to think of a situation where Pakistan will compromise over Kashmir, especially in a nuclear environment. As Muchkund Dubey states, "Solving the Kashmir issue has become more intractable with the possession of nuclear weapons."[68] This was further elaborated by Sahadevan, who stated,

> Nuclear weapons have maintained deterrence, but not conflict resolution. Nuclear weapons have actually increased the frequency of crisis situations. The crises emanate more from the Pakistani side. Pakistan obviously is the weaker side and triggers the crises. The frequency of crises has increased since 1998. The Prime Minister and President directly accuse each other these days (after 1998–9) – after Musharraf took over power. This was not happening in Zia's period. This explains that there is mounting pressure for creating crises. There is tension, which is reflected in their words.[69]

This implies that the leaders in the two countries do not care much about conflict resolution. If they did, they would create an atmosphere propitious for peacemaking. On a general note, Uday Bhaskar states, "The conflict can't be resolved. There can be prudent management. Any abiding conflict where contiguous neighbors have attained hostility, by and large, have to go through wars."[70] Since wars are a remote possibility in the India–Pakistan context, resolution of the conflict is difficult, if not impossible. Not all Pakistanis share this view. In discussing the role of nuclear weapons in conflict resolution, Nasim Zehra states, "If anything, nuclear weapons have created space for conflict resolution."[71]

But Pakistanis may express such views because they are the weaker side and they know that the nuclear shield may provide them with the opportunity to make short-term territorial gains during crises, to internationalize the problem and attract the attention of the US by generating crises that have the potential for escalation to nuclear level, or to convince India to hold dialogue since war is out of the question. Additionally, nuclear weapons have given Pakistan more negotiating strength vis-à-vis India, and this should help to resolve the conflict fairly. Thus Zehra states, "Nuclear weapons also established parity of sorts in terms of negotiating power. That is something that is a plus."[72] But whatever negotiating strength Pakistan may have derived from the acquisition of nuclear weapons, even Pakistanis agree that "nuclear weapons have jeopardized the atmosphere of the dialogue"[73] because in addition to frequent crises and constant low-intensity violence, Pakistanis have threatened to use nuclear weapons in future crises, upholding a first-use policy. Samina Ahmed states, "At times of heightened diplomatic and military tension with India, Pakistan's decision makers have resorted to nuclear threats, implying a willingness to use nuclear weapons in case of Indian aggression."[74] Similarly, Indians have threatened pre-emptive strikes against Pakistan. These threats and counterthreats in a nuclear environment are definitely not conducive to constructive dialogue.

Both New Delhi and Islamabad realize there is no military solution to the problem. As Niaz Naik states, "The acquisition of nuclear weapons does not enhance security."[75] In 2003, five years into the nuclear period, Pakistan understands that none of its new military strategies – proxy wars, terrorist attacks, or low–medium-intensity violence – will enable it to achieve its goal of resolving the Kashmir problem. Musharraf also changed his strategy, relying increasingly on less religiously oriented constituents, for two reasons: US pressure to fight the war on terror has antagonized fundamentalists, forcing Musharraf to seek political support elsewhere; there is a rising consensus among business groups that they would have much to gain if tensions with India were reduced.[76] India, too, understands that it cannot win a war against a conventionally weaker but nuclear-armed Pakistan. It is also realized that South Asian prosperity depends to a large extent on India Pakistan conflict resolution, and this cannot be accomplished with military options in a nuclear environment. Non-military mechanisms of resolution need to be investigated and used for the benefit of both states. The US should act as a facilitator of bilateral discussions. India and Pakistan should focus on the fact that ultimately peace is a product of a peaceful environment.

## Summary

This chapter's primary concern has been to show that peace initiatives made by the policy-makers of India and Pakistan have been mainly unproductive because each time, before a peace process was consolidated another crisis erupted, jeopardizing any chance for progress toward peace to be institutionalized. Frequent crises resulting from low-intensity attacks and counterattacks in the India–Pakistan conflict theater, generated distrust, mounting every time a crisis erupted after a peace initiative had been undertaken. As the initiator of crises, Pakistan was considered treacherous and it was hard for India to build up trust again. Pakistan was likewise suspicious of Indian motives and actions. The next chapter shows how this situation has transformed the India–Pakistan conflict.

# 9  Conflict transformed

This chapter discusses how the negative effects of nuclear proliferation eventually bring a lasting transformation to the conflict. It underscores the connection between the lack of freedom from violence in the conflict setting, lack of trust, and cooperation between the adversaries on non-security levels. The aim is to demonstrate that although constructive peacemaking cannot be sustained in the India–Pakistan conflict, cooperation in affairs other than security has been established through dialogue, even against a continuous low-level violence-prone background but in the absence of serious crises. This has ultimately protracted the conflict indefinitely.

One of the first points to note is that the India–Pakistan conflict has been frozen at the third phase, escalation, of the four-phase life-cycle of a protracted conflict, ever since the two parties acquired nuclear weapons. This means that the conflict has not been able to advance from the escalation phase to the final phase – de-escalation – due to its overall instability. As Amitabh Mattoo states, "Nuclear weapons freeze the relationship."[1] Wars are avoided, and this should make the conflict stable and bring the parties to the negotiating table and eventually to mutual understanding. But these consequences do not follow because lower-level violence and crises continue to maintain the hostilities. These crises lead to military confrontation which affects the relationship negatively. Thus, Mattoo states that just "because war is not a viable instrument of policy, it does not mean that they [India and Pakistan] will be instant friends. It just means that on one level the relationship is frozen."[2] The absence of war and presence of crises create a situation non-conducive to conflict resolution in which the nature of the protracted conflict changes in such a way that it is protracted indefinitely.

India and Pakistan seem to be comfortable in the present situation of no war and no peace. Since stability is a function of no war and no crisis, and crisis still characterizes the conflict, the parties have become quite accustomed to the situation. They sense that wars are unlikely and crises and violence will continue; they are prepared to face low–medium-intensity violence and are unsure about the permanence of any peace process. Kanti Bajpai wonders, since deterrence works at the war level, why the countries need to try to settle their differences.[3] In the India–Pakistan case, they have not abandoned efforts to settle their differences, as discussed in the previous chapter. They have made serious efforts to initiate a peace process at least twice in the nuclear period. As Kenneth Waltz states, "India and Pakistan, however, did not reach agreement on Kashmir or on other issues when neither had nuclear weapons; now both have at least an incentive to discuss their problems."[4] The problem is not their intentions, but an environment that militates against conflict settlement. That induces them to concentrate on dialogue to improve the situation as much as possible and form a better understanding of each other. But in the absence of an environment conducive to conflict resolution, they focus not on any peace process as such but on bilateral cooperation in non-controversial areas. The protracted conflict changes its nature as a result.

Futile peace initiatives made in the midst of violence and crisis have made the parties feel that they cannot be at peace for long. Although each perceives the causes of the failures of these initiatives differently and, as might be expected, blames the other for jeopardizing peace efforts, both realize one thing: that hostility needs to be contained if they are to achieve prosperity in, for example, the economic and commercial spheres. So they talk in an atmosphere of tension and suspicion; conflict resolution is ignored. Some people in Pakistan believe that this is the best possible route to a positive relationship between India and Pakistan since the most effective policy, secret diplomacy, also failed prior to the Kargil crisis. According to Niaz Naik, India and Pakistan were on the verge of reaching agreement on Kashmir in 1999, using the secret diplomacy preferred by the leaders of both democratic states. He said that since peace initiatives were generally jeopardized by crises and misunderstandings, it was felt that secret diplomatic efforts would be the best way of settling the root problem, Kashmir, once and for all. According to him, at the Lahore Summit, Vajpayee and Nawaz Sharif met at least three times. They agreed that one person from each side should hold talks. Naik states,

> Nawaz Sharif called me to talk on his behalf to the Indians on March 25, 1999. Even my High Commissioner didn't know that I was there. R. K. Misra, Chairman of the Observer Group, was authorized by Vajpayee to talk on his behalf. Our mandate was to look to the future. Four basic elements were highlighted: (1) both sides should move beyond publicly stated positions (rigid positions taken); (2) India and Pakistan and the Kashmiri people's interests must be taken into account; (3) solutions must be agreeable and implementable; and (4) the solutions must be final and not partial.[5]

On the basis of these four elements, Naik and Misra discussed three proposals:

> (1) Convert the LoC [line of control] to an international border. I said that must be rejected. (2) On the question of plebiscite, India said, "no plebiscite." So that was left aside. We discussed a regional plebiscite. India didn't accept. (3) Partition could be based on how it was partitioned in 1947 – based on religion. That was not acceptable to the Indians because the communal aspect would be disastrous to India. Other examples that could be applicable to the India–Pakistan situation were also discussed. None was accepted. We reached a dead-end.[6]

Seeing that no solution was acceptable to both parties, Misra went to Vajpayee and asked him to speak to Naik directly. Naik states,

> Vajpayee conveyed to me that all these have been experienced and discussed from time to time and that he wants me to come up with an innovative solution. "A territorial division of the state of Jammu and Kashmir" could be made. The Chenab river could be used to demarcate the two Kashmirs.[7]

Naik continues,

> I was coming back on the night of the 31st [March]. The Prime Minister wanted to meet me. He asked when Misra could go to Islamabad. It was set for April 9th. He also told me to get the map of the Chenab river and to go into details. He said please convey this message to Mr Nawaz Sharif. He also told me that whenever it is April, your army starts to come to the LoC and then we deter them. Shelling goes on. Now we will be in a new situation this summer. Tell Mr Sharif to control the army. We are not worried about the Kashmiris – it is their cause.[8]

The situation was very positive. Then, Naik states,

> Mr Misra came to Islamabad not to talk about Kashmir, but to know whether or not I had conveyed the message to Mr Sharif. This was because there was serious cross-border terrorism by this time. Vajpayee was influenced by the hawkish people who did not believe that Nawaz Sharif was to be trusted. Thus, Kargil started.[9]

Naik's detailed account of the initiation of the secret diplomacy to resolve the Kashmir problem, showing the two leaders' interest in it and the subsequent misunderstanding, is indicative of why both India and Pakistan have lost all hope of conflict resolution and instead have focused on short-term cooperation on less controversial issues which will benefit both parties and will not cause domestic problems. The government of Pakistan undeniably faces domestic problems when it joins peace talks. As Shireen Mazari states, "Pakistan's policy [pertaining to India] is hostage to domestic policy."[10] The failure of the Naik-Misra secret diplomacy similarly shows that India's policies cannot disregard hawkish domestic constituencies. Mushahid Hussain stated, "Musharraf and Vajpayee are hostage to the domestic constituencies."[11] Rasheed Khalid stated, "There are certain forces within these two countries who don't want the conflict to be resolved. The defense forces are important in this context. They need disputes to justify the size of the army."[12] This is especially true of Pakistan, which has been ruled by the military for most of its history. Military rulers in Pakistan have strengthened the power of the military in every domain, particularly since Zia-ul-Haq's presidency. Civilians in Pakistan have also felt the necessity of maintaining a large standing army to safeguard national integrity and sovereignty. The military, the only competent institution in the country, feels that Pakistan's international and external stability is dependent on it alone and that it has the best understandings of the national interest since it is close to the people. It also believes that it must play a major role in decision-making as the country's politicians are corrupt.[13] Khalid further states that other elements make conflict resolution difficult. For example, "The Mullahs do not want any serious dialogue. They try to sabotage [peace efforts]."[14] Their understanding is that peace efforts will mainly serve state interests, and the interests of different elements in the society, such as theirs, will not be reflected in arrangements made by state officials. Religious and rightist parties in Pakistan have always been the most rigid on the Kashmir issue.[15] They support the insurgency in Kashmir and are unlikely to accept compromise strategies on the issue.

The unprecedented level of cooperation reached by India and Pakistan since 2003 is encouraging, but begs the question: What are the consequences of cooperation for the protracted conflict? The conflict has not ended, but cooperation on different levels has transformed it permanently. As states cooperate in a conflict setting, they grow accustomed to the situation and may lose interest in ending it. Although the states in conflict intend to resolve their basic difference, they realize the difficulty of doing so. But they feel that trade and cultural links between them should not be stalled by bilateral disputes and cooperation could alleviate some aspects of the conflict. Cooperation within the parameters of the conflict becomes the norm. India and Pakistan have realized that it may be extremely difficult to resolve their long-running conflict, given their domestic political situations and the Kashmiris' own interests. Additionally, they cannot trust each other enough to cooperate on security matters, especially Kashmir. Consequently, they have decided to cooperate during the protracted conflict, thereby permanently transforming it.

There are three important ideas here: that protracted conflict states may tend to cooperate during the conflict; that their cooperation centers on soft issues in the hope that spillover effects will result, enabling the parties to resolve the outstanding issues and terminate the conflict; that even though both parties may intend to settle their differences on all issues through this cooperation, in fact they tend to learn to live with the conflict indefinitely. Thus, the central questions that are addressed in the following section are: When and why do states in long-running conflicts introduce cooperation into their relations and what are the consequences for the conflict? Nuclear detonations and their impact on cooperation are analyzed. The consequences for the conflict of the cooperative moves taken by the parties since the Twelfth South Asian Association for Regional Cooperation (SAARC) Summit are explained. Evidence supporting the idea that the parties have abandoned attempts at conflict termination owing to cooperation in non-security arenas is presented.

## Cooperation during protracted conflict

Protracted conflict states are generally unlikely to cooperate with each other owing to mutual hatred and distrust, which accentuate during crises and wars, undoing any improvement there may have been in peaceful interludes. However, as states acquire deterrent capabilities, especially nuclear weapons, and wars become unlikely, they may realize that cooperation offers a workable strategy for the improvement of the relationship. During this phase, exchange of intentions is generally done through summits and informal meetings between state officials or heads of state. Moves toward cooperation are made when both parties understand each other's intentions and neither side imposes its terms on the other. Cooperation is not sought for relative gains, where if one side gains, the other loses. Absolute gain is sought, meaning mutual gain is the ultimate aim. The parties select areas where they "can make agreements to choose strategies jointly,"[16] and cooperation will be positive-sum. Although initiatives must be taken by states, this can only be done when crises are absent and wars are a remote possibility.[17] Summits are the best places to start a conversation about cooperation for mutual benefit. Great power pressures can also facilitate such cooperative moves.

Cooperation generally begins in the less controversial areas such as trade, communications, and culture. It is initiated through dialogue between government and non-government officials at different meetings and sessions. These continue for a number of years until the proposals are implemented and institutionalized. Track-one and track-two dialogues are productive because meetings of different levels of government officials offer a range of views on the issues. Finally, heads of state can meet to sign the final agreements or end formalities. As progress is made on these non-controversial issues and cooperation begins, the parties come to feel they can trust each other more. This encourages them to expand their cooperation to other soft issues to their mutual benefit. These cooperative ventures gradually institutionalize. But the downside is that by cooperating on some levels and not on others, the parties keep the root cause of their conflict alive indefinitely. They probably avoid dealing with it as it is not only sensitive but could also jeopardize the benefits of cooperation on other levels, especially the commercial and economic levels. Once states grow used to economic interaction they tend to avoid at all costs anything that might disrupt it. Whatever brings economic prosperity and development becomes acceptable. It is a question not of reluctance to solve the root cause of the conflict, but of reluctance to disturb the soft issues on which cooperation has been established. The reason is simple: ultimately, the development of a country depends on economic prosperity and the infrastructure of the state. People want food, shelter, and clothing, all of which they can obtain if they have enough income; income is generated by and primarily dependent on national economic development, which in turn is largely dependent on bilateral and multilateral trade.

A few years after their nuclear tests India and Pakistan began to realize the negative impact for the conflict of having a deterrent capability and to understand that the possession of nuclear weapons would in fact extend the protracted conflict further.[18] To break out of this unending cycle, India made special efforts to initiate cooperation with its rival, Pakistan. The Indian Prime Minister A. B. Vajpayee's bus trip to Lahore in 1999, just one year after the nuclear tests, was the first confidence-building measure taken by one of the contending parties. This visit resulted in the remarkable Lahore Declaration, a series of agreements between the two states. Pakistani President General Pervez Musharraf's visit to

India for the Agra Summit was another breakthrough in the relationship. Although both these visits failed to achieve anything very positive, and the Kashmir issue was highlighted in the inter-state crises that followed, especially during the Kargil crisis of 1999, since 2003 India and Pakistan have again shown strong interest in moving forward with a new dialogue which would allow them to cooperate on multiple levels.

The Twelfth SAARC Summit in 2003 saw a new turn in the history of the India–Pakistan conflict. Specific suggestions were made by the Prime Minister of Pakistan in the context of SAARC and bilateral relations, including the resumption of civil aviation links, road and rail links, sports contracts, and so on. Pakistan also assured India that it would take specific measures against cross-border terrorism and would dismantle the infrastructure of support to terrorism. The two leaders believed that constructive dialogue would promote progress toward the common objective of peace, security, and economic development for both countries. The idea was that conflict resolution is only possible through confidence-building measures, but before that, "people to people contact must be established," which can only happen if there is freedom for the people in Pakistan. Therefore, "democratization of the Pakistani polity is important,"[19] although that was not on the agenda of India. Interestingly, even Pakistanis feel that democracy is the key to successful dialogue. Matiur Rahman states, "India has democracy and that is their advantage. Pakistan has a tarnished image due to its political institution. There is a need to have a democratic culture in Pakistan."[20] The main idea was to have continuous dialogue, which would be instrumental in solving the issues. As Mazari states, "Let's find a solution through dialogue."[21]

Both states have shown interest in making substantial progress on trade and economic cooperation. The central idea was to remain committed to resolving all issues between them bilaterally, as provided for by the Simla Agreement[22] and the Lahore Declaration. Both remained fully committed to improving bilateral relations. Most liberals have stressed

> the importance of commerce in reinforcing the web of interdependence spun by international institutions. Free trade creates material incentives to resolve disputes peacefully. The cosmopolitan business elites who benefit most from trade are seen as comprising a powerful transnational interest group with a stake in promoting amicable solutions to festering disagreements.[23]

However, India made it clear on several occasions that a sustained dialogue would necessarily require an end to cross-border terrorism and the dismantling of its infrastructure. It believed that discussions on nuclear issues and other confidence-building measures (CBMs) could be held in the context of composite dialogue. Pakistan responded positively to the initiatives taken by India. It was quite clear that specific steps had to be taken by Pakistan to advance this process meaningfully. Both sides attached importance to the process of normalization of bilateral links and to moving ahead in a step-by-step manner, building on the successes achieved and the confidence generated.

To advance the process of normalization of relations, both leaders agreed to commence the composite dialogue in February 2004. The two leaders also believed that this would lead to peaceful settlement of all bilateral issues, including Jammu and Kashmir, to the satisfaction of both sides.

Expert Level talks on Nuclear Confidence Building Measures were held in New Delhi from 19–20 June 2004. Both states agreed on the following:

The existing hotline between the DGMOs [Director Generals of Military Operations] would be upgraded, dedicated and secured.

A dedicated and secure hotline would be established between the two Foreign Secretaries, through their respective Foreign Offices to prevent misunderstandings and reduce risks relevant to nuclear issues.

Both countries will work towards concluding an Agreement with technical parameters on pre-notification of flight testing of missiles, a draft of which was handed over by the Indian side.

Each side reaffirmed its unilateral moratorium on conducting further nuclear test explosions unless, in exercise of national sovereignty, it decides that extraordinary events have jeopardized its supreme interests.

Both countries would continue bilateral discussions and hold further meetings to work towards the implementation of the Lahore MoU [Memorandum of Understanding] of 1999.

Both countries will continue to engage in bilateral consultations on security and non-proliferation issues within the context of negotiations on these issues in multilateral fora.

Both countries called for regular working level meetings to be held among all the nuclear powers to discuss issues of common concern.

Both sides agreed to report the progress of the talks to the respective Foreign Secretaries who would meet on 27–28 June 2004.[24]

As part of the composite dialogue process, discussions were held on economic and commercial cooperation in Islamabad on August 11–12, 2004. This was not surprising, given the need for cooperation on the economic level and given that cooperation on the security level required more trust and confidence. The former Indian Prime Minister I. K. Gujral states, "Cooperation basically in modern times is economic cooperation. In the subcontinent we think politics comes first, economy then. We have not changed our minds."[25] The economic level is the easiest one on which to launch cooperation because it makes absolute gains achievable. It is generally believed by liberal theorists that "the flow of trade between former enemies increases communication, erodes parochialism, and encourages both sides to construct new institutions to coordinate their behavior in other issue areas."[26] Track-two diplomacy, various confidence-building measures, and similar efforts have been intended "to increase regional cooperation and trust, and to moderate, if not transform, a relationship that seems to be based on fear, hatred, and distrust."[27]

By December 2004 expert-level talks on conventional confidence-building measures and a second round of talks on nuclear confidence-building measures had taken place. The first meeting of the India–Pakistan Joint Study Group (JSG) on Trade and Economic Cooperation was held on February 22–23, 2005. The JSG had detailed discussions on the promotion of trade and economic cooperation for the mutual benefit of both countries. It constituted two working or sub-groups on customs cooperation and trade facilitation and on non-tariff barriers (NTBs). The two sides identified problems relating to bilateral trade. It was also decided to hold the second meeting of the JSG on mutually agreed dates. The recommendations of the JSG would be submitted to the respective governments for consideration under the framework of the composite dialogue.[28]

Throughout 2005 expert-level talks continued on different topics including the opening of crossing points across the LoC, operationalization of the Amritsar-Lahore and Amritsar-Nankana bus service, economic and commercial cooperation, nuclear confidence-building measures, and opening rail links between Munnabao and Khokhrapar. In 2006, the two foreign secretaries reviewed the second round of the composite dialogue process and looked forward to having a third round. Amongst the positive developments were the overall improvement in relations between the two countries, the development of confidence and trust and the reduction of what has been called the "trust deficit," increased people-to-people contacts, and several CBMs in the nuclear and conventional realms. In terms of the nuclear CBMs, one of the successes of the second round of the composite dialogue was the completion of the Pre-notification of Ballistic Missiles Agreement. India had presented to Pakistan a draft for an MoU on the reduction of nuclear accidents and unauthorized use of nuclear weapons. The successful inauguration of the hotline between the foreign secretaries was also discussed. The existing DGMO link between the two Director Generals of Military Operations was upgraded. An optical fibre hotline was also established between them. They looked at some military CBMs, for example banning any fresh construction within 500 meters of the LoC, and allowing only the improvement of existing structures but not the creation of new posts along the LoC. Media products and their free movement between India and Pakistan were also discussed, as were other major issues like terrorism and drug-trafficking. Civil aviation links were discussed. On a general level, a large number of people had been traveling between the two countries, many more visas were being issued, people were crossing the border for pilgrimages, and bus and rail connections had been established.[29] One of the most important and encouraging topics discussed was that the ceasefire had been observed by both states for more than two years. However, Jammu and Kashmir were not discussed until 2006.

The flexibility shown by both sides in reaching agreement on the arrangements for the Srinagar-Muzaffarabad bus service or on the opening of certain crossing points on the LoC indicates that they have been able to develop a degree of mutual trust and confidence. It is important for analysts and practitioners of conflict resolution to be "aware of how communication and language influence the process of conflict and its resolution."[30] The India–Pakistan composite dialogue process reveals that India made it transparent that its ability to carry on with the peace process is very much related to the creation of a violence-free atmosphere.

Manmohan Singh said in 2006 that Musharraf "has not done enough" to control terrorist elements like Lashkar-e-Taiba and Jaish-e-Mohammed who operate out of Pakistan. In the India–Pakistan joint statement of January 2004, "Pakistan made a commitment to curbing terror groups in Pakistan that is the cornerstone for any meaningful advance of bilateral ties."[31] Singh further stated that if "Musharraf isn't doing enough about this after over two years, it simply means that the General is not inspiring much confidence in New Delhi."[32] Some Pakistanis also feel that their government has not done enough and India has the right to make the dialogue on Kashmir and security issues conditional. Farooq Hassan stated, "India rightly feels aggrieved by actions and tragedies emanating from Pakistan."[33] No matter how some Pakistanis feel about it, the language used by the Indians to undervalue Pakistan's effort to stop cross-border terrorism has negatively impacted the conflict. Some in Pakistan feel that it has done everything possible to stop cross-border terrorism. Aga Shahi stated, "We have done our best. India tries to dictate us and wants to have conditional talks,"[34] which is unacceptable. Matiur Rahman made the interesting comment that "There isn't substantial cross-border terrorism. India has such a big armed force. If they can't control it, how can Pakistan control it?"[35] He further stated that Pakistan had been trying very hard to control it, but the "people who are still going there, are going on their own."[36] Some Indians feel that they have no choice but to consider raising the costs of the terrorist operations, which has not yet happened. S. D. Muni states, "You have to tell Pakistan that there are certain costs to operations. It [India] has not increased the cost of Pakistan's operations. It must be done."[37] He further states that although "this is not a structural part of India's foreign policy,"[38] the terrorist operations make it essential for this to be integrated into India's foreign policy. Nevertheless, the leaders of India and Pakistan still meet, even after terror strikes such as the Mumbai blasts. After the Parliament Attack K. Subrahmanyam described India and Pakistan as in an "eyeball to eyeball confrontation. It is the biggest confrontation in the past few decades. In spite of that the two nations shake hands in the summit. There is a different kind of chemistry in which they move."[39] It is difficult to understand why they do what they do under conditions of animosity in the conflict. External pressure could make them understand that "they can't have permanent hostility."[40] The Indian Prime Minister gave a realistic picture of why he still meets his counterpart if promises are not met. He said, "You can't choose your neighbors and Pakistan happens to be India's." Given that the "destinies of the two countries are (thus) interlinked," there is no option but to keep the dialogue alive.[41] The ultimate purpose is to continue the dialogue with Pakistan.

Prime Minister Manmohan Singh has described his vision of peace and friendship between India and Pakistan, a departure from the history of conflict and mutual recrimination between the two sides. The two countries would cooperate not only for the welfare of their own people but for the prosperity of the South Asian region as a whole. However, there are political limitations on both sides. Manmohan Singh believes that India is not in a position to redraw boundaries or look at territorial adjustments. But short of that, India is willing to do whatever is required to give comfort to the people on both sides of the LoC, allow the free movement of people, goods, and ideas, and create opportunities for the celebration of the natural cultural affinity which exists between the people of the two sides.[42] This evidently means that India is primarily looking for ways to have an ordinary working relationship with its neighbor, Pakistan, on all levels except the security/ territorial dimension. India wants constructive engagement, primarily because its development depends on its neighbors. It understands that it is unlikely to be like China or Russia, but its further development and economic success are conditional on its undertaking constructive and flexible engagement policies toward its neighbors – especially Pakistan.[43] Some people argue, however, that India–Pakistan cooperation is superficial, limited to "dialogue about dialogue" and with no major breakthrough.[44] Although this may be true to some extent, substantial progress has certainly been made in cultural and communications cooperation since the Twelfth SAARC Summit. As Gaddam Dharmendra said, there is a "tremendous thawing of the atmosphere of distrust and suspicion [in India–Pakistan relations]. . . . We may agree to disagree, but we are committed to dialogue."[45] He added that what cannot be discussed in structured settings can be discussed over dinner.[46]

India has made it perfectly clear that cross-border terrorism has to be eliminated before any progress can be made on the security dynamics in the region, including Kashmir. This policy has remained constant across the Vajpayee and Singh periods. While policy differences exist between Bharatiya Janata Party the (BJP) and Congress, "neither supports significant concessions on Kashmir,"[47] and both believe that the ending of cross-border terrorism must be a precondition for any discussion on Kashmir. This is a condition that Pakistan cannot fulfill in the near future. R. R. Subramanian argues, "The relationship is highly complicated as far as India is concerned. India will not compromise on Kashmir. There is no meeting point on that. There can be no compromise on the part of India."[48] However, flexible views are also expressed on Kashmir. Muni contends, "For stable peace in the subcontinent, we [the Indians] would like to go half way as well, but the Kashmir struggle has now been made into an Islamic struggle."[49] This has further complicated an already contentious issue, making resolution even more difficult. On the Pakistani side, Shahi stated, "We cannot give up our stand on Kashmir. We cannot accept the Line of Control in Kashmir. We will have a lot of problems in Pakistan. We will be totally destabilized."[50] The statement indicates that for Pakistan, settlement of the Kashmir problem is difficult and the purpose of the dialogue is simply to improve better relations with India on different levels which benefit both parties. In similar vein, Stephen P. Cohen states, "The obstacles to peace are even greater on the Pakistani side. The intellectual and political debate there is dominated by hard-liners and the military-security establishment, and moderate voices either go unheard or are routinely suppressed."[51]

Unfortunately, in Pakistan the mullahs and the militants are in the ascendant, which makes it difficult for the government to make serious efforts to resolve the Kashmir issue with India. As for India, it perhaps prefers to manage the conflict rather than solve it. Management is the key word. Autonomy will probably be given to the Kashmiris in the course of time. The soft border and cease-fire line will be protected.[52] Pakistan has to take into account the interests of the army and the people – both opposed to compromising on Kashmir. The militants in Pakistan have their own interests and agenda and so has the Inter-Services Intelligence (ISI). Consequently, the government has to safeguard the interests of all sectors and this may become an impediment to accommodation with India on the security level. The following statement by P. R. Chari represents of a section of Indian opinion:

> Both India and Pakistan are actually concerned about domestic political constituencies. Musharraf is more [concerned]. Since Bhutto's time using the Islamic card was common. Musharraf said he was a modern man. He has used the *mujahidin* in Kargil. He used the ISI in Afghanistan, Taliban, and Kashmir. You can't suddenly reverse 180 degrees.[53]

The Indian Ministry of Foreign Affairs resists the idea of reconciliation with Pakistan. In its view, "India is always right," which implies that its neighbors are always wrong. Suspicion of neighbors has been a primary impediment to constructive cooperation,[54] and as a result, although there has been progress on soft issues, strategic issues have not been followed-up.

Although at the time of writing in 2007–8, it is four years since the beginning of the composite dialogue, the participants have not clearly stated what needs to be done with the overall Kashmir problem and how to set about solving it. It is quite clear that India and Pakistan have learned to live in a situation in which the conflict is overlaid by cooperation on the economy, culture, and communications. Farooq Hassan, an advisor to four former prime ministers of Pakistan – Nawaz Sharif, Benazir Bhutto, Moin Qureshi, and Muhammad Khan Junejo – stated in an interview in 2006 about the ongoing dialogue that "Pakistan articulates the needs of the regime in power and doesn't contemplate a wider visionary goal of peace in the region."[55] "Many problems are under the carpet and this may be such a case. If there is no war, this [the conflict] may continue," stated Mostafa Faruque Mohammed.[56] While the conflict remains "under the carpet," development on different levels can be focused on.[57] India thinks this should continue until cooperation on different levels eventually paves the way to a solution.[58] However, the former Secretary General of SAARC argues that Pakistan is suspicious of this Indian intention. He stated that even though at the Twelfth SAARC Summit in Islamabad seven member nations agreed to strengthen the Secretariat, a year later he had been unable to arrange a meeting of experts to implement the decision. In his view, they do not want the Secretariat to be strengthened and cooperation to flourish because it would mean that Kashmir had to be forgotten.[59]

Mohammed thinks that even the Kashmiris may learn to live in this situation indefinitely if the economy develops successfully. Ultimately, who cares where they live? How one lives in financial terms is more important. If this is correct then perhaps India's intention of prioritizing development, not the conflict, may yield good results on the security/strategic dimension.[60]

What then is the connection between nuclear weapons and conflict resolution? P. Sahadevan thinks that "nuclear weapons have not done much for conflict resolution. Both [countries] are comfortable with the present state of the conflict – so they don't feel the need to negotiate."[61] According to Raj Chengappa, "The rationale for developing [nuclear weapons] was not conflict resolution. It was not like you had an option. It was forced on India."[62] Savita Pande makes much the same point: "They [nuclear weapons acquisition] were not supposed to help in initiating negotiation between India and Pakistan."[63] From this perspective, there was no expectation that India and Pakistan would benefit in terms of conflict resolution from the acquisition of nuclear weapons.

How should conflict resolution be achieved? Muni argues that the LoC should be accepted as an international border. Territory is not the issue for the Indians, but Pakistan has to accept the LoC.

> There are limits beyond which no compromise is possible. Nobody in Pakistan should have any illusion. That is the beauty of democracy. No government shall ever be able to seek any territory of PoK [Pakistan-occupied Kashmir] – according to the Constitution. I can easily say that that is the best solution.[64]

While Indians may think that is the best solution, Pakistanis do not agree. Stephen P. Cohen states, "Many Indians would like to draw the international boundary along the cease-fire line, with minor adjustments. Pakistan rejects this idea, although it keeps cropping up in Indian discussions and in proposals by third parties."[65] If this situation continues and the issue remains unresolved, what will be the conflict relations in the future? Mattoo maintains that nuclear weapons have shown India and Pakistan that they cannot fight a war. Now they have to think about every possibility short of war. Since war is not possible in the India–Pakistan conflict, resolution is also difficult.[66]

The India–Pakistan conflict has coexisted with cooperation in trade, culture, and communications since 2003 and this has continued to strengthen good relations between the contending parties. However, both have refrained from making any serious progress on the salient issue, Kashmir, which could mitigate the conflict permanently. Both believe that cooperation on different levels might pave the way to conflict resolution. However, in the four intervening years the central issue has not been thoroughly discussed, and India intentionally refrains from dealing with it seriously. It is unlikely that Pakistan will be able to eliminate terrorism, which remains one of India's conditions for the settlement of all outstanding security issues with Pakistan. Each side has its own agenda and it seems unlikely that either will be willing to compromise on this important territorial issue. As a result, they have almost closed off discussion on the root security cause of the conflict and are dealing with other soft issues. This process has primarily restructured the relationship into one where the states are cooperating within the parameters of the conflict – aware that the conflict has no end in sight although war is no longer an option and new dimensions of cooperation have emerged. Thus the conflict has undergone a permanent transformation. Does this mean there is no possibility of it being resolved? The next chapter analyzes some actor and situational attributes that could be instrumental in resolving the transformed India–Pakistan conflict.

## Summary

This chapter has looked at one of the salient implications of nuclear weapons acquisition for conflict resolution, investigating what happened to the India–Pakistan conflict when the two sides started cooperation in different spheres but could not address the central issue in dispute. It argued that this cooperation has transformed the conflict permanently. Having learned to cooperate in an environment of conflict, the two sides learn to live with the situation indefinitely and lose interest in terminating the conflict. They may realize the urgency of resolving the root issue, but they also realize the difficulties involved. Consequently, they tend to cooperate within the parameters of the conflict.

# 10 Potential for conflict termination

This book's primary purpose is to demonstrate the negative ramifications of nuclear weapons acquisition for the India–Pakistan protracted conflict. However, it also aims to highlight the salient roles of actor attributes and situational attributes in resolving the conflict. The purpose is to illustrate that a conflict is likely to become protracted when the two sides acquire nuclear weapons, a unit-level attribute, unless there is a significant change in an actor attribute such as leadership or political/ economic capability, or in a situational attribute, such as third-party intervention in order to terminate the conflict. The chapter discusses whether there is still any possibility of terminating the conflict despite its crisis-prone environment. The roles of external powers, in particular the US, bold leaders, and political/economic capabilities are analyzed in this regard. The connection between all three attributes is also discussed.

How valuable is a thaw – which can be brought about by an external power, strong leadership, or domestic aspects – for conflict termination? A thaw in a conflict means a relaxation of tension between the actors. It may be a function of a cease-fire after a crisis or war, or it may simply be a distinct or unique period in a conflict. During a thaw, the overall relationship between the parties in conflict tends to be stable. Thaws may be imposed on the contending parties by powerful states with an interest in managing the conflict or they may be achieved by the parties themselves. Some thaws are more positive or productive than others, and so have a better chance of bringing the parties to the negotiating table. How do states create positive/productive thaws?

A combination of systemic, domestic, and leadership elements may bring a thaw in a long-running conflict with the potential of terminating it. One of the principal factors conducive to a thaw is a systemic change, which has impacts at the regional level. Where the stability and security of the world system are associated with regional security, great powers may focus on regional security dynamics to obtain global stability. Thus a systemic change attracts the attention of the great powers to regional conflicts. When a great power takes a special interest in a regional conflict for its own security reasons, its first step is to pressure the parties to create a thaw. Its role here is not that of a mediator but simply that of a facilitator with its own interests in seeing a thaw in the regional conflict. Once the stage for a thaw is set by a great power, the parties are in a position to move forward and focus on the real issues in dispute between them. In such a case, one of the parties may take conciliatory moves as proposed by the Graduated Reduction in Tension (GRIT) strategy, discussed on pp. 18–19. This is further facilitated if the leadership is motivated by a personal or domestic political agenda. As one of the leaders initiates and consolidates the process, it becomes increasingly difficult for the other side not to change the enemy's negative image which is now being contradicted by new information, as explained by Janis Gross Stein and analyzed on p. 18. That the enemy state is evil and cannot be friendly or good is always at the back of the leader's mind, but the change in its policies proves otherwise. Reciprocity is dependent on the words of the enemy being followed up by deeds, so that trust develops. The process is facilitated by the great power's constant oversight of the security dynamics of the conflict for its own reasons. Consequently, although a thaw may be initiated by a leader – whether following the GRIT strategy or not – and although the leader's motive could be domestic or personal, it is unlikely to happen without a facilitator. However, no country ever wants to take on this role because it means serious and active involvement, cost, and sometimes taking sides. As mentioned before, the facilitator is often not interested in specific regional security dynamics unless they are directly connected to its own security. Although it is rare, such a connection could emerge due to systemic changes. Where that is the case, it is likely that the great power will take a special interest in regional security matters.

The great power has the important role of it focusing on regional stability and putting pressure on whichever party is disrupting it. A situation is thus created in which the other party to the conflict is not afraid to make overtures of friendship. The troublemaker in the region abides by the norms set by the great power, even if unwilling to give in to its pressure permanently. Compliance is all the more likely if in the context of other regions the great power has shown previously that intransigence is followed by negative consequences. Although the party under pressure from the great power may dislike the way things are going, as it reaps the benefits of a stable environment in the region it comes to value the role the facilitator has played. After all, no party wants to entertain violence and instability, but no one knows where to start the peace process and what the consequences might be. Interestingly, where a great power has set the stage, a thaw may be productive. This is partially because rivals can begin to trust each other and consequently confidence-building measures can be developed. The thaw is likely to be institutionalized if the great power continues to be the regional watchdog on account of its own security needs. Although thaws in protracted conflicts tend not to last, it is not impossible to create a durable one if leaders take conciliatory steps in different realms.

A propitious environment, generated by a facilitator, is the main precondition for a thaw. If this environment can be made to last, the initial trust it generates will be institutionalized, favouring the development of a peace process that will lead to conflict resolution.

As discussed throughout this study, the India–Pakistan conflict has proved intractable, and the efforts made to end it have been generally unsuccessful. The conflict has witnessed three wars and a large number of inter-state crises. There have been few peaceful periods except the Lahore Peace Process in 1999 and the

Agra Summit in 2001 (see pp. 116–27). The Simla Agreement concluded at the end of the 1971 Bangladesh war, that marked the break-up of Pakistan, was not a peace process but primarily a post-war settlement which stipulated that all disputes between India and Pakistan would be settled bilaterally.

The Indian Parliament Attack of December 2001 triggered an unprecedented level of hostility between the contending powers. As discussed in previous chapters, in the post-attack period the conflict severely intensified As tension decreased with the de-escalation of the crisis, both sides started considering other options for improving relations, and in just a few months their relationship calmed down, and the atmosphere seemed propitious for a dialogue to start. India and Pakistan began a new round of initiatives to settle their disputes in a comprehensive manner, as discussed in chapter 9. The results of a set of planned meetings were also promising. The media on both sides put an optimistic slant on the dialogue because they were encouraged not to convey unnecessary hate messages and provoke anti-peace attitudes.

In this context, it is important to analyze the present cooperation endeavor and compare it with the last two peace initiatives to see whether this one is any more promising. The comparison should shed light on whether the dialogue will survive and what is likely to help it to do so. It will also demonstrate the connections between unit-level and situational attributes. All this will show whether there is potential for the India–Pakistan conflict to be resolved and what forces, independently or interconnectedly, would help to attain that goal.

## The systemic shock: the role of 9/11 in setting the stage for the thaw

Unlike the previous ones, the present thaw is a direct product of the 9/11 attacks, which constituted a systemic shock that impacted almost every region of the world, including South Asia. It is a systemic shock because although the end of the cold war brought an end to the two-power/bipolar international system, the US, now the sole superpower, only consolidated its power after the 9/11 attacks, and only then was American supremacy legitimized. Robert Kagan argues that "the struggle to define and obtain legitimacy in this new era may prove to be among the critical contests . . . in some ways as significant in determining the future of the international system and America's place in it."[1] America's legitimacy as a world leader had been at stake since the end of the cold war. Javier Solana states that legitimacy "depends on creating a wide international consensus," but there is no universal consensus on who will decide how wide is wide and when it is wide enough.[2] Prior to the attacks, America was called the lonely superpower[3] that did not have the support or respect of not only minor regional powers but major powers as well. However, after the attacks, most states in the international system bandwagoned with the US in its war on terror. Every country was able to comprehend the power of the US and how far it was willing to go to clamp down on terrorists. Terrorism of any form had to be eliminated. Almost every country in the world felt the need to support the US in its drive to uproot terrorism. Perhaps for the first time since the US emerged from the cold war as the only superpower, it enjoyed unconditional support and cooperation from most states in the world.

Generally external shocks, such as world wars and the end of the cold war, are supposed to bring systemic changes. The terrorist attacks on New York and Washington on September 11, 2001 likewise changed the world. Friends, allies, and former enemies or not-so-friendly states came forward to cooperate with the US in its war on terror. Terrorism was a serious concern not only of the US but of almost every other state as well. It was also understood by most states including the US that containing terrorism required global cooperation. Only if no state allowed terrorists time, space, and support, they could be defeated. Now South Asia became a focus because of Pakistan's connections with Al Qaeda. From being a pariah state, Pakistan became a front-line state when, within the first few days, the US realized its importance in the fight against terror. The Bush administration announced it would "hunt down the terrorists" and "smoke them out" of their holes. Afghanistan became the key country in this new war since it was giving shelter to the primary suspect, Bin Laden, and his terrorist organization Al Qaeda. The Taliban government of Afghanistan was asked to hand over Bin Laden but it refused to do so. Pakistan, Saudi Arabia, and the United Arab Emirates were the only three countries to have recognized the Taliban as the legitimate government of Afghanistan. Pakistan, a country sharing a long border with Afghanistan, had financed and militarily supported the Taliban which was giving shelter to Bin Laden and enabling him to remain actively involved in terrorist activities. Thus Pakistan was seen as a crucial partner in the war on terrorism. This was not a traditional war which can be won by military might, but a war in which strategy, intelligence, and information were all-important weapons. In addition, fighting terrorists, a non-state actor, is very different from fighting a state with defined borders. It became crystal-clear that Pakistan could be an extremely strong partner in this state versus non-state actor war. Overnight Washington made the first move in compelling Islamabad to cooperate fully with the US in its fight against terrorism. Under enormous US pressure, Pakistan had to make a prompt decision as to whether to be part of this endeavor. Left with the choice of either siding with the US or becoming known as a state supporting terrorism, Pakistan agreed to join the US-led coalition against international terrorism. Any leader in President Pervez Musharraf's position would have chosen alliance with the US. Since then, there has been intense pressure on Islamabad to dismantle terrorist camps and any terrorist training facility that may have existed on its soil. Pakistan's military ruler, General Musharraf, with little domestic support, has gone all the way in cooperating with the US to combat terrorism.

Musharraf tried, as no other Pakistani leader had, to eradicate terrorism from the country, using deeds, not mere words, to satisfy the US demands. In the wake of 9/11, the US had become a much stronger and more confident hegemonic power, which felt it not only had the right but also the power to change the policies of regional states, even a nuclear state such as Pakistan. Just a few days after the Indian Parliament Attack, Brahma Chellaney stated, "Pakistan is a failed state, but Americans have a contingency plan for Pakistan."[4] By this time, India was expecting the US to deal with Pakistan's terrorist activities. Prior to 9/11, the US either was not motivated to compel Pakistan to address the problem of terrorism or did not feel such pressure was justified, even though the connection between Al Qaeda and Pakistan was quite well known.

While the Americans witnessed a terrorist attack of a massive scale in 2001, India has endured terrorist activities on its soil since the 1980s when Kashmiri militants began low–medium-intensity violence in the Indian part of Kashmir. The Indians believed that Pakistanis were giving these terrorists/militants moral, diplomatic, and, most importantly, military support. After the Indian Parliament Attack of December 2001, the US could no longer ignore Pakistan's complicity in the terrorist activities of militant Kashmiris.[5] The Bush administration then launched its "two-pronged strategy," which "counseled restraint on the part of India while placing Lashkar-i-Taiba and Jaish-i-Mohammed [two Pakistani extremist groups] on the State Department's list of terrorist organizations and freezing their assets in the United States."[6] As Pakistan implemented its anti-terrorist policies, one of India's main South Asian security concerns was addressed. For India, it did not matter why Pakistan's policies had changed, it was more important to see whether or not the new policies were enforced. With Musharraf's implementation of some of those policies, India began to trust Pakistan and the regional climate improved. India was in an advantageous position in this equation because the US had taken on the role of overseer of terrorist activities in Pakistan. India could be less nervous than it had been in earlier periods when Pakistan said one thing and did something else. This set the stage for a thaw between India and Pakistan, facilitated by the US as a result of the external shock of the 9/11 attacks.

It must be borne in mind, however, that the Indian Parliament was attacked after 9/11, on December 13, 2001, and the ensuing crisis in South Asia lasted for eighteen months. The thaw only started during the spring of 2003, so the exogenous shock did not have an immediate impact on the South Asian region. This does not contradict Goertz and Diehl's systemic shock theory, discussed on p. 17, because they allow that the impact of an external shock on a conflict may not be immediate. After the 9/11 attacks, the Pakistani government needed time to change its policies on terrorism and implementing them took even more time. Although Musharraf was under pressure from the US to eliminate Pakistan's connections with terrorism, nothing could be done overnight. Under US pressure, Musharraf in an address to the nation on January 12, 2002 – a month after the Indian Parliament Attack – stated that Pakistani soil would not be utilized to export terror to any part of the world. With this statement, he made it his official policy to terminate cross-border terrorism in South Asia. He also announced a new policy of reform of *madrassas* by broadening their curriculum and banned the two terrorist organizations – Lashkar-e-Taiba and Jaish-e-Mohammed – that were supposedly responsible for the Indian Parliament Attack.[7] These policy changes were significant because before 9/11, Musharraf himself insisted that there was a need to distinguish *jihad* (holy war) from terrorism, and argued that *jihad* was "a legitimate instrument of the Kashmiris' freedom struggle."[8] However, implementation of these policy changes was not easy, given the serious domestic pressures he was faced with. Whereas India was critical because the new policies were taking too long to implement to have a positive impact on the India–Pakistan conflict, in the domestic sphere Musharraf was condemned for abandoning the militants.[9] It took him about two years to call for a *jihad* against the *jihadis* (holy warriors) – a step change from his earlier policy shifts – in his first address to the Pakistani Parliament in early 2004. Such decisions took time to garner the support of the people who were bewildered by this drastic shift to a policy that went against their ideology, doctrine, and understanding of South Asian security dynamics. The US war on Iraq of March 2003 also helped Musharraf to convince his people that Pakistan must not support radical militants because continuing its previous policies on terrorism could invite a US attack. After all, the US-led war was waged not simply to rid Iraq of weapons of mass destruction, but also to put a stop to alleged Iraqi connections with terrorism.[10] Although some segments of the society may have supported the changes in the interests of greater security, Musharraf continued to face tremendous domestic pressure, demonstrated by the three assassination attempts he escaped when he first decided to clamp down on terrorists and cooperate with America in its war on terror. By January 2003, India had understood that Pakistan's transformation would be instrumental in bringing "qualitative change" in India–Pakistan relations.[11]

## Image change leading to use of the GRIT strategy: Vajpayee's unilateral peace initiative

India was the main beneficiary of the US–led drive to create a Pakistan free of the scourge of terrorism. Vajpayee, who had already twice tried unsuccessfully to make peace with Pakistan during his term of office, saw another opportunity to extend the hand of friendship. He made the peace overture in April 2003, but it was not until October 2003 when he decided to back it up with a renewed package of confidence-building measures, that the initiative received a new momentum.[12] He waited to see if Musharraf's new policies would actually be implemented. He attended the South Asian Association for Regional Cooperation (SAARC) Summit in Islamabad in January 2004 as a good will gesture and offered to hold talks with Pakistan on outstanding issues in the conflict. The significance of Vajpayee's personal and party interests cannot be overestimated in this context. On a personal level, he wanted his tenure to leave its mark. An India–Pakistan peace initiative was likely to have a positive impact on the upcoming national elections, which would bring Vajpayee to power again if the Bharatiya Janata Party (BJP) won. He expected India's large Muslim community to understand his positive role in the search for peace and the BJP's respect for India's secular policies. Stephen Saideman states, "Politicians will do what is necessary to stay in power even if it means supporting policies likely to hurt the country. The key is to consider upon whom leaders depend for support and what their supporters want."[13] Pervaiz Iqbal Cheema maintained in 2003, "The BJP can win the next election if it maintains friendly relations with Pakistan and the neighbors."[14] Although these considerations may have influenced Vajpayee to start a new round of initiatives, he only did so after Musharraf announced his changed views and policies on terrorism. India had long insisted that a new round of talks could only start if Pakistan ended its support for the terrorists in Kashmir, dismantled their infrastructure of terror, and stopped cross-border terror. Thus it would have been difficult for Vajpayee to undertake this new move had Musharraf not cracked down on the terrorists.[15]

Musharraf's policy changes influenced Vajpayee for two reasons: first the image of Pakistan changed, even if only temporarily, when Musharraf announced his new policy on terrorism. As stated earlier, hostile images of the enemy are serious obstacles to conflict resolution or even reduction. Musharraf's government's decisions to uproot the extremist groups, ban the most radical terrorist organizations, arrest their leaders,[16] and call on the nation not to help people who use violence and terror in the name of Islamic *jihad*, were highly significant, and not even India could fail to acknowledge their importance. These big policy shifts and their implementation meant a lot to the Indians who had waited for decades for a day when the leaders of Pakistan, especially the military, would understand the value of not aiding terrorists in South Asia. Vajpayee, who considered Musharraf to be untrustworthy due to his earlier support for Islamic militants,[17] could not ignore these policy changes because they were not trivial. In fact, even before Musharraf made commitments to cut off Islamabad's connections with Kashmiri terrorists, India observed Pakistan's policy changes in the realm of terrorism in Afghanistan very closely. James Clad argues that

> India was caught unprepared for General Musharraf's about-face opportunism over Taliban. Pakistan's willingness to step aside and watch the destruction of its Taliban ally – installed in Afghanistan after years of the Pakistani military's patient work and overt backing on the battlefield – showed strategic pragmatism at its best and worst.[18]

Pakistan's policy changes were all the more significant to the Indians because it was Musharraf, a military man who had orchestrated the Kargil conflict as Pakistan's army chief, who undertook them. Pakistan's military, which has ruled the country for most of its history, has always been sympathetic to the Kashmiri militants and has engaged in violent activities in the disputed Kashmir region. As Major General V. K. Srivastava puts it, the "Pakistan army has a very authoritative control in the political affairs of the state. Half the time the army has controlled the country. For them an anti-India stance is good."[19] What General Musharraf did was remarkable, as the Pakistanis acknowledged. Mushahid Hussain stated, "General Musharraf has been extremely flexible considering the fact that he is a military ruler."[20] Thus, positive and dramatic policy changes by a military leader changed India's image of Pakistan and signaled a better future, even though India had always believed that it could only establish friendly relations with a democratic Pakistan.

Vajpayee's decision to visit Pakistan for the second time in his tenure was extremely valuable for the dialogue process. While he may also have been motivated by a domestic political and personal agenda,[21] his decision was a direct response to Pakistan's dramatic change of policy. Though acting under US pressure, Pakistan realized that "a conflict simmering endlessly is not helping" and "Vajpayee means business when he talks about peace."[22] When India decided to retaliate the terrorist attacks in 2001, Washington "extracted a pledge" from President Musharraf to stop infiltration across the line of control (LoC).[23] India had never previously wanted the US or any other external power to mediate in the conflict. The Simla Accord of 1972 and the Lahore Process both stipulated that the disputed issues should be resolved through bilateral negotiations. However, after the 9/11 attacks, India realized it could make the US understand what it had had to face since the 1980s. It was quick to express its support for the US war on terror, although the US needed Pakistan rather than India to defeat the Taliban and Al Qaeda in Afghanistan. Raja Mohan states that "New Delhi calculated that the events of September 11 would finally clinch the much-vaunted natural alliance, which India had hoped to build since the late 1990s, and take it to new levels."[24] India's relations with the US had begun to improve under the Clinton administration. In May 2001 Stephen P. Cohen observed that New Delhi and Washington "have moved from a near-alliance in the late 1950s, to apathy in the 1970s, to estrangement by the 1990s. The two countries may not be natural allies, but they are now natural friends."[25] The new friendship had emerged in the late 1990s and early 2000, and was consolidated when President Clinton helped to defuse the Kargil conflict and pressured Pakistan to retreat from Kargil unconditionally, when he visited South Asia and Washington addressed issues of religious extremism and international terrorism. However, the 9/11 attacks "brought a new energy and purpose to US engagement."[26] South Asian security had become a global concern and the US could not longer avoid the issue of cross-border terrorism there. India and the US had a shared interest in dismantling the *jihadi* network in South Asia.[27] Conditions for friendship with the US had been created and India wanted the Kashmiri militants to be "objects of the ongoing US anti-terror campaign."[28]

New Delhi understood that an "American role could work to India's advantage."[29] There can be no doubt that US involvement in South Asia is closely linked to the nuclear issue. First, as this study has proved, a peace process is unlikely to take place where there are nuclear weapons. Thus, the US played an essential role in setting the stage for a thaw. Second, the US became involved because the crisis had the potential to escalate to nuclear level. Third, US engagement was a result of the terrorist attacks of 2001 and its concern to eliminate terrorism from South Asia, where the perpetrators had hitherto found refuge. There was also the fear that the terrorists might gain access to Pakistan's nuclear weapons in their campaign against the US.

A crucial factor in resolving the India–Pakistan conflict is the role of the leadership, an actor attribute. Leadership can provide a major breakthrough in diplomacy for a peace agreement.

> Specific new policies, which involve the end of hostility with an enemy, need to be formulated and implemented in order for conflict resolution to occur.

Major policy changes require new ideas, and these usually come in the form of new people. New leadership is frequently divorced from past policies, often comes into power because past policies have failed, and is not inhibited by the sunk costs of old leadership.[30]

Although Vajpayee had not just come to power in 2003, he introduced new policies that marked a major break from his predecessor's policies, as evidenced by the two peace endeavors he initiated after the nuclear tests, his path-breaking bus journey to Lahore, and the subsequent invitation to Musharraf for the Agra Summit. Vajpayee was serious about making peace with Pakistan and resolving the intractable conflict. His words were respected in India and people understood that he was serious when he spoke of peace and, equally, when he said firm measures against Pakistan were needed, for example when he felt betrayed after Kargil and the Parliament Attack. K. K. Nayyar stated after the Indian Parliament Attack, "When Vajpayee says something – that is final. His name is 'Atal' and he is stubborn. Pakistan needs to realize that. When Vajpayee says, 'Enough is enough,' that's it."[31] Vajpayee was respected and taken seriously even in Pakistan. Referring to Vajpayee, Nasim Zehra maintained in 2003, "It is easier to deal with hawkish policy makers and easier to understand them."[32] When the leader of a hawkish Hindu party wants to make peace with a Muslim Pakistan, the people there take the initiative seriously. Zehra added, "It wouldn't be wise for Pakistan to wait" till another government comes to power.[33] Vajpayee's personal wish for peace with Pakistan to be his historical legacy was a strong influence on the process.

His quest for peace may have been connected to domestic political considerations, as indicated by the timing of his moves for dialogue prior to the Indian election. Economic factors may also influence and shape peacemaking. Leaders may want to mitigate economic problems by making peace with rivals. Richard Ned Lebow argued that a leader, committed to domestic reforms which are dependent on foreign cooperation, is likely to initiate accommodation strategies with its rival.[34] Democratic states can further economic reform and national development by encouraging openness to international trade and investment.[35] Vajpayee focused on economic reform during his tenure and his search for peace with Pakistan was influenced by the economic benefits interdependent trade would bring. On the Pakistani side, although many think Pakistan was compelled to make peace by US pressure, domestic political and economic considerations were also important. Musharraf wanted to preserve his military regime by showing that he was interested in peace. He also wanted to disprove the general belief that military leaders are less inclined to peace and to improve civil-military relations on the domestic front. Farooq Hassan states that "Musharraf is desperate to have good relations with India because he wants stability for his regime and not because he is interested in peace. India and Pakistan are proceeding in a direction which can't be called friendly."[36] As Pakistan's economy has not been doing well since the end of the cold war, peace could encourage international economic aid and "lessen the crushing defense burden."[37]

## Comparison with past thaws

The present thaw should be compared with similar thaws in the past so as to assess the potential for long-term conflict termination. The most important thaws in the past were the period leading up to the Lahore Peace Process and the period just prior to the Agra Summit. Both were very different from the thaw lasting from 2003 to the present. One of the most important components missing from both of them was an external power willing to oversee security dynamics in South Asia. The Lahore *yatra* was at best a GRIT strategy initiated by Vajpayee in the hope of reciprocation. Although Vajpayee came to power with bold Hindu religious rhetoric and soon afterwards India conducted a series of nuclear tests, he took a bolder step when he offered friendship to Pakistan. He did this without external pressure, nor was there any pressure on Pakistan to reciprocate. May 1998 to February 1999 was the period when US-India relations reached their lowest ebb in the post-cold war era because of India's nuclear tests and the sanctions then imposed on India by the US and the international community. There was no question of US involvement in mediating or in facilitating the peace process then. Pakistan's relations with the US had also deteriorated as a result of its nuclear tests and the imposition of sanctions.

Vajpayee made his journey to Lahore not because his image of Pakistan had changed or because he believed that Pakistan had stopped supporting the Kashmiri militants, or because he was under pressure. It was a simple act on the part of a leader who believed in peace. Consequently, the peace did not last long. Although the cold war had ended in 1990, the implications for South Asian security were minimal. The US, now the only superpower, was busy inventing new threats, having lost its foe of forty years standing. Consequently, the focus was more on rogue states than on South Asia. Although both India and Pakistan were then on the verge of becoming nuclear states, they were never considered threats to the US.

The Lahore Peace Process did not even last three months because one of the worst crises ever between India and Pakistan erupted in Kargil. Pakistan took advantage of the GRIT strategy Vajpayee adopted in February 1999. Islamabad could not play a new game in an old context, as already stated. The old context was very much predominant and the old pattern of crisis and conflict continued. Consequently, the Indian image of Pakistan still remained the same or even deteriorated as a result of Kargil.

US pressure was not a factor in the period leading up to the Agra Summit of July 2001 either. There was no change in Pakistan's policies on terrorism, nor any serious US pressure to change the South Asian security situation. After General Musharraf took power in Pakistan in October 1999, there was little hope in India for a peace initiative with the architect of the Kargil attack. Violence continued in the Kashmir region and showed no sign of abatement. Although President Clinton visited South Asia in March 2000 and discussed terrorism with both India and Pakistan, as mentioned earlier, his visit did not change Pakistan's support for militancy in Kashmir. When Vajpayee declared a unilateral cease-fire at the start of Ramadan in November 2000 and extended it after the holy month had ended, violence in Kashmir did not decrease and, in fact, Jaish-e-Mohammed and Hizbul Mujahideen disregarded the cease-fire.[38] Vajpayee came under increasing pressure from his own party to change his policies and lift the cease-fire because it was not bringing any benefit to India.[39] Although the cease-fire was revoked by May 2001, he showed his willingness to discuss bilateral issues with Pakistan by inviting General Musharraf to the summit in Agra which was held in July 2001. However, on both sides of the border, people did not expect much from the summit.[40]

One of the reasons for pessimism was that this ground-breaking decision taken by Vajpayee was not related to a policy change in Pakistan that could have made the thaw stable. At the summit, while Vajpayee insisted on discussing the insurgency in Kashmir and Pakistan's support for it, Pakistan insisted that the LoC could not be the international border. India reiterated that a compromise on Kashmir was not possible because it would cause a domino effect in the rest of India.[41] The summit ended in Indian dissatisfaction because the Pakistanis underestimated the importance of the Kashmiri insurgency and would not discuss the matter seriously enough. Pakistan was likewise unhappy because India still seemed to believe that Jammu and Kashmir was not in dispute. Thus, the Agra Summit merely proved that the two leaders could not even agree "on the language for a joint communiqué."[42]

The reasons for this unsatisfactory outcome were obvious: India's image of Pakistan was unchanged because its adversary had never admitted its support for cross-border terrorism and was not willing to change its policies on Kashmir. India insisted that Pakistan must stop cross-border terrorism whereas Pakistan insisted that it was only providing moral and diplomatic support to the Kashmiris. There was no common ground, each side took a tough stance on Kashmir, and the talks stalled. The conditions for fruitful dialogue were absent. Both parties repeated the statements they had made already and failed to exploit the opportunity to discuss issues face to face.

Stephen P. Cohen hypothesized that to resolve the central issues between India and Pakistan, the "process would require major policy changes on the part of India and Pakistan . . . and on the part of the most likely outside 'facilitator' of such a process, the United States."[43] As mentioned earlier, both India and Pakistan changed their policies in South Asia in the aftermath of 9/11 and the facilitator – the US – also changed its stance toward South Asia as it wanted to eliminate terrorism. But prior to 9/11 all attempts at peacemaking were unproductive.

If the US had taken on its present role a few decades ago, the situation in South Asia would have been very different and the conflict might not have become so intractable. As Ashok Kapur rightly argues, the US and other great powers have played a role in institutionalizing the India–Pakistan rivalry.[44]

Although hopes for conflict resolution are still premature, it is quite possible that if the US continues to act as a facilitator in the India–Pakistan dialogue, peace may ultimately ensue.

What does this imply? This chapter has emphasized the differences between the present India–Pakistan thaw and similar situations in the past to assess the outlook for conflict termination. The new thaw was the result of an external shock, 9/11, which made the US see South Asian security as a serious aspect of the war on terror. Pakistan's attempts to comply with US requests to uproot terror created a better environment in South Asia, by changing India's image of Pakistan. This congenial setting was used by India to initiate a dialogue. The Pakistanis, like the Indians, believe that conflict resolution can be "arrived at by intensive dialogue."[45] A new situation has been created. The comparison indicates that although the conflict seemed to have become indefinitely protracted, there is room for optimism if the US continues to take a special interest in resolving the conflict. As Cohen puts it, "India and Pakistan may not be able to arrive at a comprehensive peace without the help of an outside power or powers. The only outsider that could initiate such a process at this time would be the United States."[46]

The comparison reveals some interesting points. First, the idea that only democratic states are able to terminate a long-running conflict could be spurious. Pakistan's case demonstrates that with pressure, support, and cooperation from a great power, especially the US, a non-democratic state may initiate a peace process or reciprocate to overtures launched by its adversary. Second, the Indian notion that no external involvement would be required to terminate the bilateral India–Pakistan conflict has also been disproved. Although the US has not mediated in the conflict, it has facilitated the dialogue process as a result of the better security environment created in South Asia by its pressure on Pakistan to uproot terrorism. Cross-border terrorism has been brought under some degree of control, even if it has not stopped altogether. Pakistanis are wrong when they say that "the American sponsored dialogue will not be favorable to the Pakistanis,"[47] because this implies that the US is a mediator, which is not its role in the India–Pakistan conflict since 2003. Third, the belief among some scholars that conflicts can be ended if leaders make bold peace initiatives, Anwar Sadat of Egypt did in the context of the Arab-Israeli conflict, is also debatable. While leaders' efforts and initiatives are required for any peace process to start, they can only succeed in a conducive environment, not in a crisis-and violence-prone setting of the kind analyzed in this study. A leader must believe that the enemy will reciprocate if he/she takes the first step. This belief will only come about if the enemy state has shown signs of a positive policy change. A leader cannot make a bold gesture toward peace without domestic approval. This is more likely in a democratic environment and India, one of the largest democracies in the world, is no exception. Domestic approval is more likely when a favorable environment has been created already, either through bilateral efforts unusual where the states in conflict have nuclear weapons – or through the action of a great power – possibly more effective in a protracted conflict.

Even though the present thaw seems more genuine than the earlier ones, there is room for skepticism because a thaw does not automatically lead on to the termination of a conflict. Conflict termination requires the resolution of all the issues in contention. Since this difficult task still faces India and Pakistan, it is impossible to conclude that the enduring rivalry will end just because a more convincing thaw has been created. The results of the composite dialogue will determine the fate of the conflict. It will also be important for the US to maintain its oversight of the South Asian security situation, especially as regards militancy and terrorism, so that any progress made by the states in conflict is not jeopardized.

## Summary

This chapter has compared the present India–Pakistan thaw, which has allowed the composite dialogue to take place, with previous periods of thaw, investigating whether there is any potential for the resolution of this intractable conflict. It revealed that the actor attribute of leadership, whether motivated by personal, domestic-political, or economic factors, is not likely to establish a permanent thaw which could actually end the conflict. Past thaws have all been of this kind, and have consequently not endured. The present thaw has the new factor of the US role of facilitator, motivated by the 9/11 attacks which made America especially interested in South Asian security as a result of its goal of ending terrorism. With US oversight and Pakistan changing its policies on terrorism, India could change its image of Pakistan and participate in a new dialogue process. Given the US role, dialogue could be sustained. Whether it will produce positive results in terms of conflict termination remains uncertain.

# Conclusion

This book sought to expose the negative effects of nuclear weapons acquisition on conflict resolution. It made a causal connection between nuclear weapons acquisition by two warring states and the indefinite intractability of a protracted conflict. It defined protracted conflicts as high conflict situations without termination points where crises are embedded and wars remain a probability largely because territory is at stake. It maintained that each protracted conflict has a life-cycle which encompasses several phases: beginning, escalation, de-escalation, and cessation. Each is affected by the others and each phase has to be crossed for the conflict to end. A conflict begins as a result of one or more triggers and escalates in crises and wars. Escalation may be high, medium, or low depending on the level of violence, whether war, crisis, or some other violent event. De-escalation is a function of agreement, compromise, settlement, third-party mediation, and leadership initiative. Cessation reflects the end of the conflict with the establishment of peace. Unless a conflict reaches the cessation phase, it cannot be said to have terminated.

The book has argued that in the absence of nuclear weapons, a conflict usually reaches the cessation phase as a result of war, the traditional conflict termination mechanism used by most belligerent states in the world. Wars decide winners and losers and at the termination of a conflict the winning side dictates the terms of the settlement to the loser. As states acquire nuclear weapons to deter war in a protracted conflict setting – and this is likely to involve conflict over territory – they can no longer manage crises through full-scale war for fear of escalation to the nuclear level; thus a crisis management technique has become unusable. Consequently, they tend to use other means of crisis management such as violent clashes and low–medium-intensity violence. Additionally, as escalation to war becomes less likely, more crises are initiated by the weaker side to make small territorial gains and change the status quo. Therefore, while the deterrent effect of nuclear weapons creates a no-war situation, heated crises and low–medium-intensity violence may become more likely. The occurrence of frequent crises and low–medium-intensity violence – functions of the absence of war – changes the nature of the protracted conflict, perhaps even keeping it alive indefinitely. Peace initiatives may be taken by leaders during periods of calm but cannot be institutionalized due to the eruption and recurrence of crises. Meanwhile, continuing low-intensity violence causes a general deterioration in the environment, precluding the possibility of successful peace initiatives. In these conditions, the conflict is indefinitely prolonged. This is a result not only of the adverse climate for peace initiatives but also of the fact that the parties learn to live in an environment of violence where they cooperate on less controversial issues, not addressing the root cause of the conflict. Thus India and Pakistan have embarked on cooperation on less controversial, positive-sum issues, and hesitate to address the root cause or the tangible territorial issue, Kashmir. However, the book has argued that such cooperation has the potential to produce positive results in conflict resolution if major powers, in particular the US, become involved and if leaders are prepared to make bold, dramatic moves.

The book applied the theoretical framework to test its value and strength against the India–Pakistan protracted conflict case. The case study shows that the India–Pakistan rivalry, which began in 1947 and has lasted ever since, went through the first two phases of the life of a protracted conflict – beginning and escalation – but could not get beyond the second phase. Instead, it froze at this stage. It has also been shown that this near-stagnation has been a result of the acquisition of nuclear weapons by the warring parties after 1986. The conflict encompassed two periods – pre-nuclear and nuclear – which have been different in terms of their crises and the use of the crisis management strategy, war. The pre-nuclear period saw crises which escalated to wars in 1947–8, 1965, and 1971, whereas the nuclear period has seen more serious crises which never escalated, even though they all had the potential to do so. The weaker party in the conflict, Pakistan, initiated all four serious crises in the nuclear period, the Brasstacks crisis, the Kashmir crisis of 1990, the Kargil crisis, and the Parliament Attack crisis. Given the presence of nuclear weapons, Pakistan knew these crises were unlikely to escalate and hoped to make small territorial gains and internationalize the conflict by attracting the attention of the US. It believed that Washington would be concerned about possible nuclear escalation of a crisis in the India–Pakistan conflict and become diplomatically involved.

The study also established that peace talks were held by India and Pakistan during periods of calm in the conflict despite its generally crisis-prone nature. The evidence suggests that the recurrence of crises prevented all these peace initiatives from being consolidated, for example the Lahore Peace Process and the Agra Summit. Thus all efforts were futile. It also confirmed that constant low-intensity violence has made it difficult for the parties to trust each other as hatred has resurfaced with every new violent incident. Such a situation is not conducive to undertaking peace initiatives and institutionalizing those already undertaken. Although under US pressure the parties began a dialogue two years after the Parliament Attack in 2004, they have discussed not the crisis-prone India–Pakistan conflict but less controversial issues where positive-sum results may be expected – such as trade, communications, and cultural affairs. The root cause of the conflict, Kashmir, has not been addressed. The study has shown that the parties deliberately decided to avoid discussion of the salient issue, which is zero-sum, because the attempt would be doomed to failure, given the suspicion and hatred between the two sides. The study also showed that any discussion of Kashmir would jeopardize the actual and potential benefits of cooperation in other realms. Thus, it is in the interest of both states to deal with non-controversial issues and let the overall conflict drag on. The Kashmir issue is complicated not only because it is in dispute between the two parties – India and Pakistan – but also because the Kashmiris themselves have a legitimate role to play, an additional factor reducing yet further the chances of resolution. The study reveals that according to the Indians, their precondition – that Pakistan should stop cross-border terrorism before substantive dialogue on Kashmir and other important security issues – has not been met. The Pakistanis feel they have done enough and anyway there is no point in dialogue based on precondition. Consequently, a solution looks unlikely. The study also shows that both India and Pakistan seem quite comfortable with the present situation. They know resolution is a remote possibility under the circumstances and have found ways of living with each other by cooperating on other levels in the midst of violence.

To shed light on whether the conflict has any chance of being terminated, the study made a comparative analysis of the thaw between India and Pakistan in 1999 and 2001 – when the leaders of the two states made attempts to launch cooperation which did not last as new and more serious crises arose in the conflict – and the new thaw which began in 2003 and has led to the dialogue process. It proved that thaws and steps toward cooperation have been effective and enduring when the US has taken a special interest in bringing the parties together to discuss disputed issues. It highlighted the crucial role of US involvement. Under US pressure, India and Pakistan have had no choice but to hold dialogue and improve their mutual understanding. US pressure on Musharraf to crack down on terrorism, and the steps he took towards this goal, have helped to change the Indians' image of the Pakistanis. This shows the importance of great power influence in bringing about dramatic policy change in a country like Pakistan: change which is difficult for political leader to make but which helps to promote peace. The lesson to be drawn is that the great power does not have to be in the role of mediator – a third-party role which India has rejected ever since the beginning of the India–Pakistan conflict – but can simply help to create a so propitious environment for conflict resolution between the parties. While any conclusions would be premature, this substantiates the point that situational attributes – major power involvement, especially facilitation – may be instrumental in creating an atmosphere conducive to resolving the India–Pakistan conflict.

The value of actor attributes was also proven by the study: bold leaders like Vajpayee can take positive steps toward resolving the conflict; likewise, Musharraf took steps to uproot terrorism against strong domestic opposition and participated in the dialogue process. The study also showed that leaders generally want to initiate a peace process for domestic political and economic reasons. Whatever inspires the leaders to work for peace, their individual roles are extremely important, as shown by both Vajpayee and Musharraf. The study proved that the future of the India–Pakistan conflict resolution will to a large extent depend on bold leadership and courageous initiatives.

## Theoretical implications

The study has major theoretical implications. It disproves the realist theoretical paradigm that states are more secure when they build up their military capabilities.[1] The acquisition of nuclear weapons has not made India and Pakistan secure. Although at the strategic level they avoided war, serious crises erupted more frequently in nuclear period of the conflict, each of these could have escalated, increasing insecurity. The constant low-intensity violence also challenges the notion that overall security and stability in a conflict are enhanced by the acquisition of nuclear weapons. States are generally more insecure in a nuclear environment. Although they acquire nuclear weapons for security enhancement, they may thereby become more insecure in their long-term relations with protracted conflict adversaries. Thus, realism, a major International Relations theory which holds that the security of states is maximized through military capabilities, fails to explain why states face insecurity for extended periods following the acquisition of the most advanced weaponry, nuclear weapons.

Deterrence, a debated and complex paradigm, does prevent wars between protracted conflict states which possess nuclear weapons. However, the study establishes that by deterring wars and thereby generating more crises, nuclear weapons acquisition jeopardizes comprehensive stability where two states are in conflict. Additionally, nuclear weapons may help to maintain immediate deterrence but not general deterrence.[2] The eruption of a serious crisis that has the potential to escalate goes against the basic notion of general deterrence. The non-escalation of a crisis, however, demonstrates the success of immediate deterrence. Thus, the idea that nuclear weapons acquisition is driven by the need for deterrence must be reconsidered in the light of real world cases.

The case-study implies that peace theory should understand peace as absence of war and absence of crisis. Stability cannot be attained where crises are embedded and have become chronic. If stability equals peace and peace equals absence of war and crisis, then nuclear weapons acquisition does not ensure peace or stability.

Crisis theorists need to redefine crisis between parties which have acquired nuclear weapons. The definition of crisis as "threat to basic values, time pressure for response, and heightened probability of war" should be changed in the case of states that possess nuclear weapons: "heightened probability of low–medium intensity violence" should replace "heightened probability of war." The definition, as well as excluding war between nuclear states, should also make a clear distinction between crisis between nuclear states and between non-nuclear states.

Conflict theorists should recognize that the concept of conflict transformation may have a negative connotation as well as its usual positive connotation. Transformation means "a change in the relationship," which may be positive or negative, and nuclear weapons acquisition transforms a conflict negatively. This understanding is likely to generate new thinking and studies on conflict transformation, broadening the horizon of knowledge in the field.

## Policy implications

The study has substantial policy implications. It implies that acquiring nuclear weapons may not be all that helpful for states faced with insecurity and threats. States considering acquiring nuclear weapons for deterrence should rethink their decisions and those that have already acquired them should consider rolling back their capabilities. A state facing a revisionist opponent in a nuclear context may be more insecure as a result of frequent provocation of crises by its opponent seeking to change the status quo and attract third-party intervention. The India–Pakistan case study shows why nuclear weapons acquisition is not a wise option.

There are major policy implications for India and Pakistan. They need to end their long-drawn-out conflict by finding ways to deal with the most important issue, Kashmir. Whatever the benefits of their current cooperation, leaving the central issue aside is not helping to resolve the conflict. They need to realize that they must work to create an atmosphere propitious to starting a peace process. Bold leaders are required who can ignore domestic opposition and come forward with new peacemaking strategies, offering friendship and compromise. They also need to believe in peace and get beyond the hatred and suspicion which plague the conflict.

For the individual states, the implications of the study are different. India should raise the cost of crises and low–medium-intensity violence for Pakistan, as policy-makers proposed after the Parliament Attack. Pakistan must realize that it will not be able to change the status quo by trying to grab territory and involve third parties in the conflict by provoking crises. The lesson for Pakistan is that it should comprehend that frequent crises will not resolve the central problem keeping the conflict alive. If the conflict cannot be resolved because of the crisis-prone environment created by Pakistan, its government will be pressured by the US to make dramatic political changes and it will be compelled to abide by the rules set by the hegemonic power which has already tilted toward India post-9/11, as demonstrated by the projected US-India nuclear cooperation deal.

Lessons are also there for the international community, especially the US, which tends to believe that democracy is the key to peace. Ultimately, peace is a function of conflict resolution, and has little to do with democracy; conflict resolution is a product of a peace process which can only be initiated in a peaceful environment, which in turn is a product of absence of war and crisis between the contending states. Contrary to western expectations, the military government of Musharraf showed remarkable determination in cracking down on terrorism; only a military leader could have had the power and authority to do so. This has helped to build confidence between the two states. Thus, democracy may not be the solution to the problems the world faces.

Finally, this study has major policy implications for the US. The India–Pakistan conflict and similar protracted conflicts in the world need the US as a facilitator helping to create a congenial atmosphere for conflict resolution purposes. Unless the US understands this fully and takes a special interest in South Asian affairs, the conflict is unlikely to change from its present indefinite protraction.

**Potential for further studies**

The study is expected to encourage new endeavors along similar lines. First, the theoretical framework of this study can be tested against other protracted conflicts to establish whether it can be generalized across similar cases. This would help to strengthen or weaken the theory. Second, new studies on Pakistan could be conducted into why its policy-makers do not understand the negative impacts of crises on the overall India–Pakistan conflict and what might change their crisis-oriented policies. Third, more work needs to be done on the causal linkage between domestic politics and crisis initiation by the weaker revisionist state, Pakistan, against the stronger opponent, India. Fourth, a case study could be conducted on how far India is really ready to compromise on Kashmir if Pakistan creates a crisis-free environment. Fifth, further studies are required to test the value of nuclear weapons for conflict resolution. For example, studies could be conducted on whether or not the present India–Pakistan dialogue process, and the associated hope for conflict resolution, could be a function of nuclear weapons acquisition.

# Notes

## Introduction

1  See Rodney W. Jones and Mark G. McDonough, *Tracking Nuclear Proliferation: A Guide in Maps and Charts* (Washington, DC: Carnegie Endowment for International Peace, 1998), pp. 273–5.
2  Ibid., p. 307.
3  For a causal connection between protracted conflicts and nuclear proliferation, see Saira Khan, *Nuclear Proliferation Dynamics in Protracted Conflict Regions: A Comparative Study of South Asia and the Middle East* (Aldershot: Ashgate, 2002).

## 1  Studies on conflict transformation

1  Graham Evans and Jeffrey Newnham, *Dictionary of International Relations* (New York: Penguin Books, 1998), p. 94.
2  Morton Deutsch, *The Resolution of Conflict: Constructive and Destructive Processes* (New Haven, Conn.: Yale University Press, 1973).
3  D. Bloomfield and Ben Reilly, "The Changing Nature of Conflict and Conflict Management," in Peter Harris and Ben Reilly, eds, *Democracy and Deep-rooted Conflict* (Stockholm: Institute for Democracy and Electoral Assistance, 1998), p. 18.
4  Evans and Newnham, *Dictionary of International Relations*, p. 94.
5  William O. Staudenmaier, "Conflict Termination in the Nuclear Era," in Stephen J. Cimbala and Keith A. Dunn, eds, *Conflict Termination and Military Strategy: Coercion, Persuasion, and War* (Boulder, Colo., and London: Westview Press, 1987), p. 26.
6  Ibid., p. 26, fn. 22.
7  Raymond L. Garthoff, "Conflict Termination in Soviet Thought," in Cimbala and Dunn, *Conflict Termination and Military Strategy, p. 43.*
8  Ibid., pp. 43–4.
9  Thomas L. Saaty and Joyce M. Alexander, *Conflict Resolution: The Analytic Hierarchy Approach* (New York: Westport, Conn., and London: Praeger, 1989), p. 3.
10  See Raimo Vayrynen, "To Settle or to Transform? Perspectives on the Resolution of National and International Conflicts," in Raimo Vayrynen, ed., *New Directions in Conflict Theory* (London: Sage, 1991).
11  Peter Wallensteen, "The Resolution and Transformation of International Conflicts: A Structural Perspective," in Vayrynen, *New Directions in Conflict Theory*, p. 129.
12  E. F. Dukes, "Why Conflict Transformation Matters: Three Cases," www.gmu.edu/academic/pcs/Dukes61PCS.html.
13  Quincy Wright, *A Study of War* (Chicago: University of Chicago Press, 1965).
14  See R. Vayrynen, ed., *The Quest for Peace: Transcending Collective Violence and War Among Societies, Cultures, and States* (London: Sage Publications, 1986); L. Kriesberg,

T. A. Northrup, and S. J. Thorson, eds, *Intractable Conflicts and their Transformation* (Syracuse NY: Syracuse University Press, 1989).

15 Vayrynen, "To Settle or to Transform?," p. 4.

16 Ibid.

17 R. Vayrynen, "From Conflict Resolution to Conflict Transformation: A Critical Review." in H. W. Jeong, ed., *The New Agenda for Peace Research* (Aldershot: Ashgate, 1999).

18 J.D. Leatherman, W. DeMars, P. D. Gaffney, and R. Vayrynen, *Breaking Cycles of Violence* (West Hartford, Conn.: Kumarian Press, 1999), p. 50.

19 Ibid., p. 73.

20 J. P. Lederach, *The Little Book of Conflict Transformation* (Intercourse, Pa.: Good Press, 2003), p. 15; "Conflict Transformation," www.beyondintractability.org/essay/trans formation.

21 J. P. Lederach, *Building Peace: Sustainable Reconciliation in Divided Societies* (Washington, DC: United States Institute of Peace Press, 1997).

22 Ron Kraybill, "Facilitation Skills for Interpersonal Transformatic in *Berghof Handbook for Conflict Transformation*, undated, www.berghof-handbook.net/uploads/downloads/ kraybill_handbook.pdf p. 2.

23 Stephen Ryan, *The Transformation of Violent Intercommunal Conflict* (Aldershot: Ashgate, 2007), p. 32.

24 Hugh Miall, "Conflict Transformation: A Multi-Dimensional Task," Berghof Research Center for Constructive Conflict Management, http://www.berghof-handbook.net/ articles/miall_handbook.pdf, pp. 3–4.

25 Ryan, *The Transformation of Violent Intercommunal Conflict*, p. 22.

26 Ibid.; Edward Azar, The Management of *Protracted Social Conflict* (Abershot: Dartmouth, 1990).

27 Johan Galtung, *Peace by Peaceful Means* (London: Sage Publications, 1996), p. 96.

28 D. Francis, *People, Peace, and Power: Conflict Transformation in Action* (London: Pluto, 2002), p. 40.

29 A. Tidwell, *Conflict Resolved? A Critical Assessment of Conflict Resolution* (New York: Pinter, 1998), pp. 72–4.

30 Staudenmaier, "Conflict Termination in the Nuclear Era," pp. 17–18.

31 Miall, "Conflict Transformation," p. 4.

32 K. Clements, "Peace Building and Conflict Transformation," *Peace and Conflict Studies*, 4, 1997, www.gmu.edu/academic/pcs/clements.htm.

33 Saaty and Alexander, *Conflict Resolution*, pp. 3–4.

34 Steven L. Spiegel, "Introduction," in Steven L. Spiegel and Kenneth N. Waltz, eds, *Conflict in World Politics* (Cambridge, Mass.: Winthrop Publishers, 1971), p. 6.

35 See Stuart J. Thorson, *Intractable Conflicts and Their Transformation* (Syracuse, NY: Syracuse University Press, 1989).

36 Ibid.

37 See Gary Goertz and Paul F. Diehl, "The Initiation and Termination of Enduring Rivalries: The Impact of Political Shocks," *American Journal of Political Science*, 39, 1, February 1995, pp. 35–9.

38 Janice Gross Stein, "Image, Identity, and Conflict Resolution," in Chester A. Crocker, Fen Osler Hampson and Pamela R. Aall, eds, *Managing Global Chaos: Sources of and Responses to International Conflict* (Washington, DC: US Institute of Peace Press, 1996), p. 93.

39 Ibid., p. 99.

40 Ibid., pp. 99–102.

41 See Charles Osgood, *An Alternative to War or Surrender* (Urbana: University of Illinois Press, 1962).

42 Ibid.

43 Ibid.

44  S. Lindskold, P. S. Walters, and H. Koutsourais, "Cooperators, Competitors, and Response to Grit," *Journal of Conflict Resolution*, 27, 1983, pp. 521–32.
45  See Amitai Etzioni, "The Kennedy Experiment," *Western Political Quarterly*, 20, June 1967, pp. 361–380; Joshua S. Goldstein and John R. Freeman, *Three-Way Street: Strategic Reciprocity in World Politics* (Chicago: University of Chicago Press, 1990).
46  Susan Heitler, *From Conflict to Resolution* (London: W. W. Norton, 1990).
47  Tidwell, *Conflict Resolved?*, p. 147.
48  Robert Axelrod, *The Evolution of Cooperation* (New York: Basic Books, 1984), p. 173.
49  Ibid., p. 176.
50  John Burton, *Conflict: Resolution and Provention* (New York: St Martin's Press, 1990), p. 7.
51  Saaty and Alexander, *Conflict Resolution*, p. 5.
52  Burton, *Conflict: Resolution and Pròvention*, p. 195.
53  Tidwell, *Conflict Resolved?*, p. 165.
54  Georg Schwarzenberger, *International Law and Order* (London: Stevens and Sons, 1971), pp. 8–26.
55  Staudenmaier, "Conflict Termination in the Nuclear Era," p. 19.
56  Saaty and Alexander, *Conflict Resolution*, p. 10.
57  Keith A. Dunn, "The Missing Link in Conflict Termination Thought: Strategy," in Cimbala and Dunn, *Conflict Termination and Military Strategy, p. 26, fn 22.*
58  Miall, "Conflict Transformation: A Multi-Dimensional Task," p. 3.
59  Ryan, *The Transformation of Violent Intercommunal Conflict*, p. 77.
60  Ibid., p. 80.
61  Raymond L. Garthoff, "Conflict Termination in Soviet Thought," in Cimbala and Dunn, *Conflict Termination and Military Strategy*, p. 34.

## 2  Ramifications of nuclear weapons acquisition

1  For the linkage between protracted conflicts and proliferation, see Saira Khan, *Nuclear Proliferation Dynamics in Protracted Conflict Regions: A Comparative Study of South Asia and the Middle East* VT.. (Aldershot and Burlington, Vt.: Ashgate, 2002).
2  For a detailed analysis of motivations for nuclear weapons acquisition, see Khan, *Nuclear Proliferation Dynamics in Protracted Conflict Regions*, pp. 11–34; Stephen J. Cimbala, *Nuclear Weapons and Strategy: U.S. Nuclear Policy for the Twenty-First Century* (London and New York: Routledge, 2005), pp. 58–75; Stephen M. Meyer, *The Dynamics of Nuclear Proliferation* (Chicago: University of Chicago Press, 1984); Scott D. Sagan, "Why Do States Build Nuclear Weapons?: Three Models in Search of a Bomb," *International Security*, 21, 3, Winter 1996/97; Ted Greenwood, *Nuclear Proliferation: Motivations, Capabilities and Strategies for Control* (New York: McGraw Hill, 1977); George Quester, *The Politics of Nuclear Proliferation* (Baltimore, Md.: Johns Hopkins University Press, 1973); William C. Potter, *Nuclear Power and Nonproliferation: An Interdisciplinary Perspective* (Cambridge, Mass.: Gunn and Hain, 1982); T.V. Paul, *Power versus Prudence: Why Nations Forgo Nuclear Weapons* (Montreal and Kingston: McGill-Queen's University Press, 2000).
3  Andy Butfoy, *Disarming Proposals: Controlling Nuclear, Biological and Chemical Weapons* (Sydney: UNSW Press, 2005), p. 29.
4  Ibid., p. 38.
5  Ibid., p. 42.
6  Ibid., p. 43.
7  Ibid., p. 44.
8  Sidney D. Drell and James E. Goodby, *The Gravest Danger: Nuclear Weapons* (Stanford, Calif.: Hoover Institution Press, 2003), pp. 88–93.
9  Butfoy, *Disarming Proposals*, pp. 31–3.
10  Ibid., pp. 30–3.

11 Cimbala, *Nuclear Weapons and Strategy*, p. 4.
12 Drell and Goodby, *The Gravest Danger*, p. 7.
13 Ibid., p. 10.
14 Jed C. Snyder, "The Non-Proliferation Regime: Managing the Impending Crisis," in Neil Joeck, ed., *Strategic Consequences of Nuclear Proliferation in South Asia* (London: Frank Cass, 1986), p. 12.
15 Ibid.
16 Butfoy, *Disarming Proposals*, p. 44.
17 Gary K. Bertsch and William C. Potter, "Introduction: The Challenge of NIS Export Control Developments," in Gary K. Bertsch and William C. Potter, eds, *Dangerous Weapons, Desperate States: Russia, Belarus, Kazakstan, and Ukraine* (New York and London: Routledge, 1999), p. 6.
18 Gary K. Bertsch and William C. Potter, "Conclusion," in Bertsch and Potter, eds, *Dangerous Weapons, Desperate States*, pp. 235–6.
19 George Quester, *Deterrence Before Hiroshima: The Airpower Background of Modern Strategy* (New Brunswick, NJ: Transaction, 1986).
20 Bernard Brodie, ed., *The Absolute Weapon* (New York: Harcourt, Brace, 1946).
21 For a detailed explanation and analysis on deterrence and how it works, see Patrick Morgan, *Deterrence: A Conceptual Analysis* (Beverly Hills, Calif., and London: Sage, 1977).
22 Albert Wohlstetter, "Nuclear Sharing: NATO and the N+1 Country," in Richard N. Rosecrance, ed., *The Dispersion of Nuclear Weapons: Strategy and Politics* (New York: Columbia University Press, 1964), p. 204.
23 Lewis A. Dunn, "Nuclear Proliferation and World Politics," *Annals of the American Academy of Political and Social Science*, 430, March 1977, p. 97.
24 Scott D. Sagan and Kenneth N. Waltz, *The Spread of Nuclear Weapons: A Debate Renewed* (New York and London: W. W. Norton, 2003), p. 91.
25 Ibid., p. 93.
26 Ibid., p. 102.
27 Ibid., p. 106.
28 Ibid., p. 131.
29 See Bruce Bueno de Mesquitta and William H. Riker, "An Assessment of the Merits of Selective Nuclear Proliferation," *Journal of Conflict Resolution*, 26, 2, June 1982, pp. 290–1; Steven J. Rosen, "A Stable System of Mutual Nuclear Deterrence in the Middle East," *American Political Science Review*, 71, 4, December 1977, pp. 1367–83; Devin T. Hagerty, *Consequences of Nuclear Proliferation,: Lessons from South Asia* (Cambridge, Mass., and London: MIT Press, 1998); and John. J. Weltman, "Nuclear Devolution and World Order," *World Politics*, 32, 2, January 1980, p. 190.
30 William C. Potter, "On Nuclear Proliferation," in Edward A. Kolodziej and Patrick M. Morgan, eds, *Security and Arms Control*, vol. 2: *A Guide to International Policy-making* (New York: Greenwood, 1989), p. 321.
31 Lewis A. Dunn, "Containing Nuclear Proliferation," *Adelphi Paper*, 263 (London: International Institute of Strategic Studies, 1991), p. 4.
32 Cimbala, *Nuclear Weapons and Strategy*, p. 71.
33 Ibid.
34 See, among others, John Lewis Gaddis, "Great Illusions, the Long Peace, and the Future of the International System," in Charles W. Kegley, ed., *The Long PostWar Peace*, (New York: HarperCollins, 1991), chapter 2.
35 Michael Brecher and Jonathan Wilkenfeld, "International Crises and Global Instability," in Kegley, *The Long PostWar Peace*, pp. 85–104.
36 Ibid.
37 Ibid.
38 Glenn Snyder, "Balance of Power or Balance of Terror," in Paul Seadbury, ed., *Balance of Power* (San Francisco: Chandler Publishing, 1965).

39  Sumit Ganguly, *Conflict Unending: Indo-Pakistan Tensions Since 1947* (New York: Columbia University Press, 2001), p. 108.
40  Jeffrey W. Knopf, "Recasting the Optimism-Pessimism Debate," *Security Studies*, 12, 1, Autumn 2002, p. 52.
41  Lowell Dittmer, "South Asia's Security Dilemma," *Asian Survey*, 41, 6, November/December 2001, p. 903.
42  Paul Kapur, "India and Pakistan's Unstable Peace: Why Nuclear South Asia Is Not Like Cold War Europe," *International Security*, 30, 2, Fall 2005, pp. 127–52.
43  Michael Krepon, "The Stability-Instability Paradox, Misperception, and Escalation Control in South Asia" (Washington, DC: The Henry L. Stimson Center Paper, May 2003).
44  Feroz Hassan Khan, "Challenges to Nuclear Stability in South Asia," *Nonproliferation Review*, 10, 1, Spring 2003, p. 60.
45  Scott D. Sagan, "Rethinking the Causes of Nuclear Proliferation: Three Models in Search of a Bomb," in Victor A. Utgoff, ed., *The Coming Crisis: Nuclear Proliferation, US Interests and World Order* (Cambridge, Mass.: MIT Press, 2000), pp. 17–50; Robert A. Strong, "The Nuclear Weapon States: Why They Went Nuclear?," in W. H. Kincade and C. Bertram, eds, *Nuclear Proliferation in the 1980s*, (New York: St Martin's Press, 1982), pp. 3–26; Mitchell Reiss, *Without the Bomb: The Politics of Nuclear Non-Proliferation* (New York: Columbia University Press, 1988), pp. 247–69; George Quester, "Reducing the Incentives to Proliferation," *Annals*, 430, March 1977, pp. 70–81; Mitchell Reiss, *Bridled Ambition: Why Countries Constrain Their Nuclear Capabilities* (Washington, DC: Woodrow Wilson Center Press, 1995), pp. 7–43; Paul, *Power Versus Prudence*; David J. Karl, "Proliferation Pessimism and Emerging Nuclear Powers," *International Security*, 21, 3, Winter 1996/97, pp. 87–119; Peter D. Fever and Scott D. Sagan, "Proliferation Pessimism and Emerging Nuclear Powers," *International Security*, 22, 2, Fall 1997, pp. 185–207; Kenneth N. Waltz, "The Spread of Nuclear Weapons: More May Be Better," *Adelphi Papers*, 171, Autumn 1981, pp. 1–32; Scott D. Sagan and Kenneth N. Waltz, *The Spread of Nuclear Weapons: A Debate* (New York: W. W. Norton, 1995), pp. 47–91.
46  Louis Kriesberg, "The Growth of the Conflict Resolution Field," in Chester A. Crocker, Fen Osler Hampson, and Pamela R. Aali eds, *Turbulent Peace: The Challenges of Managing International Conflicts* (Washington, DC: The United States Institute of Peace Press, 2001), pp. 407–26; Bruce Russett, *Grasping the Democratic Peace: Principles for a Post-Cold War World* (Princeton, NJ: Princeton University Press, 1993), pp. 24–42; Janice Gross Stein, "Image, Identity, and Conflict Resolution," in Chester A. Crocker, Fen Osler Hampson, and Pamela R. Aali, eds, *Managing Global Chaos: Sources of and Responses to International Conflict* (Washington, DC. United States Institute of Peace Press, 1996), pp. 93–111; Chester A. Crocker, "Intervention: Toward Best Practices and a Holistic View," in Crocker *et al.*, *Turbulent Peace*, pp. 229–48; Ken Booth, "War, Security and Strategy: Toward a Doctrine for Stable Peace," in Ken Booth, ed., *New Thinking about Strategy and International Security* (London: HarperCollins, 1991), pp. 335–76; Charles W. Kegley and Gregory A. Raymond, *How Nations Make Peace* (New York: St Martin's Press, 1999), pp. 3–25, 225–54.
47  Walter Laqueur, *The Age of Terrorism* (Boston: Little Brown, 1987), p. 72.
48  United States, Code, Title 22, Section 2656f(d).
49  Dan Cadwell and Robert E. Williams Jr., *Seeking Security in an Insecure World* (Boulder, Colo., New York, and Oxford: Rowman & Littlefield, 2006), p. 175.
50  Ibid., p. 174.
51  Some of these works are: Michael Klare, *Rogue States and Nuclear Outlaws* (New York: Hill and Wang, 1995); Stephen M. Walt, "Containing Rogues and Renegades: Coalition Strategies and Counterproliferation," in Utgoff, *The Coming Crisis*, pp. 191–226; Carolyn C. James, "Iran and Iraq as Rational Crisis Actors: Dangers and Dynamics of Survivable Nuclear War," in Eric Herring, ed., *Preventing the Use of Weapons of Mass*

*Destruction* (London: Frank Cass, 2000), pp. 52–73; Richard Butler, *The Greatest Threat: Iraq, Weapons of Mass Destruction, and the Growing Crisis of Global Security* (New York: Public Affairs, 2000); James M. Lindsay and Michael E. O'Hanlon, *Defending America: The Case for Limited National Missile Defense* (Washington, DC: Brookings Institution Press, 2001), chapter 3; John Mueller and Karl Mueller, "The Methodology of Mass Destruction: Assessing Threats in the New World Order," in Herring, *Preventing the Use of Weapons of Mass Destruction*, pp. 163–187; Eric Herring, "Rogue Rage: Can We Prevent Mass Destruction," in Herring, *Preventing the Use of Weapons of Mass Destruction*, pp. 188–212; Graham Allison, *Nuclear Terrorism: The Ultimate Preventable Catastrophe* (New York: Times Books, 2004); Richard A. Falkenrath, "Confronting Nuclear, Biological, and Chemical Terrorism," *Survival*, 40, 3, Autumn 1998; Cimbala, *Nuclear Weapons and Strategy*.

52 Cimbala, *Nuclear Weapons and Strategy*, p. 74.
53 Ibid., p. 73.
54 Ibid., p. 74.
55 See Walt, "Containing Rogues and Renegades," pp. 221–5; Marc Dean Millot, "Facing the Emerging Reality of Regional Nuclear Adversaries," *Washington Quarterly*, 17, 3, 1994, p. 57.
56 Vladimir A. Orlov, "Export Controls and Nuclear Smuggling in Russia," in. Bertsch and C. Potter, *Dangerous Weapons, Desperate States*, p. 164.
57 Matthias Dembinski, "The Threat of Nuclear Proliferation to Europe," in K. Bailey and Robert Rudney, eds, *Proliferation and Export Controls* (London: University Press of America, 1993), p. 1.
58 William C. Potter, "Russia's Nuclear Entrepreneurs," *New York Times*, November 7, 1991, p. A29.
59 Orlov, "Export Controls and Nuclear Smuggling in Russia," p. 171.
60 Drell and Goodby, *The Gravest Danger: Nuclear Weapons*, p. 44.
61 For information on this see William C. Potter, "Improving Nuclear Materials Security in the Former Soviet Union," *Arms Control Today*, January–February 1993; James E. Doyle, "Improving Nuclear Material Security in the Former Soviet Union, Next Steps for the MPC & A Program," *Army Control Today* March 1998.
62 Allison, *Nuclear Terrorism*, pp. 61–3.
63 Cimbala, *Nuclear Weapons and Strategy*, p. 77.

## 3 Elucidating conflict transformation with nuclear weapons

1 For a better understanding of conflict of interest and conflict behavior, see Michael Nicholson, *Rationality and the Analysis of International Conflict* (Cambridge: Cambridge University Press, 1992), pp. 11–24.
2 Steven L. Spiegel, "Introduction," in Steven L. Spiegel and Kenneth N. Waltz, eds, *Conflict in World Politics* (Cambridge, Mass.: Winthrop Publishers, 1971), p. 4.
3 Edward E. Azar, P. Sureidini, and R. Mclaurin, "Protracted Social Conflict: Theory and Practice in the Middle East," *Journal of Palestine Studies*, 8, 1, 1978, p. 50.
4 See Saira Khan, *Nuclear Proliferation Dynamics in Protracted Conflict Regions: A Comparative Study of South Asia and the Middle East* (Aldershot: Ashgate, 2002), p. 42.
5 Michael Brecher, *Crises in World Politics* (Oxford: Pergamon Press, 1993).
6 For the termination of a conflict, see Frank Whelon Wayman, "Recurrent Disputes and Explaining War," in John A. Vasquez, ed., *What Do We Know about War?* (London, Boulder, Colo., New York, and Oxford: Rowman & Littlefield, 2000), pp. 219–34.
7 For a detailed analysis of the connection between territorial issues and war, see Khan, *Nuclear Proliferation Dynamics in Protracted Conflict Regions*, pp. 39–40. Also see Harvey Starr, "Territory, Proximity, and Spatiality: The Geography of International Conflict," *International Studies Review*, 7, 3, September 2005, pp. 387–406.

8  John Vasquez, "Distinguishing Rivals That Go to War from Those That Do Not: A Quantitative Comparative Case Study of Two Paths to War," *International Studies Quarterly*, 40, 1996, pp. 531–58.

9  Hemda Ben-Yahuda, "Territoriality and War in International Crises: Theory and Findings, 1918–2001," *International Studies Review*, 6, 4, December 2004, p. 103.

10  Khan, *Nuclear Proliferation Dynamics in Protracted Conflict Regions*.

11  Interestingly Arnold Toynbee developed another theory of war-weariness that suggests that political leaders who have experienced repeated wars and devastation have a strong aversion to wars. Also, at the nation-state level, war-weariness becomes part of the national character or political culture. In other words, the feeling is shared by the population. This essentially means that such states do not need to make use of the deterrence strategy because they are deterred from waging wars by being war-weary. See Arnold Toynbee, *A Study of History*, Vol. IX (London: Oxford University Press, 1954).

12  Although Kargil is often called a fourth war between India and Pakistan, this study considers it a serious crisis only. War does not only require 1000 or more battle deaths, it also involves regular armed forces of sufficient magnitude crossing an internationally recognized border with the potential to inflict catastrophic defeat on the opponent.

13  Hans J. Morgenthau, *Politics Among Nations: The Struggle for Power and Peace*, 6th edn, revised by Kenneth W. Thompson (New York: Alfred A. Knopf, 1985), p. 52.

14  Michael Brecher, "Crisis Escalation: A New Model and Findings," in Frank Harvey and Ben D. More, eds, *Conflict in World Politics* (New York: St Martin's Press, 1998), p. 124.

15  See, among others, Bernard Brodie, ed., *The Absolute Weapon* (New York: Harcourt, Brace, 1946); T. V. Paul, Richard K. Harknett, and James J. Wirtz, eds, *The Absolute Weapons Revisited: Nuclear Arms and the Emerging International Order* (Ann Arbor: University of Michigan Press, 1998).

16  William O. Staudenmaier, "Conflict Termination in the Nuclear Era," in Stephen J. Cimbala and Keith A. Dunn, eds, *Conflict Termination and Military Strategy: Coercion, Persuasion, and War* (Boulder, Colo., and London: Westview Press, 1987), p. 21.

17  Staudenmaier, "Conflict Termination in the Nuclear Era," p. 21. Walter Mills states, A continuation of the present state of international affairs is bound sooner or later to produce a catastrophe in which most civilized values and all the present warring value systems must perish . . . [war] can no longer serve its greatest social function – that of ultima ratio in human affairs – for it can no longer decide. Walter Mills, *A World Without War* (Santa Barbara, Calif.: Center for the Study of Democratic Institutions, 1961), p. 405)

18  Glenn Snyder, "Balance of Power or Balance of Terror," in Paul Seadbury, ed., *Balance of Power* (San Francisco: Chandler Publishing, 1965), pp. 185–6.

19  Glenn Snyder and Paul Diesing, *Conflict Among Nations: Bargaining, Decision-Making and System Structure in International Crises* (Princeton, NJ: Princeton University Press, 1977), p. 455.

20  J. David Singer and Melvin Small define war as "a conflict involving at least one member of the interstate system on each side of the war, resulting in a total of 1000 or more battle deaths." See J. David Singer and Melvin Small, *The Wages of War 1816–1965: A Statistical Handbook* (New York: John Wiley, 1972), p. 381.

21  Michael Brecher and Jonathan Wilkenfeld, *A Study of Crisis* (Ann Arbor: University of Michigan Press, 1997), pp. 3–4, 8–11; Brecher, *Crises in World Politics*, p. 3; Snyder and Diesing, *Conflict Among Nations*, p. 7; Glenn H. Snyder, "Crisis Bargaining," in Charles F. Hermann, ed., *International Crises: Insights from Behavioral Research* (New York: Free Press, 1972), p. 217.

22  Brecher, *Crises in World Politics*, p. 3; Michael Brecher and Jonathan Wilkenfeld, *Crisis, Conflict and Instability* (Oxford: Pergamon Press, 1989), pp. 5 and 19.

23  Snyder and Diesing, *Conflict Among Nations*, p. 7.

24 Brecher and Wilkenfeld, *A Study of Crisis*, p. 3.
25 By this I mean that the parties are not expected to go through this conflict phase once they acquire nuclear weapons.
26 T. V. Paul, "Causes of the India–Pakistan Enduring Rivalry," in T. V. Paul, ed., *The India–Pakistan Conflict: An Enduring Rivalry* (Cambridge: Cambridge University Press, 2005), p. 15.
27 Paul Kapur, *Dangerous Deterrent: Nuclear Weapons Proliferation and Conflict in South Asia* (Stanford, Calif.: Stanford University Press, 2007), p. 32.
28 Russell J. Leng, "Realpolitik and Learning in the India–Pakistan Rivalry," in Paul, *The India–Pakistan Conflict*, p. 117.
29 Charles W. Kegley and Gregory A. Raymond, *How Nations Make Peace* (New York: St Martin's Press, 1999), p. 244.
30 Ibid., p. 243.
31 Ibid.
32 Michael Brecher, "Crisis Escalation: A New Model and Findings," in Frank Harvey and Ben D. More eds, *Conflict in World Politics* (New York: St Martin's Press, 1998), p. 125.
33 Alan Tidwell, *Conflict Resolved: A Critical Assessment of Conflict Resolution* (London and New York: Pinter, 1998), p. 144.
34 Stephen Ryan, *The Transformation of Violent Intercommunal Conflict* (Aldershot: Ashgate, 2007), p. 122.

## 4 Life-cycle of the protracted conflict

1 John J. Vasquez and Christopher Leskiw, "The Origins and War Proneness of Interstate Rivalries," *Annual Review of Political Science*, 4, 2001, pp. 295–316.
2 John A. Vasquez, "The India–Pakistan Conflict in Light of General Theories of War, Rivalry, and Deterrence," in T.V. Paul, ed., *The India–Pakistan Conflict: An Enduring Rivalry* (Cambridge Mass.: Cambridge University Press, 2005), p. 61.
3 Ibid.
4 Interview with Muchkund Dubey, former foreign Secretary of India, New Delhi, December 27, 2001.
5 Saira Khan, *Nuclear Proliferation Dynamics in Protracted Conflict Regions: A Comparative Study of South Asia and the Middle East* (Aldershot: Ashgate, 2002), pp. 42–3.
6 Stephen M. Saideman, "At the Heart of the Conflict: Irredentism and Kashmir," in Paul, ed., *The India–Pakistan Conflict*, pp. 212–3.
7 Ibid., p. 213.
8 See Sumit Ganguly, *Conflict Unending: India–Pakistan Tensions since 1947* (New York: Columbia University Press, 2001).
9 International Crisis Group Report, "Kashmir: Learning from the Past," *ICG Asia Report*, 70, Islamabad/New Delhi/Brussels, December 4, 2003, pp. 1 and 6.
10 Gabriella Blum, *Islands of Agreement: Managing Enduring Armed Rivalries* (Cambridge, Mass.: Harvard University Press, 2007), p. 57.
11 See Khan, *Nuclear Proliferation Dynamics in Protracted Conflict Regions*, p. 133.
12 Interview with Zafar Iqbal Cheema, former Chairman, Defense and Strategic Studies Department, Quaid-e-Azam University, Islamabad, February 12, 1997.
13 For more information on the Kashmir issue, see, among others, Iffat Mailk, *Kashmir: Ethnic Conflict, International Dispute* (Karachi: Oxford University Press, 2001), Robert G. Wirsing, *India, Pakistan, and the Kashmir Dispute: On Regional Conflict and its Resolution* (New York: St Martin's Press, 1994), Raju G. Thomas, ed., *Perspectives on Kashmir: The Roots of Conflict in South Asia* (Boulder, Colo.: Westview Press, 1992), and Victoria Schofield, *Kashmir in Conflict: India, Pakistan, and the Unfinished War*, (London: I.B. Taurus, 2002).

14  Blum, *Islands of Agreement*, p. 59.
15  Resolution 91, 1951, Concerning the India–Pakistan Question, United Nations Security Council, March 30, 1951, UN Doc.S/201/Rev.1 (March 30, 1951).
16  Blum, *Islands of Agreement*, p. 59.
17  Sumit Ganguly, *The Crisis in Kashmir: Portents of War, Hopes of Peace* (Cambridge: Cambridge University Press, 1997), p. 3.
18  Ibid., p. 20.
19  Sumantra Bose, *The Challenge in Kashmir: Democracy, Self Determination and a Just Peace* (New Delhi: Sage Publications, 1997), p. 106.
20  Ganguly, The *Crisis in Kashmir*, p. 3.
21  Daniel S. Geller, "The India–Pakistan Rivalry: Prospects for War, Prospects for Peace," in Paul, *India–Pakistan Conflict*, p. 86.
22  Robert G. Wirsing, *Kashmir in the Shadow of War: Regional Rivalries in a Nuclear Age* (New York and London: M.E. Sharp, 2003), p. 135.
23  Personal interview with K. K. Nayyar, former Vice Admiral of India and member of the National Security Council Advisory Board, New Delhi, December 27, 2001.
24  Ganguly, *The Crisis in Kashmir*, pp. 39–42.
25  See Ashutosh Varshney, "India, Pakistan, and Kashmir: Antinomies of Nationalism," *Asian Survey*, 31, November 1991, pp. 997–1007.
26  See Leonard Binder, *Religion and Politics in Pakistan* (Berkeley: University of California Press, 1961).
27  Marvin Weinbaum, *Pakistan and Afghanistan: Resistance and Reconstruction* (Boulder, Colo.: Westview Press, 1994).
28  Stephen M. Saideman, "At the Heart of the Conflict: Irredentism and Kashmir," in Paul, *India–Pakistan Conflict*, p. 224.
29  Blum, *Islands of Agreement*, p. 66.
30  Ibid., pp. 67–8.
31  Smruti S. Pattanaik, "Indo-Pak Relations: Need for a Pragmatic Approach," *Strategic Analysis*, 23, 1, April 1999, pp. 85–110.
32  Frank Whelon Wayman, "Rivalries: Recurrent Disputes and Explaining War," in John J. Vasquez, ed., *What Do We Know about War?* (Lanham, Md.: Rowman and Littlefield, 2000), p. 230.
33  J. N. Dixit, *India–Pakistan in War and Peace* (London and New York: Routledge, 2002), p. 309.
34  Michael Brecher and Jonathan Wilkinfeld, *A Study of Crisis* (Ann Arbor: University of Michigan Press, 1997), p. 171.
35  For detailed information on the crisis and war, see ibid., pp. 171–2.
36  Ibid., pp. 172–3.
37  See Dennis Kux, *The United States and Pakistan, 1947–2000: Disenchanted Allies* (Washington, DC: Woodraw Wilson Center Press, 2002).
38  See Sumit Ganguly and Devin T. Hagerty, *Fearful Symmetry: India–Pakistan Crises in the Shadow of Nuclear Weapons* (Seattle: University of Washington Press, 2005), pp. 69–70.
39  See Robert Horn, *Soviet-Indian Relations: Issues and Influence* (New York: Praeger, 1982).
40  Interview with Major General V. K. Srivastava, Deputy Director of the Institute for Defense Studies and Analysis (IDSA) in 2002, New Delhi, January 3, 2002.
41  Interview with Major General V. K. Srivastava.
42  Interview with Savita Pande, proliferation scholar, New Delhi, January 7, 2002.
43  Ganguly and Hagerty, *Fearful Symmetry*, p. 191.
44  For more information on the India–Pakistan asymmetric conflict, see TV. Paul, *Asymmetric Conflicts: War Initiation by Weaker Powers* (Cambridge: Cambridge University Press, 1994).
45  This does not imply that the conflict lasted from 1947 to 2001. The last serious crisis

erupted in 2001, which is important for this study, which considers negotiation endeavors between the adversaries until 2007.

46 T.V. Paul, "Causes of the India–Pakistan Enduring Rivalry," in Paul, *The India–Pakistan Conflict*, p. 12.
47 Ibid.
48 Ibid., p. 13.
49 Ibid.
50 Personal interview with Pervaiz Iqbal Cheema, President of the Islamabad Peace Research Institute (IPRI), Islamabad, April 25, 2003.
51 Interview with Pervaiz Iqbal Cheema.
52 Paul, "Causes of the India–Pakistan Enduring Rivalry," p. 13.
53 Paul Diehl, Gary Goertz, and Daniel Saeedi, "Theoretical Specifications of Enduring Rivalries: Applications to the India–Pakistan Case," in Paul, *The India–Pakistan Conflict*, p. 39.
54 Vasquez, "The India–Pakistan Conflict in Light of General Theories of War, Rivalry, and Deterrence," p. 62.
55 Personal interview with Brahma Chellaney, proliferation scholar, New Delhi, December 28, 2001.
56 Interview with Major General V. K. Srivastava.
57 Interview with P. Sahadevan, proliferation scholar, Jawaharlal Nehru University, New Delhi, January 4, 2002.
58 Interview with P. Sahadevan.
59 Interview with Air Commodore Jasjit Singh, New Delhi, December 29, 2001.
60 Personal interview with the former Indian Prime Minister I. K. Gujral, New Delhi, December 31, 2001.
61 Interview with the former Indian Prime Minister I. K. Gujral.
62 Interview with Bhabani Sen Gupta, columnist, New Delhi, January 4, 2002.
63 Interview with Bhabani Sen Gupta.
64 Interview with K. Santhanam, Director, IDSA, in 2002, New Delhi, January 4, 2002.
65 Interview with Niaz Naik, former Foreign Secretary of Pakistan, Islamabad, April 23, 2003.
66 Interview with Niaz Naik.
67 Interview with Niaz Naik.
68 Ashley J. Tellis, C. Christine Fair, and Jamison Jo Medby, *Limited Conflicts Under the Nuclear Umbrella: Indian and Pakistani Lessons from the Kargil Crisis* (Santa Monica, Calif.: Rand, 2001), p. 48.
69 Ganguly, *The Crisis in Kashmir*, p. 103.
70 Diehl *et al.*, "Theoretical Specifications of Enduring Rivalries: Applications to the India–Pakistan Case," in Paul, *The India–Pakistan Conflict*, p. 46.
71 Personal interview with Shireen Mazari, Director of the Islamabad Institute of Strategic Studies (IISS), Islamabad, April 22, 2003.
72 Interview with Nasim Zehra, columnist in Pakistan, Islamabad, April 25, 2003.
73 Interview with Nasim Zehra.
74 Tellis *et al.*, *Limited Conflicts Under the Nuclear Umbrella*, p. 49.
75 Interview with Pervaiz Iqbal Cheema.
76 Interview with Pervaiz Iqbal Cheema.
77 Ganguly and Hagerty, *Fearful Symmetry*, p. 192.

## 5 Introduction of nuclear weapons into the conflict

1 Brij Mohan Kaushik, *Pakistan's Nuclear Bomb* (New Delhi: Sopan Publishing House, 1980), p. 12.
2 K. Subrahmanyam, *Security in a Changing World* (New Delhi: B. R. Publishing Corporation, 1990), p. 123.

3  Sumit Ganguly, *Conflict Unending: India–Pakistan Tensions Since 1947* (New York: Columbia University Press, 2001), p. 103.
4  Gabriella Blum, *Islands of Agreement: Managing Enduring Armed Rivalries* (Cambridge, Mass.: Harvard University Press, 2007), p. 71.
5  For more information on the India–Pakistan nuclear and missile programs, see, among others, Sumit Ganguly, "Nuclear Proliferation in South Asia: Origins, Consequences, and Prospects," in Shalendra Sharma, ed., *The Asia-Pacific in the New Millennium* (Berkeley, Calif.: Institute of East Asian Studies, University of California, 2000); Itty Abraham, *The Making of the Indian Atomic Bomb* (London: Zed Books, 1998); George Perkovich, *India's Nuclear Bomb* (New Delhi: Oxford University Press, 2001); Samina Ahmed, "Pakistan's Nuclear Weapons Program: Turning Points and Nuclear Choices," *International Security*, 23, 1999, pp. 178–204; and Stephen P. Cohen, ed., *Proliferation in South Asia: The Prospects of Arms Control* (Boulder, Colo.: Westview Press, 1991).
6  See Nazir Kamal and Pravin Sawhney, "Missile Control in South Asia and the Role of Cooperative Monitoring Technology," SAND98-0505/4 (Albuquerque, NM: Sanda National Laboratories, October 1998); Federation of American Scientists, September 9, 2000, www.fas.org/nuke/guide/India/missile/prithvi.htm; "India to Make 300 Prithvi Missiles," *Hindu*, September 8, 2000; "Developing a Delivery System," *Frontline*, 16, 9, April 24–May 7, 1999).
7  "Ghauri Missiles," September 9, 2000, http///www.pakmilitary.com/army/missiles/ghauri.html.
8  See, among others, "India Bombs the Ban," *Bulletin of the Atomic Scientists*, 54, 4, July/August 1998.
9  Perkovich, *India's Nuclear Bomb*, p. 412.
10  Interview with the former Indian Prime Minister I. K. Gujral, New Delhi, December 31, 2001.
11  Interview with former Prime Minister I. K. Gujral.
12  Perkovich, *India's Nuclear Bomb*, p. 412.
13  See Gary Goertz and Paul Diehl, "The Empirical Importance of Enduring Rivalries," *International Interactions*, 18, 1992, pp. 151–63.
14  Even though crisis may not be terminated by war, adversaries tend to use war to manage crisis where war-deterrent capabilities are absent. Michael Brecher considers war to be one of the several crisis management techniques. For a detailed discussion on this, see Michael Brecher, *Crises in World Politics* (Oxford: Pergamon Press, 1993), pp. 6–7.
15  Lewis A. Dunn, "India, Pakistan, Iran – A Nuclear Proliferation Chain," in William H. Overholt, ed., *Asia's Nuclear Future* (Boulder, Colo.: Westview Press, 1977), p. 202.
16  Sisir Gupta, in M. S. Rajan and Sumit Ganguly, eds, *India and the International System* (New Delhi: Vikas, 1981), p. 1.
17  K. Subrahmanyam, "India: Keeping the Option Open," in Robert Lawrence and Joel Laurus, eds, *Nuclear Proliferation Phase II* (Lawrence: Published for the National Security Education Program by University Press of Kansas, 1974), p. 133.
18  Personal interview with I. K. Gujral.
19  Interview with Raj Chengappa, editor, *India Today*, New Delhi, December 29, 2001.
20  Ganguly, *Conflict Unending*, p. 102.
21  Ashok Kapur, *Pakistan's Nuclear Development* (London: Croom Helm, 1987), p. 146.
22  Zulfiqar Ali Bhutto, *The Myth of Independence* (London: Oxford University Press, 1969).
23  Interview with P. Sahadevan, proliferation scholar, New Delhi, January 4, 2001.
24  Interview with Shireen Mazari, Director of the Islamabad Institute of Strategic Studies, Islamabad, February 14, 1997.
25  Interview with Aga Shahi, former Foreign Secretary, Islamabad, February 14, 1997.
26  Sumit Ganguly and Devin T. Hagerty, *Fearful Symmetry: India–Pakistan Crises in the Shadow of Nuclear Weapons* (Seattle: University of Washington Press, 2005), p. 10.

27 See Scott D. Sagan and Kenneth N. Waltz, *The Spread of Nuclear Weapons: A Debate* (London and New York: WW. Norton, 2003), pp. 90–108.

28 See Saira Khan, *Nuclear Proliferation Dynamics in Protracted Conflict Regions: A Comparative Study of South Asia and the Middle East* (Aldershot: Ashgate, 2002), pp. 151–65.

29 K. Sundarji, "India's Nuclear Weapons Policy," in Jorn Gjelstad and Olav Njolstad, eds, *Nuclear Rivalry and International Order* (Oslo: International Peace Research Institute, 1996), p. 178.

30 Quoted in George Perkovich, "A Nuclear Third Way in South Asia," *Foreign Policy*, 91, Summer 1993, pp. 88–9.

31 See Khan, *Nuclear Proliferation Dynamics in Protracted Conflict Regions*, pp. 155–7.

32 Ganguly and Hagerty, *Fearful Symmetry*, p. 57.

33 Milton R. Benjamin, "India Said to Eye Raid on Pakistan's A-Plant," *Washington Post*, December 20, 1982.

34 Perkovich, *India's Nuclear Bomb*, p. 241.

35 Ganguly and Hagerty, *Fearful Symmetry*, p. 60.

36 Ibid., p. 61.

37 Michael Brecher and Jonathan Wilkenfeld, *A Study of Crisis* (Ann Arbor: The University of Michigan Press, 1997), pp. 174–8.

38 Interview with Brahma Chellaney, proliferation scholar, New Delhi, December 28, 2001.

39 Interview with K. K. Nayyar, former Vice Admiral of India and member of the National Security Council Advisory Board, New Delhi, December 27, 2001.

40 Interview, with R.R. Subramanian, Senior Research Associate, Institute for Defense Studies and Analyses, New Delhi, January 3, 2002.

41 Personal interview with Uday Bhaskar, Deputy Director, Institute for Defense Studies and Analyses, New Delhi, January 5, 2002.

42 P. R. Chari, "Nuclear Restraint, Nuclear Risk Reduction, and the Security-Insecurity Paradox in South Asia," in Michael Krepon and Chris Gagne, eds, *The Stability-Instability Paradox: Nuclear Weapons and Brinkmanship in South Asia* (Washington, DC: Stimson Center), report no. 38, June 2001, p. 21.

43 Interview with P. R. Chari, Director, Institute of Peace and Conflict Studies, New Delhi, January 7, 2002.

44 Interview with Air Commodore Jasjit Singh, December 29, 2001.

45 Interview with P. R. Chari.

46 Interview with P. R. Chari.

47 Personal interview with Pervaiz Iqbal Cheema, President of the Islamabad Peace Research Institute, Islamabad, April 25, 2003.

48 Personal interview with Pervaiz Iqbal Cheema.

49 Personal interview with Pervaiz Iqbal Cheema.

50 Interview with Raj Chengappa.

51 Interview with Raj Chengappa.

52 Interview with Savita Pande, proliferation scholar, January 7, 2002.

53 Personal interview with Pervaiz Iqbal Cheema.

54 Personal interview with Pervaiz Iqbal Cheema.

55 Personal interview with Mushahid Hussein, Senator of Pakistan, Islamabad, April 24, 2003.

56 Interview with P. R. Chari.

57 Interview with Amitabh Mattoo, member, National Security Council Advisory Board, New Delhi, January 7, 2002.

58 Personal interview with Pervaiz Iqbal Cheema.

59 Personal interview with Pervaiz Iqbal Cheema.

60 Personal interview with K. Subrahmanyam, former Defense Secretary of India and head of the Kargil Commission, New Delhi, January 6, 2002.

## 6  Crises and wars in the pre-nuclear period

1  Michael Brecher and Jonathan Wilkenfeld list nine inter-state crises between 1947 and 1990, including two very serious crises in the nuclear period – the Brasstacks crisis and the 1990 Kashmir/nuclear crisis. While their research ends in 1990, two other crises occurred after 1990 – the Kargil crisis of 1999 and the Indian Parliament Attack crisis of 2001. Thus, the conflict has actually witnessed eleven inter-state crises during its sixty-year history. See Michael Brecher and Jonathan Wilkenfeld, *A Study of Crisis* (Ann Arbor: The University of Michigan Press, 1997), p. 164.
2  Ibid., pp. 165–6.
3  Ibid., p. 167.
4  Paul Kapur, *Dangerous Deterrent: Nuclear Weapons Proliferation and Conflict in South Asia* (Stanford, Calif.: Stanford University Press, 2007), p. 95.
5  Brecher and Wilkenfeld, *A Study of Crisis*, p. 167.
6  Sumit Ganguly, *Conflict Unending: India–Pakistan Tensions Since 1947* (New York: Columbia Press, 2001), p. 19.
7  Sumit Ganguly and Devin T. Hagerty, *Fearful Symmetry: India–Pakistan Crises in the Shadow of Nuclear Weapons* (Seattle: University of Washington Press, 2005), p. 35.
8  Personal interview with P. R. Chari, Director of Peace and Conflict Studies, New Delhi, January 7, 2002.
9  See Brecher and Wilkenfeld, *A Study of Crisis*, p. 168.
10  Ibid., p. 173.
11  Ibid., p. 169.
12  Ibid.
13  Ganguly, *Conflict Unending*, p. 41.
14  Brecher and Wilkenfeld, *A Study of Crisis*, p. 170.
15  See Iffat Malik, *Kashmir: Ethnic Conflict, International Dispute* (Oxford: Oxford University Press, 2002), pp. 113–14, 121.
16  Kapur, *Dangerous Deterrent*, p. 97.
17  Gabriella Blum, *Islands of Agreement: Managing Enduring Armed Rivalries* (Cambridge, Mass.: Harvard University Press, 2007), p. 60.
18  J. N. Dixit, *India–Pakistan in War and Peace* (London and New York: Routledge, 2002), p. 148.
19  Blum, *Islands of Agreement*, pp. 60–1.
20  Stephen P. Cohen, *India: Emerging Power* (New Delhi: Oxford University Press, 2002), p. 218.
21  See Saira Khan, "Nuclear Weapons and the Prolongation of the India–Pakistan Rivalry," in T. V. Paul. ed., *The India–Pakistan Conflict: An Enduring Rivalry* (Cambridge, Mass.: Cambridge University Press, 2005), pp. 162–3.
22  Dixit, *India–Pakistan in War and Peace*, p. 149.
23  Ibid., pp. 149–50.
24  Personal interview with K. Subrahmanyam, New Delhi, January 28, 1997.
25  Ganguly, *Conflict Unending*, p. 31.
26  Blum, *Islands of Agreement*, pp. 59–60.
27  Timothy D. Hoyt, "Strategic Myopia: Pakistan's Nuclear Doctrine and Crisis Stability in South Asia," in Lowell Dittmer, ed., *South Asia's Nuclear Security Dilemma: India, Pakistan, and China* (London and New York: M. E. Sharpe, 2005), p. 129.
28  Scott D. Sagan, "More Will Be Worse," in Scott D. Sagan and Kenneth N. Waltz, *The Spread of Nuclear Weapons: A Debate* (New York: W. W. Norton, 2003), p. 62.
29  Ganguly, *Conflict Unending*, p. 39.
30  Hoyt, "Strategic Myopia," p. 130.
31  Ganguly, *Conflict Unending*, pp. 40–2.
32  Dixit, *India–Pakistan in War and Peace*, p. 149.

33  Ibid., p. 148.
34  Interview with Bhabani Sen Gupta, columnist, January 4, 2002.
35  Sumit Ganguly, *The Crisis in Kashmir: Portents of War, Hopes of Peace* (Cambridge, Mass.: Cambridge University Press, 1997), p. 59.
36  Brecher and Wilkenfeld, *A Study of Crisis,* pp. 172–4.
37  Ibid., p. 173.
38  Raj Changappa, *Weapons of Peace: The Secret Story of India's Quest to be a Nuclear Power* (New Delhi: HarperCollins Publishers, 2000), p. 57.
39  Stephen P. Cohen, *India: Emerging Power* (New Delhi: Oxford University Press, 2002), p. 201.
40  Kapur, *Dangerous Deterrent*, p. 66.
41  Neil Joeck, "Pakistani Security and Nuclear Proliferation in South Asia," in Neil Joeck, ed., *Strategic Consequences of Nuclear Proliferation in South Asia* (London: Frank Cass, 1986), p. 88.
42  Scott Sagan, "Indian and Pakistani Nuclear Weapons: For Better or Worse," in Sagan and Waltz, *The Spread of Nuclear Weapons;* p. 93.
43  Ganguly and Hagerty, *Fearful Symmetry*, p. 59.
44  Ibid.
45  Personal interview with Pakistan's former Army Chief General Aslam Beg, Islamabad, February 13, 1997
46  Interview with General Aslam Beg.
47  Kapur, *Dangerous Deterrent*, p. 94.

## 7  Crises and non-escalation in the Nuclear period

 1  J. Manuel Andreu, Takehiro Fujihara, Takaya Kohyama, and J. Martin Ramirez, "Justification of Interpersonal Aggression in Japanese, American, and Spanish Students," *Aggressive Behavior*, 25, 1998, pp. 185–95.
 2  Gabriella Blum, *Islands of Agreement: Managing Enduring Armed Rivalries* (Cambridge, Mass.: Harvard University Press, 2007), p. 65.
 3  In 1984 Prime Minister Indira Gandhi ordered the initiation of Operation Bluestar, a full-scale military operation, to wipe out the Sikh fundamentalists who had taken control of the revered Golden Temple shrine. The fundamentalist leader was killed in this operation which triggered outrage among the Sikhs in Punjab and ultimately led to Indira Gandhi's assassination. It is believed that many of these terrorists left for Pakistan in the wake of the operation to receive support and training from Pakistan and in particular from the Inter Services Intelligence (ISI). It is argued that the violence these fundamentalists were able to create and the military operations they conducted for the establishment of Khalistan, an independent Sikh theocratic state, had much to do with the military assistance they received from Pakistan. Indira Gandhi publicly accused Pakistan of supporting the terrorists in Khalistan. For more information on Pakistan's role in the Punjab problem, which was partly responsible for the Brasstacks crisis, see Praveen Swami, "Failed Threats and Flawed Fences: India's Military Responses to Pakistan's Proxy War," *India Review*, 3, 2, April 2004 pp. 147–70; Harish K. Puri, Paramjit Singh Judge, and Jagrup Singh Sekhon, *Terrorism in Punjab: Understanding Grassroots Reality* (New Delhi: Har Anand Publications, 1999); Satyapal Dang, *Genesis of Terrorism: An Analytical Study of Punjab Terrorists* (New Delhi: Patriot Publishers, 1988); Sharda Jain, *Politics of Terrorism in India: The Case of Punjab* (Delhi: Deep and Deep Publications, 1995).
 4  For a detailed discussion on the Brasstacks crisis, see Kanti Bajpai, P. R. Chari, Pervaiz Iqbal Cheema, Stephen P. Cohen, and Sumit Ganguly, *Brasstacks and Beyond: Perception and Management of Crisis in South Asia* (New Delhi: Manohar, 1995).
 5  Blum, *Islands of Agreement*, p. 65.
 6  Bajpai *et al., Brasstacks and Beyond*.

7 Sumit Ganguly, *Conflict Unending: India–Pakistan Tensions Since 1947* (New York: Columbia University Press, 2001), pp. 86–7.
8 C. Raja Mohan and Peter Lavoy, "Avoiding Nuclear War," in Michael Krepon and Amit Sevak, eds, *Crisis Prevention, Confidence-Building, and Reconciliation in South Asia* (New York: St Martin's Press, 1995), p. 32.
9 Ganguly, *Conflict Unending*, p. 86.
10 Ibid., pp. 86–8.
11 Sumit Ganguly and Devin T. Hagerty, *Fearful Symmetry: India–Pakistan Crises in the Shadow of Nuclear Weapons* (Seattle: University of Washington Press, 2005), p. 78.
12 Ibid.
13 Kuldip Nayar, "We Have the A-Bomb, Says Pakistan's Dr. Strangelove," *Observer*, London, March 1, 1987.
14 N. Dixit, *India–Pakistan in War and Peace* (London and New York: Routledge, 2002), p. 261.
15 "Bomb Controversy," *Muslim*, March 3, 1987.
16 Ganguly and Hagerty, *Fearful Symmetry*, p. 76.
17 Dixit, *India–Pakistan in War and Peace*, p. 260.
18 Ibid.
19 Ganguly and Hagerty, *Fearful Symmetry*, p. 76.
20 Saira Khan, *Nuclear Proliferation Dynamics in Protracted Conflict Regions: A Comparative Study of South Asia and the Middle East* (Aldershot: Ashgate, 2002), pp. 151–65.
21 Dixit, *India–Pakistan in War and Peace*, p. 261.
22 Saira Khan, "Nuclear Weapons and the Prolongation of the India–Pakistan Enduring Rivalry," in T. V. Paul, ed., *The India–Pakistan Conflict: An Enduring Rivalry* (Cambridge: Cambridge University Press, 2005), pp. 164–5.
23 Dixit, *India–Pakistan in War and Peace*, p. 261.
24 Ibid., p. 262.
25 The Kargil Review Committee Report, *From Surprise to Reckoning* (New Delhi: Sage Publications, 2000), pp. 90–1.
26 Chris Gagne, "Nuclear Risk Reduction in South Asia: Building on Common Ground," in Michael Krepon and Chris Gagne, eds, *The Stability-Instability Paradox: Nuclear Weapons and Brinkmanship in South Asia*, Report No. 38 (Washington, DC: Stimson Center, 2001), p. 44.
27 Ibid.
28 Seymour Hersh, "On the Nuclear Edge," *New Yorker*, March 29, 1993, pp. 56–67; Devin T. Hagerty, *Consequences of Nuclear Proliferation: Lessons from South Asia* (Cambridge, Mass.: The MIT Press, 1998), p. 154; George Perkovich, *India's Nuclear Bomb: The Impact on Global Proliferation*, (Berkeley: University of California Press, 1999), pp. 293, 308–9.
29 See Michael Brecher and Jonathan Wilkenfeld, *A Study of Crisis* (Ann Arbor: University of Michigan Press, 1997), p. 176.
30 Hersh, "On the Nuclear Edge," pp. 56–67.
31 Personal interview with General Aslam Beg, Islamabad, February 13, 1997.
32 For non-traditional nuclear deterrence, see Khan, *Nuclear Proliferation Dynamics in Protracted Conflict Regions*, pp. 151–65.
33 Hagerty, *Consequences of Nuclear Proliferation*, p. 166.
34 Perkovich, *India's Nuclear Bomb*, p. 293.
35 William R. Doerner, "Knocking at the Nuclear Door," *Time*, March 30, 1987, p. 42.
36 Perkovich, *India's Nuclear Bomb*, p. 295.
37 "If Pushed Beyond a Point by Pakistan, We Will Retaliate," *India Today*, April 30, 1990, p. 76.
38 Ganguly and Hagerty, *Fearful Symmetry*, p. 83.
39 Ibid., p. 104.

40 Personal interview with K. Subrahmanyam, former Defense Secretary of India and head of the Kargil Commission, New Delhi, January 28, 1997.
41 Ganguly and Hagerty, *Fearful Symmetry*, p. 106.
42 Ibid., p. 107.
43 Russell J. Leng, "Realpolitik and Learning in the India–Pakistan Rivalry," in Paul, *The India–Pakistan Conflict*, pp. 103–27.
44 Ganguly and Hagerty, *Fearful Symmetry*, p. 143.
45 Interview with Air Commodore Jasjit Singh, New Delhi, December 29, 2001.
46 Interview with Air Commodore Jasjit Singh.
47 Scott D. Sagan and Kenneth N. Waltz, *The Spread of Nuclear Weapons: A Debate Renewed* (New York and London: W. W. Norton, 2003), p. 115.
48 Interview with Nasim Zehra, columnist in Pakistan, Islamabad, April 25, 2003.
49 Interview with Nasim Zehra.
50 Interview with Nasim Zehra.
51 Leng, "Realpolitik and Learning in the India–Pakistan Rivalry," pp. 103–27.
52 Sagan and Waltz, *The Spread of Nuclear Weapons*, p. 96.
53 Ibid.
54 See P. R. Chari, *Nuclear Crisis, Escalation Control, and Deterrence in South Asia*, Stimson Working Paper (Washington, DC: Henry L. Stimson Center, 2003), pp. 18–20; Ashok Krishna and P. R. Chari, eds, *Kargil: The Tables Turned* (New Delhi: Manohar Press, 2001).
55 Ganguly, *Conflict Unending*, p. 122.
56 Sagan and Waltz, *The Spread of Nuclear Weapons*, p. 97, footnote 19.
57 See The Kargil Review Committee Report, *From Surprise to Reckoning*, p. 77; Maleeha Lodhi, "The Kargil Crisis: Anatomy of a Debacle," *Newsline*, July 1999, p. 1.
58 Leng, "Realpolitik and Learning in the India–Pakistan Rivalry," p. 115.
59 Ibid.
60 Daniel Geller, "Nuclear Weapons, Deterrence, and Crisis Escalation," *Journal of Conflict Resolution*, 34, 1990, pp. 291–310.
61 Leng, "Realpolitik and Learning in the India–Pakistan Rivalry," pp. 116.
62 Ganguly, *Conflict Unending*, p. 121.
63 Samina Ahmed, "Nuclear Weapons and the Kargil Crisis: How and What Have Pakistanis Learned?," in Lowell Dittmer, ed., *South Asia's Nuclear Security Dilemma: India, Pakistan, and China* (New York and London: M. E. Sharpe, 2005), p. 145.
64 Ganguly, *Conflict Unending*, p. 121.
65 Ahmed, "Nuclear Weapons and the Kargil Crisis: How and What Have Pakistanis Learned?," p. 145.
66 Interview with K. Subrahmanyam, New Delhi, January 6, 2002.
67 "Indian Envoy Rules Out Full-scale War," *Dawn*, May 18, 1999.
68 Interview with K. Subrahmanyam.
69 See Kargil Review Committee Report, *From Surprise to Reckoning*.
70 Ganguly, *Conflict Unending*, p. 122.
71 Interview with Raj Changappa, editor, *India Today*, New Delhi, December 29, 2001.
72 Sagan and Waltz, *The Spread of Nuclear Weapons*, p. 115.
73 Raja Menon, *A Nuclear Strategy for India* (New Delhi: Sage Publishing, 2000), p. 116.
74 Interview with Major General V. K. Srivastava, New Delhi, January 3, 2002.
75 Interview with S. D. Muni, Professor of South Asian Security and Proliferation, Jawaharlal Nehru University, New Delhi, January 4, 2002.
76 Interview with S. D. Muni.
77 Ganguly, *Conflict Unending*, p. 127.
78 See Khan, "Nuclear Weapons and the Prolongation of the India–Pakistan Rivalry," pp. 168–72.
79 Barry Bearak, "26 Die as Suicide Squad Bombs Kashmir Legislative Building," *New York Times*, October 1, 2001, p. B3.

80 Economist Global Agenda, "Terror in India," December 19, 2001, www.economist. com.
81 Ganguly and Hagerty, *Fearful Symmetry*, p. 168.
82 Interview with Mushahid Hussain, Senator of Pakistan, Islamabad, April 24, 2003.
83 Interview with Mushahid Hussain.
84 Interview with Pervaiz Iqbal Cheema, President of the Islamabad Peace Research Institute, Islamabad, April 25, 2003.
85 Interview with Nasim Zehra, Islamabad, April 25, 2003.
86 Interview with Aga Shahi, former Foreign Secretary, Islamabad, April 21, 2003.
87 Interview with Khalid Mahmud, Institute of Regional Studies, Islamabad, April 25, 2003.
88 Interview with Mushahid Hussain.
89 Interview with Mushahid Hussain.
90 Interview with P. Sahadevan, proliferation scholar, Jawaharlal Nehru University, New Delhi, January 4, 2002.
91 Interview with Air Commodore Jasjit Singh, New Delhi, December 29, 2001.
92 Interview with Amitabh Mattoo, member, National Security Council Advisory Board, New Delhi, January 7, 2002.
93 Interview with Brahma Chellaney, proliferation scholar, New Delhi, December 28, 2001.
94 Bhavdeep Kang, "Tempers Tempered," *Outlook*, December 31, 2001, p. 24.
95 Raj Chengappa and Sisir Gupta, "In Cold Pursuit," *India Today*, December 24, 2001, p. 37.
96 Interview with K. Subrahmanyam.
97 Interview with Vice Admiral K. K. Nayyar, New Delhi, December 27, 2001.
98 Interview with Vice Admiral K. K. Nayyar.
99 Interview with Muchkund Dubey, former Foreign Secretary of India, New Delhi, December 27, 2001.
100 Interview with the former Indian Foreign Secretary, S. K. Singh, New Delhi, December 27, 2001.
101 Interview with P. Sahadevan.
102 Interview with the former Indian Prime Minister I. K. Gujral, December 31, 2001.
103 Interview with Prime Minister I. K. Gujral.
104 Interview with Rasheed Khaled, city correspondent, *The News* (Rawalpindi), Islamabad, April 23, 2003.
105 Ahmed, "Nuclear Weapons and the Kargil Crisis: How and What Have Pakistanis Learned?," p. 139.
106 Kargil Review Committee Report, *From Surprise to Reckoning*, p. 56.
107 Interview with K. Santhanam, Director, IDSA, New Delhi, January 4, 2002.
108 Interview with Bhabani Sen Gupta, columnist, New Delhi, January 4, 2002.
109 Interview with Air Commodore Jasjit Singh.
110 Interview with Pervaiz Iqbal Cheema.
111 Lawrence Saez, "The Political Economy of the India–Pakistan Nuclear Standoff," in Dittmer, *South Asia's Nuclear Security Dilemma*, p. 13.
112 Major General Ashok Krishna, "The Kargil War," in Krishna and Chari, *Kargil: The Tables Turned*, p. 82.

**8 Futile peace initiatives in the midst of violence**

1 Eqbal Ahmed, "A Kashmiri Solution for Kashmir," *Himal*, South Asia, 1997.
2 Michael Brecher, "Crisis Escalation: A New Model and Findings," in Frank Harvey and Ben D. Mor, eds, *Conflict in World Politics: Advances in the Study of Crisis, War, and Peace* (New York: St Martin's Press, 1998), p. 125.

3 See "The Highway Beyond Agra," *Strategic Analysis*, special issue, 25, 7, October 2001.

4 Brahma Chellaney, "Patience Overstretched," *Hindustan Times*, October 2, 2002

5 Stephen Kinzer, "Kashmir Gets Scarier," *New York Times*, June 29, 1999, p. 5.

6 Sumit Ganguly, *Conflict Unending: India–Pakistan Tensions since 1947* (New York: Columbia University Press, 2001), p. 114.

7 Quoted in *Dawn*, December 3, 1998.

8 *Hindustan Times*, February 22, 1999.

9 J. N. Dixit, *India–Pakistan in War and Peace* (London and New York: Routledge, 2002), p. 367.

10 Ibid.

11 *Hindu*, February 22, 1999.

12 The Lahore Declaration, February 21, 1999, Peace Agreements Digital Collections: India–Pakistan, United States Institute of Peace, www.usip.org.

13 Ganguly, *Conflict Unending*, p. 115.

14 Dixit, *India–Pakistan in War and Peace*, p. 367.

15 Gabriella Blum, *Islands of Agreement: Managing Enduring Armed Rivalries* (Cambridge, Mass.: Harvard University Press, 2007), p. 73.

16 Ibid.

17 Dixit, *India–Pakistan in War and Peace*, p. 367.

18 D. Suba Chandran, "Why Kargil? Pakistan's Objectives and Motivation," in P. R. Chari and Major General Ashok Krishna, eds, *Kargil: The Tables Turned* (New Delhi: Manohar Publishers, 2001), p. 37.

19 Ashley J. Tellis, C. Christine Fair, and Jamison Jo Medby, *Limited Conflicts Under the Nuclear Umbrella: Indian and Pakistani Lessons from the Kargil Crisis* (Santa Monica, Calif.: RAND, 2001), p. 48.

20 Personal interview with Air Commodore Jasjit Singh, New Delhi, December 29, 2001.

21 Tellis, *et al., Limited Conflicts Under the Nuclear Umbrella*, p. 16.

22 Blum, *Islands of Agreement*, p. 75.

23 Interview with Nasim Zehra, columnist in Pakistan, Islamabad, April 25, 2003.

24 Tellis *et al., Limited Conflicts Under the Nuclear Umbrella*, p. 16.

25 Dixit, *India–Pakistan in War and Peace*, p. 367.

26 Ibid., p. 368.

27 Ibid.

28 G. Parthasarathy, "How Kandahar Hijacked Us," *Indian Express*, February 6, 2008.

29 Tellis *et al., Limited Conflicts Under the Nuclear Umbrella*, p. 58.

30 *Times of India*, October 13, 1999.

31 Ganguly, *Conflict Unending*, p. 135.

32 Blum, *Islands of Agreement*, p. 75.

33 Dixit, *India–Pakistan in War and Peace*, p. 371.

34 Ibid., p. 414.

35 Ibid., p. 401.

36 For a detailed information and the situation that led the two leaders to the summit, see Dixit, *India–Pakistan in War and Peace*, pp. 401–14.

37 Ibid., p. 425.

38 "Resolve Kashmir, then Sign No-War Pact: Musharraf," *Times of India*, May 5, 2003.

39 "Kashmir: Learning from the Past," ICG Asia Report, no. 70 (Islamabad, New Delhi, and Brussels, December 4, 2003), p, 18.

40 Michael Sullivan, "Militants Attack Indian Army Base in Kashmir," *Non-Proliferation Review*, May 14, 2002.

41 "Resolve Kashmir, then Sign No-War Pact: Musharraf."

42 Blum, *Islands of Agreement*, p. 82.

43 Tellis *et al., Limited Conflicts Under the Nuclear Umbrella*, p. 77.

44 Robert G. Wirsing, *Kashmir in the Shadow of War: Regional Rivalries in the Nuclear Age* (New York and London: M. E. Sharpe, 2003), p. 57.

45 Tellis *et al., Limited Conflicts Under the Nuclear Umbrella*, p. 77.
46 Interview with Jasjit Singh.
47 Interview with Savita Pande, proliferation scholar, New Delhi, January 7, 2002.
48 Interview with Khalid Mahmud, Institute of Regional Studies, Islamabad, April 25, 2003.
49 Interview with Khalid Mahmud.
50 Stephen P. Cohen, *India: Emerging Power* (New Delhi: Oxford University Press, 2001), p. 224.
51 Interview with Mushahid Hussain, Senator of Pakistan, Islamabad, April 24, 2003.
52 Interview with Mushahid Hussain.
53 Interview with Shireen Mazari, Director of the Islamic Institute of Strategic Studies (IISS), Islamabad, April 22, 2003.
54 Interview with Raj Changappa, editor, *India Today,* New Delhi, December 29, 2001.
55 Interview with S. K. Singh, former Foreign Secretary of India, New Delhi, December 27, 2001.
56 Interview with P. Sahadevan, proliferation scholar, Jawaharlal Nehru University, New Delhi, January 4, 2002
57 Interview with K. Santhanam, Director, IOSA, New Delhi, January 4, 2002.
58 Interview with former Prime Minister I. K. Gujral, New Delhi, December 31, 2001.
59 Interview with Prime Minister I. K. Gujral.
60 Interview with Prime Minister I. K. Gujral.
61 Interview with K. Subrahmanyam, former Defense Secretary of India and head of the Kargil Commission, New Delhi, January 6, 2002.
62 Interview with Savita Pande.
63 Interview with Savita Pande.
64 Interview with Shireen Mazari.
65 Interview with Khalid Mahmud.
66 Interview with Khalid Mahmud.
67 Interview with K. K. Nayyar, former Vice Admiral of India and member of the National Security Council Advisory Board, New Delhi, December 27, 2001.
68 Interview with Muchkund Dubey, former Foreign Secretary of India, New Delhi, December 27, 2001.
69 Interview with P. Sahadevan.
70 Interview with Uday Bhaskar, Deputy Director of the Institute for Defense Studies and Analysis, New Delhi, January 5, 2002
71 Interview with Nasim Zehra, Islamabad, April 25, 2003.
72 Interview with Nasim Zehra.
73 Interview with Najam Rafique, IISS, Islamabad, April 25, 2003.
74 Samina Ahmed, "Nuclear Weapons and the Kargil Crisis: How and What Pakistanis Learned?," in Lowell Dittmer, ed., *South Asia's Nuclear Security Dilemma: India, Pakistan, and China* (London and New York: M. E. Sharpe, 2005), p. 139.
75 Interview with Niaz Naik, former Foreign Secretary of Pakistan, Islamabad, April 23, 2003.
76 Stephen M. Saideman, "At the Heart of the Conflict: Irredentism and Kashmir," in T. V. Paul, ed., *The India–Pakistan Conflict: An Enduring Rivalry* (Cambridge: Cambridge University Press, 2005), p. 223.

## 9 Conflict transformed

1 Interview with Amitabh Mattoo, member, National Security Council Advisory Board, New Delhi, January 7, 2002.
2 Interview with Amitabh Mattoo.
3 Scott D. Sagan and Kenneth N. Waltz, *The Spread of Nuclear Weapons: A Debate Renewed* (New York and London: W. W. Norton, 2003), p. 123.

4 Ibid.
5 Interview with Niaz Naik, former Foreign Secretary of Pakistan, Islamabad, April 23, 2003.
6 Interview with Niaz Naik.
7 Interview with Niaz Naik.
8 Interview with Niaz Naik.
9 Interview with Niaz Naik.
10 Interview with Shireen Mazari, Director of the Islamic Institute of Strategic Studies (IISS), Islamabad, April 22, 2003.
11 Interview with Mushahid Hussain, Senator of Pakistan, Islamabad, April 24, 2003.
12 Interview with Rasheed Khalid, Islamabad, April 23, 2003.
13 For more information on the power and role of Pakistan army, see Thathiah Ravi, "Pakistan Army and Regional Peace in South Asia," *Journal of Third World Studies*, Spring 2006.
14 Interview with Rasheed Khalid.
15 Talat Masood, "Civil-Military Relations and the 2007 Elections in Pakistan: Impact on the Regional Security Environment," *China and Eurasia Forum Quarterly*, 5, 1, 2007.
16 Anatol Rapoport and Albert M. Chammah, *Prisoner's Dilemma: A Study of Conflict and Cooperation* (Ann Arbor: The University of Michigan Press, 1965), p. 25.
17 See Saira Khan, "Nuclear Weapons and the Prolongation of the India–Pakistan Rivalry," in T. V. Paul, ed., *The India–Pakistan Conflict: An Enduring Rivalry* (Cambridge: Cambridge University Press, 2005), chapter 7.
18 See Saira Khan, "A Nuclear South Asia: Resolving or Protracting the Protracted Conflict?," *International Relations*, 15, 4, 2001. Also see Khan, "Nuclear Weapons and the Prolongation of the India–Pakistan Rivalry".
19 Interview with R. R. Subramanian, Senior Research Associate, Institute for Defense Studies and Analyses, New Delhi, January 3, 2002.
20 Interview with Matiur Rahman, Foundation for Research on International Environment, National Development, and Security (FRIENDS), April 22, 2003.
21 Interview with Shireen Mazari.
22 Naik argues that according to the Simla Agreement, dialogue should resolve the Kashmir issue. Interview with Niaz Naik.
23 Charles W. Kegley and Gregory A. Raymond, *How Nations Make Peace* (New York: St Martin's Press, 1999), p. 246.
24 Joint Statement on Indian Pakistan Expert Level Talks on Nuclear CBMs, June 20, 2004. See http://www.mea.gov.in/cgi-bin/db2www/meaxpsite/searchhome.d2w/searchstr?start=30&str=India–Pakistan&sectioncode=%20.
25 Interview with former Indian Prime Minister I. K. Gujral, New Delhi, December 31, 2001.
26 Kegley and Raymond, *How Nations Make Peace*, p. 246.
27 Stephen P. Cohen, *India: Emerging Power* (New Delhi: Oxford University Press, 2001), p. 224.
28 See http://www.mea.gov.in/speech/2005/02/23js01.htm.
29 India–Pakistan Foreign Secretary level talks in 2006, 17, January 2006. See http://www.mea.gov.in/pressbriefing/2006/01/17pb01.htm.
30 Alan C. Tidwell, *Conflict Resolved: A Critical Assessment of Conflict Resolution* (London and New York: Pinter, 1998), p. 105.
31 "Not Doing Enough: The Prime Minister Will Tell Musharraf," *Times of India*, September 13, 2006.
32 Ibid.
33 "Musharraf Desperate for Good Ties with India," *Times of India*, November 6, 2006.
34 Interview with Aga Shahi, former Foreign Secretary, Islamabad, April 21, 2003.
35 Interview with Matiur Rahman.

36  Interview with Matiur Rahman.
37  Interview with S. D. Muni, Professor of South Asian Security and Proliferation, Jawaharlal Nehru University, New Delhi, January 4, 2002.
38  Interview with S. D. Muni.
39  Interview with K. Subrahmanyam, former Defense Secretary of India and member of the Kargil Commission, New Delhi, January 6, 2002.
40  Interview with K. Subrahmanyam.
41  "Not Doing Enough: The Prime Minister Will Tell Musharraf."
42  Special Media Briefing by Indian Foreign Secretary Shri Shyam Saran on India–Pakistan Foreign Secretary level talks, January 18, 2006. See http://www.mea.gov.in/pressbriefing/2006/01/18pb01.htm.
43  Interview with Farukh Sobhan, former High Commissioner of Bangladesh to India, Dhaka, February 19, 2006.
44  Interview with Ambassador Q. A. M. A. Rahim, former Secretary General of SAARC, Dhaka, February 25, 2006.
45  Interview with Gaddam Dharmendra, Indian Political Counselor to Bangladesh, Dhaka, February 27, 2006.
46  Interview with Gaddam Dharmendra.
47  Paul F. Diehl, Gary Goertz, and Daniel Saeedi, "Theoretical Specifications of Enduring Rivalries: Applications to the India–Pakistan Case," in T. V. Paul, ed., *The India–Pakistan Conflict: An Enduring Rivalry* (Cambridge: Cambridge University Press, 2005), p. 52.
48  Interview with R. R. Subramanian.
49  Interview with S. D. Muni.
50  Interview with Aga Shahi.
51  Stephen P. Cohen, *India: Emerging Power* (New Delhi: Oxford University Press, 2002), p. 223.
52  Interview with Farukh Sobhan.
53  Interview with P. R. Chari, Director of Peace and Conflict Studies, New Delhi, January 7, 2002.
54  Interview with Farukh Sobhan.
55  "Musharraf Desperate for Good Ties with India."
56  Interview with Mostafa Faruque Mohammed, former High Commissioner of Bangladesh to India, Dhaka, February 19, 2006.
57  Interview with Mostafa Faruque Mohammed.
58  Interview with Ambassador Q. A. M. A. Rahim.
59  Interview with Ambassador Q. A. M. A. Rahim.
60  Interview with Mostafa Faruque Mohammed.
61  Interview with P. Sahadevan, proliferation scholar, Jawaharlal Nehru University, New Delhi, January 4, 2002.
62  Interview with Raj Chengappa, editor, *India Today*, New Delhi, December 29, 2001.
63  Interview with Savita Pande, proliferation scholar, January 7, 2002.
64  Interview with S. D. Muni.
65  Cohen, *India: Emerging Power*, p. 223.
66  Interview with Amitabh Mattoo.

## 10  Potential for conflict termination

 1  Robert Kagan, "A Tougher War for the US is One of Legitimacy," *New York Times*, January 24, 2004. Although Kagan speaks of a need for American legitimacy in the context of the Iraq war, the point remains that the end of the cold war did not earn the US the respect, support, and legitimacy it desired.
 2  Javier Solana, "The Future of Transatlantic Relations: Reinvention or Reform," *Progressive Governance*, July 10, 2003.

3 Samuel P. Huntington, "The Lonely Superpower," in G. John Ikenberry, ed., *American Foreign Policy: Theoretical Essays*, 4th edn (New York: Longman, 2002), pp. 586–96.
4 Interview with Brahma Chellaney, proliferation scholar, New Delhi, December 28, 2001.
5 Sumit Ganguly, "The Start of a Beautiful Friendship? The United States and India," *World Policy Journal*, 20, 1, Spring 2003.
6 David E. Sanger and Kurt Eichenwald, "Citing India Attack, US Aims at Assets of Groups in Pakistan," *New York Times*, December 21, 2001.
7 India claimed from the very beginning that these terrorist groups were responsible for the Parliament attack. Eventually even Pakistan's ISI came out in the open and admitted that Jaish-e-Mohammed was responsible. Any move by the Pakistani government to ban this and other similar organizations was important for the Indians. See B. Muralidhar Reddy, "Jaish Behind Parliament Attack: ex-ISI Chief," *Hindu*, March 7, 2004.
8 Navnita Chadna Behera, "Kashmir: Redefining the U.S. Role," *Brookings Policy Brief*, 110, November 2002, p. 2.
9 Husain Haqqani, "America's New Alliance with Pakistan: Avoiding the Traps of the Past," *Carnegie Policy Brief*, 19, October 2002, p. 6.
10 There is still no proof that Iraq had any connection with Al Qaeda or possessed weapons of mass destruction. However, that the pretext was used to launch a war against Iraq was enough to threaten other Muslim states that may have had connections with the terrorists prior to the war.
11 See Rajpal Budania, "The Emerging International Security System: Threats, Challenges and Opportunities for India," *Strategic Analysis*, 27, 1, January March 2003.
12 C. Raja Mohan, "Vajpayee's Experiment with Pakistan," *Hindu*, December 4, 2003.
13 Stephen M. Saideman, "At the Heart of the Conflict: Irredentism and Kashmir," in T. V. Paul, ed., *The India–Pakistan Conflict: An Enduring Rivalry* (Cambridge: Cambridge University Press, 2005), p. 211.
14 Interview with Pervaiz Iqbal Cheema, President of the Pakistan Peace Research Institute, Islamabad, April 25, 2003.
15 In fact, even after his Srinagar speech in April 2003 in which he offered friendship to Pakistan for the third time, Vajpayee insisted that cross-border terrorism had to stop and its infrastructure uprooted for the new peace process to proceed. See Mani Shankar Aiyar, "The Thirteenth Step," *Indian Express*, October 28, 2003.
16 Frank G. Wisner II, Nicholas Platt, and Marshall M. Bouton, *New Priorities in South Asia: U.S. Policy Toward India, Pakistan, and Afghanistan* (New York: Council on Foreign Relations, 2003), p. 47.
17 Haqqani, "America's New Alliance with Pakistan: Avoiding the Traps of the Past," p. 6.
18 James C. Clad, "An Unexpected Chance to Get Down to the Fundamentals," *Non-Proliferation Project: Global Policy Program*, 27, May 2002, p. 17.
19 Interview with Major General V. K. Srivastava, New Delhi, January 3, 2002.
20 Interview with Mushahid Hussain, Senator of Pakistan, April 24, 2003.
21 "Can India and Pakistan Seize the Moment?," *South Asia Monitor*, 60, July 1, 2003.
22 Interview with Nasim Zehra, columnist in Pakistan, Islamabad, April 25, 2003. However, others in Pakistan argued that India is under a government of fascist ideology, given the RSS's and BJP's mandates; there are modest people like Vajpayee and radicals like Advani. Interview with Aga Shahi, former Foreign Secretary, Islamabad, April 21, 2003.
23 Wisner II *et al., New Priorities in South Asia*, p. 16.
24 C. Raja Mohan, "A Paradigm Shift toward South Asia?," *The Washington Quarterly*, 26, 1, Winter 2002–3, p. 144.
25 Stephen P. Cohen, "Moving Forward in South Asia," *Brookings Policy Brief*, 81, May 2001. During Clinton's visit to India in March 2000, Washington and New Delhi formed a working group against terrorism. See Maqbool Ahmad Bhatty, "Readiness for Dialogue," *Dawn*, November 24, 2003.

26 Mohan, "A Paradigm Shift toward South Asia?," p. 142. Mohan argues that this does not mean that the US was not interested in South Asia before 9/11. During Clinton's period the US favored India, pressuring Pakistan to retreat from Kargil unconditionally.
27 Behera, "Kashmir," p. 5.
28 Teresita Schaffer, "The US and South Asia: New Priorities, Familiar Interests," *The South Asia Monitor*, 38, October 1, 2001.
29 Behera, "Kashmir," p. 5.
30 Paul F. Diehl, Gary Goertz, and Daniel Saeedi, "Theoretical Specifications of Enduring Rivalries: Applications to the India–Pakistan Case," in Paul, *The India–Pakistan Conflict: An Enduring Rivalry*, p. 52.
31 Interview with K. K. Nayyar, former Vice Admiral of India and member of the National Security Advisory Board, New Delhi, December 27, 2001.
32 Interview with Nasim Zehra, columnist, Islamabad, April 25, 2003.
33 Interview with Nasim Zehra.
34 Richard Ned Lebow, "The Search for Accommodation: Gorbachev in Comparative Perspective," in Richard Ned Lebow and Thomas Risse-Kappen, eds, *International Relations Theory and the End of the Cold War* (New York: Columbia University Press, 1995), pp. 167–86.
35 Graham Allison and Hisashi Owada, *The Responsibilities of Democracies in Preventing Deadly Conflict: Reflections and Recommendations* (New York: Carnegie Corporation, 1999), p. 19.
36 "Musharraf Desperate for Good Ties with India," *Times of India*, November 6, 2006.
37 Diehl et al., "Theoretical Specifications of Enduring Rivalries: Applications to the India–Pakistan Case," p. 53.
38 Sumit Ganguly, *Conflict Unending* (New York: Columbia University Press, 2001), p. 135.
39 Ibid.
40 Tara Shankar Sahay, "Experts Do Not Expect Much from Meeting," *India Abroad*, July 6, 2001, p. 6.
41 Sheela Bhatt, "A Compromise on Kashmir Would Have a Domino Effect on the Rest of India," India's Home Minister L.K. Advani on the India–Pakistan Summit, *India Abroad*, July 6, 2001, p. 12.
42 Ganguly, *Conflict Unending*, p. 137.
43 Stephen P. Cohen, *India: Emerging Power* (New Delhi: Oxford University Press, 2001), p. 223.
44 Ashok Kapur, "Major Powers and the Persistence of the India–Pakistan Conflict," in Paul, *The India–Pakistan Conflict: An Enduring Rivalry*, p. 131.
45 Interview with Matiur Rahman, Foundation for Research on International Environment, National Development and Security (FRIENDS), Islamabad, April 22, 2003.
46 Cohen, *India: Emerging Power*, p. 224.
47 Khalid Mahmud, research scholar, Institute of Regional Studies, Islamabad, April 25, 2003.

**Conclusion**

1 Although the concept of a security dilemma recognizes the problem that weapons may produce insecurity, the argument is about "perception" of security and not overall stability – which are functions of absence of crises and wars – in a conflict. For example, an arms race is the product of a security dilemma because when one state increases its margin of security by building armaments, its adversary feels insecure and follows suit, which makes both insecure in the end. The states in question are insecure because they "feel" insecure due to the changed balance of power. However, in the nuclear realm, the argument is different. Nuclear weapons are deterrents and security is the most important incentive that drives states to acquire them, as stated in chapter. It is argued

that states are secure because wars will not occur when states acquire these devastating and "absolute" weapons. Here "security" equals "absence of war" and "presence of stability" and "insecurity" equals "presence of war and instability." For more information on this, see Robert Jervis, "Offense, Defense, and Security Dilemma," in Robert J. Art and Robert Jervis, eds, *International Politics: Enduring Concepts and Contemporary Issues*, eighth edn (New York: Longman, 2007); Kenneth N. Waltz, "The Spread of Nuclear Weapons: More May be Better," *Adelphi Papers*, 171, Autumn 1981.

2 Nuclear weapons are assumed to deter wars in both a general and an immediate sense. General deterrence is successful when deterrent capabilities are possessed by states to regulate their adversarial relationships and neither of the opponents is seriously considering an attack. However, immediate deterrence is successful where a state successfully uses its deterrent capability as a threat to retaliate when one side is considering an attack. For a detailed discussion on general and immediate deterrence, see Patrick Morgan, *Deterrence: A Conceptual Analysis* (Beverly Hills, Calif., and London: Sage, 1977), pp. 40–3.

# Bibliography

## Books and articles

Abraham, Itty, *The Making of the Indian Atomic Bomb* (London: Zed Books, 1998).

Ahmed, Eqbal, "A Kashmiri Solution for Kashmir," *Himal*, South Asia, 1997.

Ahmed, Samina, "Nuclear Weapons and the Kargil Crisis: How and What Pakistanis Learned?," in Lowell Dittmer, ed., *South Asia's Nuclear Security Dilemma: India, Pakistan, and China* (London and New York: M. E. Sharpe, 2005).

Ahmed, Samina, "Pakistan's Nuclear Weapons Program: Turning Points and Nuclear Choices," *International Security*, 23, 1999.

Aiyar, Mani Shankar, "The Thirteenth Step," *Indian Express*, October 28, 2003.

Albin, C., "Explaining Conflict Transformation: How Jerusalem Became Negotiable," *Cambridge Review of International Affairs*, 18, 2005.

Allison, Graham, *Nuclear Terrorism: The Ultimate Preventable Catastrophe* (New York: Henry Holt, Times Books, 2004).

Allison, Graham and Hisashi Owada, *The Responsibilities of Democracies in Preventing Deadly Conflict: Reflections and Recommendations* (New York: Carnegie Corporation, 1999).

Axelrod, Robert, *The Evolution of Cooperation* (New York: Basic Books, 1984).

Azar, Edward, P. Jareidini, and R. Mclaurin, "Protracted Social Conflict: Theory and Practice in the Middle East," *Journal of Palestine Studies*, 8(1), 1978.

Bajpai, Kanti, P. R. Chari, Pervaiz Iqbal Cheema, Stephen P. Cohen, and Sumit Ganguly, *Brasstacks and Beyond: Perception and Management of Crisis in South Asia* (New Delhi: Manohar, 1995).

Ball, Desmond *et. al.*, *Crisis Stability and Nuclear War* (Ithaca, NY: Cornell University Peace Studies Program, 1987).

Bearak, Barry, "26 Die as Suicide Squad Bombs Kashmir Legislative Building," *New York Times*, October 1, 2001.

Behera, Navnita Chadna, "Kashmir: Redefining the U.S. Role," *Brookings Policy Brief*, 110, November 2002.

Benjamin, Milton R., "India Said to Eye Raid on Pakistan's A-Plant," *Washington Post*, December 20, 1982.

Ben-Yahuda, Hemda, "Territoriality and War in International Crises: Theory and Findings, 1918–2001," *International Studies Review*, 6(4), December 2004.

Bertsch, Gary K. and William C. Potter, "Conclusion," in Gary K. Bertsch and William C. Potter, eds, *Dangerous Weapons, Desperate States: Russia, Belarus, Kazakstan, and Ukraine* (New York and London: Routledge, 1999).

Bertsch, Gary K. and William C. Potter, "Introduction: The Challenge of NIS Export Control Developments," in Gary K. Bertsch and William C. Potter, eds, *Dangerous Weapons, Desperate States: Russia, Belarus, Kazakstan, and Ukraine* (New York and London: Routledge, 1999).

Bhatt, Sheela, "A Compromise on Kashmir Would Have a Domino Effect on the Rest of India," India's Home Minister L. K. Advani on the India–Pakistan Summit, *India Abroad*, July 6, 2001.

Bhatty, Maqbool Ahmad, "Readiness for Dialogue," *Dawn*, November 24, 2003.

Bhutto, Zulfiqar Ali, *The Myth of Independence* (London: Oxford University Press, 1969).

Binder, Leonard, *Religion and Politics in Pakistan* (Berkeley: University of California Press, 1961).

Bloomfield, D. and Ben Reilly, "The Changing Nature of Conflict and Conflict Management," in Peter Harris and Ben Reilly, eds, *Democracy and Deep-rooted Conflict* (Stockholm: Institute for Democracy and Electoral Assistance, 1998).

Blum, Gabriella, *Islands of Agreement: Managing Enduring Armed Rivalries* (Cambridge, Mass.: Harvard University Press, 2007).

Booth, Ken, "War, Security and Strategy: Toward a Doctrine for Stable Peace," in Ken Booth, ed., *New Thinking about Strategy and International Security* (London: HarperCollins, 1991).

Bose, Sumantra, *The Challenge in Kashmir: Democracy, Self Determination and a Just Peace* (New Delhi: Sage Publications, 1997).

Boulding, K., *The Image* (Ann Arbor: The University of Michigan Press, 1961).

Brecher, Michael, *Crises in World Politics* (Oxford: Pergamon Press, 1993).

Brecher, Michael, "Crisis Escalation: A New Model and Findings," in Frank Harvey and Ben D. More, eds, *Conflict in World Politics* (New York: St Martin's Press, 1998).

Brecher, Michael and Jonathan Wilkenfeld, *Crisis, Conflict and Instability* (Oxford: Pergamon Press, 1989).

Brecher, Michael and Jonathan Wilkenfeld, "International Crises and Global Instability: The Myth of the Long Peace," in Charles W. Kegley, ed., *The Long Post War Peace* (New York: HarperCollins, 1991).

Brecher, Michael and Jonathan Wilkenfeld, *A Study of Crisis* (Ann Arbor: The University of Michigan Press, 1997).

Brodie, Bernard, *Escalation and the Nuclear Option* (Princeton, NJ: Princeton University Press, 1966).

Brodie, Bernard, ed., *The Absolute Weapon* (New York: Harcourt Brace, 1946).

Budania, Rajpal, "The Emerging International Security System: Threats, Challenges and Opportunities for India," *Strategic Analysis*, 27(1), January–March 2003.

Burton, John, *Conflict: Resolution and Provention* (New York: St Martin's Press, 1990).

Butfoy, Andy, *Disarming Proposals: Controlling Nuclear, Biological and Chemical Weapons* (Sydney: UNSW Press, 2005).

Butler, Richard, *The Greatest Threat: Iraq, Weapons of Mass Destruction, and the Growing Crisis of Global Security* (New York: Public Affairs, 2000).

Cadwell, Dan and Robert E. Williams Jr., *Seeking Security in an Insecure World* (Boulder, Colo., New York, and Oxford: Rowman & Littlefield, 2006).

Chandran, D. Suba, "Why Kargil? Pakistan's Objectives and Motivation," in P. R. Chari and Major Gen. Ashok Krishna, eds, *Kargil: The Tables Turned* (New Delhi: Manohar Publishers, 2001).

Changappa, Raj, *Weapons of Peace: The Secret Story of India's Quest to be a Nuclear Power* (New Delhi: HarperCollins Publishers, 2000).

Chari, P. R., *Nuclear Crisis, Escalation Control, and Deterrence in South Asia*, Stimson Working Paper (Washington, DC: Henry L. Stimson Center, 2003).

Chari, P. R., "Nuclear Restraint, Nuclear Risk Reduction, and the Security-Insecurity Paradox in South Asia," in Michael Krepon and Chris Gagne, eds, *The Stability-Instability Paradox: Nuclear Weapons and Brinkmanship in South Asia* (Washington, DC: Henry L. Stimson Center, 2001).

Chari, P. R., Pervaiz Iqbal Cheema, and Stephen P. Cohen, *Perception, Politics, and Security in South Asia: The Compound Crisis of 1990* (London: RoutledgeCurzon, 2003).

Chellaney, Brahma, "Patience Overstretched," *Hindustan Times*, October 2, 2002.

Chengappa, Raj and Sisir Gupta, "In Cold Pursuit," *India Today*, December 24, 2001.

Cimbala, Stephen J., *Nuclear Weapons and Strategy: U.S. Nuclear Policy for the Twenty-First Century* (London and New York: Routledge, 2005).

Clad, James C., "An Unexpected Chance to Get Down to the Fundamentals," *Non-Proliferation Project: Global Policy Program*, 27, May 2002.

Clements, K., "Peace Building and Conflict Transformation," *Peace and Conflict Studies*, 4, 1997, www.gmu.edu/academic/pcs/clements.htm.

Cohen, Stephen P., *The Idea of Pakistan* (New Delhi: Oxford University Press, 2004).

Cohen, Stephen P., *India: Emerging Power* (New Delhi: Oxford University Press, 2002).

Cohen, Stephen P., "Moving Forward in South Asia," *Brookings Policy Brief*, 81, May 2001.

Cohen, Stephen P., *The Pakistan Army* (Karachi: Oxford University Press, 1998).

Cohen, Stephen P., ed., *Proliferation in South Asia: The Prospects of Arms Control* (Boulder, Colo.: Westview Press, 1991).

Corera, Gordon, *Shopping for Bombs: Nuclear Proliferation, Global Insecurity, and the Rise and Fall of the A. Q. Khan Network* (Oxford and New York: Oxford University Press, 2006).

Crocker, Chester A., "Intervention: Toward Best Practices and a Holistic View," in Chester A. Crocker, Fen Osler Hampson, and Pamela R. Aall, eds, *Turbulent Peace: The Challenges of Managing International Conflicts* (Washington, DC: The United States Institute of Peace, 2001).

Dang, Satyapal, *Genesis of Terrorism: An Analytical Study of Punjab Terrorists* (New Delhi: Patriot Publishers, 1988).

Dembinsk, Matthias, "The Threat of Nuclear Proliferation to Europe," in K. Bailey and Robert Rudney, eds, *Proliferation and Export Controls* (London: University Press of America, 1993).

Deutsch, Morton, *The Resolution of Conflict: Constructive and Destructive Processes* (New Haven, Conn.: Yale University Press, 1973).

Diehl, Paul F., Gary Goertz, and Daniel Saeedi, "Theoretical Specifications of Enduring Rivalries: Applications to the India–Pakistan Case," in T. V. Paul, ed., *The India–Pakistan Conflict: An Enduring Rivalry* (Cambridge: Cambridge University Press, 2005).

Dittmer, Lowell, "South Asia's Security Dilemma," *Asian Survey*, 41(6), November/December 2001.

Dixit, J. N., *India–Pakistan in War and Peace* (London and New York: Routledge, 2002).

Doerner, William R., "Knocking at the Nuclear Door," *Time*, March 30, 1987.

Drell, Sidney D. and James E. Goodby, *The Gravest Danger: Nuclear Weapons* (Stanford, Calif.: Hoover Institution Press, 2003).

Dukes, E. F., "Why Conflict Transformation Matters: Three Cases," www.gmu.edu/academic/pcs/Dukes61PCS.html.

Dunn, Keith A., "The Missing Link in Conflict Termination Thought: Strategy," in Stephen J. Cimbala and Keith A. Dunn, eds, *Conflict Termination and Military Strategy: Coercion, Persuasion, and War*, (Boulder, Colo., and London: Westview Press, 1987).

Dunn, Lewis A., "Containing Nuclear Proliferation," *Adelphi Paper*, 263, (London: International Institute of Strategic Studies, 1991).

Dunn, Lewis A., "India, Pakistan, Iran – A Nuclear Proliferation Chain," in William H. Overholt, ed., *Asia's Nuclear Future* (Boulder, Colo.: Westview Press, 1977).

Dunn, Lewis A., "Nuclear Proliferation and World Politics," *Annals of the American Academy of Political and Social Science*, 430, March 1977.

Etzioni, Amitai, "The Kennedy Experiment," *Western Political Quarterly*, 20 (June), 1967.

Evans, Graham and Jeffrey Newnham, *Dictionary of International Relations* (New York: Penguin Books, 1998).

Falkenrath, Richard A., "Confronting Nuclear, Biological, and Chemical Terrorism," *Survival*, 40(3), Autumn 1998.

Fever, Peter D. and Scott D. Sagan, "Proliferation Pessimism and Emerging Nuclear Powers," *International Security*, 22(2), Fall 1997.

Francis, D., *People, Peace, and Power: Conflict Transformation in Action* (London: Pluto Publishing, 2002).

Gaddis, John Lewis, "Great Illusions, the Long Peace, and the Future of the International System," in Charles W. Kegley, ed., *The Long Post War Peace* (New York: HarperCollins, 1991).

Gagne, Chris, "Nuclear Risk Reduction in South Asia: Building on Common Ground," in Michael Krepon and Chris Gagne, eds, *The Stability-Instability Paradox: Nuclear Weapons and Brinkmanship in South Asia*, Report No. 38, (Washington, DC: Stimson Center, 2001).

Galtung, Johan, *Peace by Peaceful Means* (London: Sage Publications, 1996).

Ganguly, Sumit, *Conflict Unending: India–Pakistan Tensions since 1947* (New York: Columbia University Press, 2001).

Ganguly, Sumit, *The Crisis in Kashmir: Portents of War, Hopes of Peace* (Cambridge: Cambridge University Press, 1997).

Ganguly, Sumit, "Nuclear Proliferation in South Asia: Origins, Consequences, and Prospects," in Shalendra Sharma, ed., *The Asia-Pacific in the New Millennium* (Berkeley: Institute of East Asian Studies, University of California, 2000).

Ganguly, Sumit, "The Start of a Beautiful Friendship? The United States and India," *World Policy Journal*, 20(1), Spring 2003.

Ganguly, Sumit and Devin T. Hagerty, *Fearful Symmetry: India–Pakistan Crises in the Shadow of Nuclear Weapons* (Seattle: University of Washington Press, 2005).

Garthoff, Raymond L., "Conflict Termination in Soviet Thought," in Stephen J. Cimbala and Keith A. Dunn, eds, *Conflict Termination and Military Strategy: Coercion, Persuasion, and War*, (Boulder, Colo., and London: Westview Press, 1987).

Geller, Daniel S., "The India–Pakistan Rivalry: Prospects for War, Prospects for Peace," in T. V. Paul, ed., *The India–Pakistan Conflict: An Enduring Rivalry* (Cambridge: Cambridge University Press, 2005).

Geller, Daniel S., "Nuclear Weapons, Deterrence, and Crisis Escalation," *Journal of Conflict Resolution*, 34, 1990.

Goertz, Gary and Paul F. Diehl, "The Empirical Importance of Enduring Rivalries," *International Interactions*, 18, 1992.

Goertz, Gary and Paul F. Diehl, "The Initiation and Termination of Enduring Rivalries: The Impact of Political Shocks," *American Journal of Political Science*, 39(1), February 1995.

Goldstein, Joshua S. and John R. Freeman, *Three-Way Street: Strategic Reciprocity in World Politics* (Chicago: University of Chicago Press, 1990).

Greenwood, Ted, *Nuclear Proliferation: Motivations, Capabilities and Strategies for Control* (New York: McGraw Hill, 1977).

Grover, Verinder and Ranjana Arora, eds, *50 Years of Indo-Pak Relations*, vol. 1, (New Delhi: BPR Publishers, 1998).

Gupta, Sisir, M. S. Rajan, and Sumit Ganguly, eds, *India and the International System* (New Delhi: Vikas, 1981).

Hagerty, Devin T., *Consequences of Nuclear Proliferation: Lessons from South Asia* (Cambridge, Mass., and London: MIT Press, 1998).

Haqqani, Husain, "America's New Alliance with Pakistan: Avoiding the Traps of the Past," *Carnegie Policy Brief*, 19, October 2002.

Heitler, Susan, *From Conflict to Resolution* (London: W. W. Norton, 1990).

Herring, Eric, "Rogue Rage: Can We Prevent Mass Destruction," in Eric Herring, ed., *Preventing the Use of Weapons of Mass Destruction* (London: Frank Cass, 2000).

Hersh, Seymour, "On the Nuclear Edge," *New Yorker*, March 29, 1993.

Horn, Robert, *Soviet-Indian Relations: Issues and Influence* (New York: Praeger, 1982).

Hoyt, Timothy D., "Strategic Myopia: Pakistan's Nuclear Doctrine and Crisis Stability in South Asia," in Lowell Dittmer, ed., *South Asia's Nuclear Security Dilemma: India, Pakistan, and China* (London and New York: M. E. Sharpe, 2005).

Huntington, Samuel P., "The Lonely Superpower," in G. John Ikenberry, ed., *American Foreign Policy: Theoretical Essays*, fourth edn (New York: Longman, 2002).

Hymans, Jacques E. C, *The Psychology of Nuclear Proliferation: Identity, Emotions, and Foreign Policy* (Cambridge, UK, and New York: Cambridge University Press, 2006).

Jain, Sharda, *Politics of Terrorism in India: The Case of Punjab* (Delhi: Deep and Deep Publications, 1995).

James, Carolyn C., "Iran and Iraq as Rational Crisis Actors: Dangers and Dynamics of Survivable Nuclear War," in Eric Herring, ed., *Preventing the Use of Weapons of Mass Destruction* (London: Frank Cass, 2000).

Jervis, Robert, "Offense, Defense, and Security Dilemma," in Robert J. Art and Robert Jervis, eds, *International Politics: Enduring Concepts and Contemporary Issues*, eighth edn (New York: Longman, 2007).

Joeck, Neil, "Pakistani Security and Nuclear Proliferation in South Asia," in Neil Joeck, ed., *Strategic Consequences of Nuclear Proliferation in South Asia* (London: Frank Cass, 1986).

Jones, Rodney W. and Mark G. McDonough, *Tracking Nuclear Proliferation: A Guide in Maps and Charts, 1998* (Washington, DC: Carnegie Endowment for International Peace, 1998).

Kagan, Robert, "A Tougher War for the U.S. is One of Legitimacy," *New York Times*, January 24, 2004.

Kamal, Nazir and Pravin Sawhney, "Missile Control in South Asia and the Role of Cooperative Monitoring Technology," SAND98-0505/4 (Albuquerque, NM: Sanda National Laboratories, October 1998).

Kang, Bhavdeep, "Tempers Tempered," *Outlook*, December 31, 2001.

Kapur, Ashok, "Major Powers and the Persistence of the India–Pakistan Conflict," in T. V. Paul, ed., *The India–Pakistan Conflict: An Enduring Rivalry* (Cambridge: Cambridge University Press, 2005).

Kapur, Ashok, *Pakistan's Nuclear Development* (London: Croom Helm, 1987).

Kapur, Paul, *Dangerous Deterrent: Nuclear Weapons Proliferation and Conflict in South Asia* (Stanford, Calif.: Stanford University Press, 2007).

Kapur, Paul, "India and Pakistan's Unstable Peace: Why Nuclear South Asia is Not Like Cold War Europe," *International Security*, 30(2), Fall 2005.

Karl, David J., "Proliferation Pessimism and Emerging Nuclear Powers," *International Security*, 21(3), Winter 1996/97.

Kaushik, Brij Mohan, *Pakistan's Nuclear Bomb* (India: Sopan Publishing House, 1980).

Kegley, Charles W. and Gregory A. Raymond, *How Nations Make Peace* (New York: St Martin's Press, 1999).

Khan, Feroz Hasan, "Challenges to Nuclear Stability in South Asia," *Nonproliferation Review*, 10(1), 2003.

Khan, Saira, *Nuclear Proliferation in Protracted Conflict Regions: A Comparative Study of South Asia and the Middle East* (Aldershot, Burlington, Vt., and Sydney: Ashgate, 2002).

Khan, Saira, "Nuclear Weapons and the Prolongation of the India–Pakistan Rivalry," in T. V. Paul, ed., *The India–Pakistan Conflict: An Enduring Rivalry* (Cambridge: Cambridge University Press, 2005).

Khan, Saira, "A Nuclear South Asia: Resolving or Protracting the Protracted Conflict?," *International Relations*, 15(4), 2001.

Kinzer, Stephen, "Kashmir Gets Scarier," *New York Times*, June 29, 1999.

Klare, Michael, *Rogue States and Nuclear Outlaws* (New York: Hill and Wang, 1995).

Knopf, Jeffrey W., "Recasting the Optimism-Pessimism Debate," *Security Studies*, 12(1), Autumn 2002.

Krepon, Michael, "The Stability-Instability Paradox, Misperception, and Escalation Control in South Asia" (Washington, DC: The Henry L. Stimson Center, May 2003).

Krepon, Michael and Ziad Haider, eds, *Reducing Nuclear Dangers in South Asia* (Washington, DC: The Henry L. Stimson Center, January 2004).

Kriesberg, Louis, "The Growth of the Conflict Resolution Field," in Chester A. Crocker, Fen Osler Hampson, and Pamela R. Aali, eds, *Turbulent Peace: The Challenges of Managing International Conflicts* (Washington, DC: The United States Institute of Peace Press, 2001).

Kriesberg, Louis, T. A. Northrup, and S. J. Thorson, eds, *Intractable Conflicts and Their Transformation* (Syracuse, NY: Syracuse University Press, 1989).

Krishna, Ashok, "The Kargil War," in Major General Krishna and P. R. Chari, eds, *Kargil: The Tables Turned* (New Delhi: Manohar, 2001).

Krishna, Ashok and P. R. Chari, eds, *Kargil: The Tables Turned* (New Delhi: Manohar Press, 2001).

Kux, Dennis, *The United States and Pakistan, 1947–2000: Disenchanted Allies* (Washington, DC: Woodrow Wilson Center Press, 2002).

Laqueur, Walter, *The Age of Terrorism* (Boston: Little Brown, 1987).

Lavoy, Peter, "Strategic Consequences of Nuclear Proliferation," *Security Studies*, 4(4), 1995.

Leatherman, J. D., W. DeMars, P. D. Gaffney, and R. Vayrynen, *Breaking Cycles of Violence* (West Hartford, Conn.: Kumarian Press, 1999).

Lebow, Richard Ned, "The Search for Accommodation: Gorbachev in Comparative Perspective," in Richard Ned Lebow and Thomas Risse-Kappen, eds, *International Relations Theory and the End of the Cold War* (New York: Columbia University Press, 1995).

Lederach, J. P., *Building Peace: Sustainable Reconciliation in Divided Societies* (Washington, DC: United States Institute of Peace Press, 1997).

Lederach, J. P., *The Little Book of Conflict Transformation* (Intercourse, Pa.: Good Press, 2003).

Leng, Russell J., "Realpolitik and Learning in the India–Pakistan Rivalry," in T. V. Paul, ed., *The India–Pakistan Conflict: An Enduring Rivalry* (Cambridge: Cambridge University Press, 2005).

Lindsay, James M. and Michael E. O'Hanlon, *Defending America: The Case for Limited National Missile Defense* (Washington, DC: Brookings Institution Press, 2001).

Lindskold, S., P. S. Walters, and H. Koutsourais, "Cooperators, Competitors, and Response to Grit," *Journal of Conflict Resolution*, 27, 1983.

Lodhi, Maleeha, "The Kargil Crisis: Anatomy of a Debacle," *Newsline*, July 1999.

Lodhi, Maleeha, "Security Challenges in South Asia," *Nonproliferation Review*, 8(2), 2002.

Maerli, Morten Bremer and Sverre Lodgaard, *Nuclear Proliferation and International Security* (London and New York: Routledge, 2007).

Mailk, Iffat, *Kashmir: Ethnic Conflict, International Dispute* (Karachi: Oxford University Press, 2001).

Manuel, Andreu, J. Takehiro Fujihara, Takaya Kohyama, and J. Martin Ramirez, "Justification of Interpersonal Aggression in Japanese, American, and Spanish Students," *Aggressive Behavior*, 25, 1998.

Masood, Talat, "Civil-Military Relations and the 2007 Elections in Pakistan: Impact on the Regional Security Environment," *China and Eurasia Forum Quarterly*, 5(1), 2007.

Mazari, Shireen, "Kashmir: Looking for Viable Options," *Defense Journal*, 3(6), 1999.

Mazari, Shireen, "Low-Intensity Conflicts: The New War in South Asia," *Defense Journal*, 3(6), 1999.

Mazari, Shireen, "Re-examining Kargil," *Defense Journal*, 3(11), 2000.

Menon, Raja, *A Nuclear Strategy for India* (New Delhi: Sage Publishing, 2000).

Mesquitta, Bruce Bueno De and William H. Riker, "An Assessment of the Merits of Selective Nuclear Proliferation," *Journal of Conflict Resolution*, 26(2), June 1982.

Meyer, Stephen M., *The Dynamics of Nuclear Proliferation* (Chicago: University of Chicago Press, 1984).

Mial, Hugh, "Conflict Transformation: A Multi-Dimensional Task," Berghof Research Center for Constructive Conflict Management, http://www.berghof-handbook.net/articles/miall_handbook.pdf.

Millot, Marc Dean, "Facing the Emerging Reality of Regional Nuclear Adversaries," *Washington Quarterly*, 17(3), 1994.

Mills, Walter, *A World Without War* (Santa Barbara, Calif.: Center for the Study of Democratic Institutions, 1961).

Mohan, C. Raja, "A Paradigm Shift toward South Asia?," *Washington Quarterly*, 26(1), Winter 2002–3.

Mohan, C. Raja, "Vajpayee's Experiment with Pakistan," *Hindu*, December 4, 2003.

Mohan, C. Raja and Peter Lavoy, "Avoiding Nuclear War," in Michael Krepon and Amit Sevak, eds, *Crisis Prevention, Confidence-Building, and Reconciliation in South Asia* (New York: St Martin's Press, 1995).

Morgan, Patrick, *Deterrence: A Conceptual Analysis* (Beverly Hills, Calif., and London: Sage, 1977).

Morgenthau, Hans J., *Politics Among Nations: The Struggle for Power and Peace*, sixth edn, revised by Kenneth W. Thompson (New York: Alfred A.Knopf, 1985).

Mueller, John and Karl Mueller, "The Methodology of Mass Destruction: Assessing Threats in the New World Order," in Eric Herring, ed., *Preventing the Use of Weapons of Mass Destruction* (London: Frank Cass, 2000).

Nayar, Kuldip, "We Have the A-Bomb, Says Pakistan's Dr. Strangelove," *Observer*, London, March 1, 1987.

Nicholson, Michael, *Rationality and the Analysis of International Conflict* (Cambridge: Cambridge University Press, 1992).

Orlov, Vladimir A., "Export Controls and Nuclear Smuggling in Russia," in Garry K. Bertsch and William C. Potter, eds, *Dangerous Weapons , Desperate States: Russia, Belarus, Kazakstan, and Ukraine* (New York and London: Routledge, 1999).

Osgood, Charles, *An Alternative to War or Surrender* (Urbana: University of Illinois Press, 1962).

Parthasarathy, G., "How Kandahar Hijacked Us," *Indian Express*, February 6, 2008.

Pattanaik, Smruti S., "Indo-Pak Relations: Need for a Pragmatic Approach," *Strategic Analysis*, 23(1), April 1999.

Paul, T. V., *Asymmetric Conflicts: War Initiation by Weaker Powers* (Cambridge: Cambridge University Press, 1994).

Paul, T. V., "Causes of the India–Pakistan Enduring Rivalry," in T. V. Paul, ed., *The India–Pakistan Conflict: An Enduring Rivalry* (Cambridge: Cambridge University Press, 2005).

Paul, T. V., ed., *India–Pakistan Conflict: An Enduring Rivalry* (Cambridge: Cambridge University Press, 2005).

Paul, T. V., *Power versus Prudence: Why Nations Forgo Nuclear Weapons* (Montreal and Kingston: McGill-Queen's University Press, 2000).

Paul, T. V., Richard K. Harknett, and James J. Wirtz, eds, *The Absolute Weapons Revisited: Nuclear Arms and the Emerging International Orde*r (Ann Arbor: University of Michigan Press, 1998).

Perkovich, George, *India's Nuclear Bomb: The Impact on Global Proliferation* (Berkeley, Calif.: University of California Press, 1999).

Perkovich, George, "A Nuclear Third Way in South Asia," *Foreign Policy*, 91, Summer 1993.

Potter, William C., "Improving Nuclear Materials Security in the Former Soviet Union," *Arms Control Today*, January–February 1993.

Potter, William C., *Nuclear Power and Nonproliferation: An Interdisciplinary Perspective* (Cambridge, Mass: Gunn and Hain, 1982).

Potter, William C., "On Nuclear Proliferation," in Edward A. Kolodziej and Patrick M. Morgan, eds, *Security and Arms Control, vol 2: A Guide to International Policy-Making* (New York: Greenwood, 1989).

Potter, William C., "Russia's Nuclear Entrepreneurs," *New York Times*, November 7, 1991.

Puri, Harish K., Paramjit Singh Judge, and Jagrup Singh Sekhon, *Terrorism in Punjab: Understanding Grassroots Reality* (New Delhi: Har Anand Publications, 1999).

Quester, George, *Deterrence Before Hiroshima: The Airpower Background of Modern Strategy* (New Brunswick, NJ: Transaction, 1986).

Quester, George, *The Politics of Nuclear Proliferation* (Baltimore, Md.: Johns Hopkins University Press, 1973).

Quester, George, "Reducing the Incentives to Proliferation," *Annals* 430, March 1977.

Raghavan, V. R., "Limited War and Nuclear Escalation in South Asia," *Nonproliferation Review*, 8(3), 2001.

Raghavan, V. R., *Siachen: Conflict Without End* (New Delhi: Viking Press, 2002).

Rapoport, Anatol and Albert M. Chammah, *Prisoner's Dilemma: A Study of Conflict and Cooperation* (Ann Arbor: The University of Michigan Press, 1965).

Ravi, Thathiah, "Pakistan Army and Regional Peace in South Asia," *Journal of Third World Studies*, Spring 2006.

Reddy, B. Muralidhar, "Jaish Behind Parliament Attack: ex-ISI Chief," *Hindu*, March 7, 2004.

Reiss, Mitchell, *Bridled Ambition: Why Countries Constrain Their Nuclear Capabilities* (Washington, DC: Woodrow Wilson Center Press, 1995).

Reiss, Mitchell, *Without the Bomb: The Politics of Nuclear Non-Proliferation* (New York: Columbia University Press, 1988).

Robinson, James A., "Crisis: An Appraisal of Concepts and Theories," in Charles F. Hermann, ed., *International Crises* (New York: The Free Press, 1972).

Rosen, Steven J., "A Stable System of Mutual Nuclear Deterrence in the Middle East," *American Political Science Review*, 71(4), December 1977.

Russett, Bruce, *Grasping the Democratic Peace: Principles for a Post-Cold War World* (Princeton, NJ: Princeton University Press, 1993).

Ryan, Stephen, *The Transformation of Violent Intercommunal Conflict* (Aldershot: Ashgate, 2007).

Saaty, Thomas L. and Joyce M. Alexander, *Conflict Resolution: The Analytic Hierarchy Approach* (New York, Westport, Conn., and London: Praeger, 1989).

Saez, Lawrence, "The Political Economy of the India–Pakistan Nuclear Standoff," in Lowell Dittmer, ed., *South Asia's Nuclear Security Dilemma: India, Pakistan, and China* (New York and London: M. E. Sharpe, 2005).

Sagan, Scott D., "Rethinking the Causes of Nuclear Proliferation: Three Models in Search of a Bomb," in Victor A. Utgoff, ed., *The Coming Crisis: Nuclear Proliferation, US Interests and World Order* (Cambridge, Mass.: MIT Press, 2000).

Sagan, Scott D., "Why Do States Build Nuclear Weapons?: Three Models in Search of a Bomb," *International Security*, 21(3), Winter 1996/7.

Sagan, Scott D. and Kenneth N. Waltz, *The Spread of Nuclear Weapons: A Debate Renewed* (New York: W. W. Norton, 2003).

Sahay, Tara Shankar, "Experts Do Not Expect Much from Meeting," *India Abroad*, July 6, 2001.

Saideman, Stephen M., "At the Heart of the Conflict: Irredentism and Kashmir," in T. V. Paul, ed., *The India–Pakistan Conflict: An Enduring Rivalry* (Cambridge: Cambridge University Press, 2005).

Sanger, David E. and Kurt Eichenwald, "Citing India Attack, US Aims at Assets of Groups in Pakistan," *New York Times*, December 21, 2001.

Schaffer, Teresita, "The US and South Asia: New Priorities, Familiar Interests," *South Asia Monitor*, 38, October 1, 2001.

Schofield, Victoria, *Kashmir in Conflict: India, Pakistan, and the Unfinished War* (London: IB Taurus, 2002).

Schwarenzenberger, Georg, *International Law and Order* (London: Stevens and Sons, 1971).

Singer, J. David and Melvin Small, *The Wages of War 1816–1965: A Statistical Handbook* (New York: John Wiley, 1972).

Singh, Jasjit, "The Fourth War," in Jasjit Singh, ed., *Kargil 1999: Pakistan's Fourth War for Kashmir* (New Delhi: Knowledge World, 1999).

Singh, Jaswant, "Against Nuclear Apartheid," *Foreign Affairs*, 77(5), 1998.

Snyder, Glenn, "Balance of Power or Balance of Terror," in Paul Seadbury, ed., *Balance of Power* (San Francisco: Chandler Publishing, 1965).

Snyder, Glenn, "Crisis Bargaining," in Charles F. Hermann, ed., *International Crises: Insights from Behavioral Research* (New York: Free Press, 1972).

Snyder, Glenn and Paul Diesing, *Conflict Among Nations: Bargaining, Decision-Making and System Structure in International Crises* (Princeton, NJ: Princeton University Press, 1977).

Snyder, Jed C., "The Non-Proliferation Regime: Managing the Impending Crisis," in Neil Joeck, ed., *Strategic Consequences of Nuclear Proliferation in South Asia* (London: Frank Cass, 1986).

Solana, Javier, "The Future of Transatlantic Relations: Reinvention or Reform," *Progressive Governance*, July 10, 2003.

Spiegel, Steven L., "Introduction," in Steven L Spiegel and Kenneth N. Waltz, eds, *Conflict in World Politics* (Cambridge, Mass.: Winthrop Publishers, 1971).

Starr, Harvey, "Territory, Proximity, and Spatiality: The Geography of International Conflict," *International Studies Review*, 7(3), September 2005.

Staudenmaier, William O., "Conflict Termination in the Nuclear Era," in Stephen J. Cimbala and Keith A. Dunn, eds, *Conflict Termination and Military Strategy: Coercion, Persuasion, and War* (Boulder, Colo., and London: Westview Press, 1987)

Stein, Janice Gross, "Image, Identity, and Conflict Resolution," in Chester A Crocker, Fen Osler Hampson, and Pamela Aali, eds, *Managing Global Chaos: Sources of and Responses to International Conflict* (Washington, DC: US Institute of Peace Press, 1996).

Strong, Robert A., "The Nuclear Weapon States: Why They Went Nuclear?," in W. H. Kincade and C. Bertram, eds, *Nuclear Proliferation in the 1980s*, (New York: St Martin's Press, 1982).

Subrahmanyam, K., "India: Keeping the Option Open," in Robert Lawrence and Joel Laurus, eds, *Nuclear Proliferation Phase II* (Lawrence: published for the National Security Education Program by University Press of Kansas, 1974).

Subrahmanyam, K., *Security in a Changing World* (New Delhi: B. R. Publishing Corporation, 1990).

Sullivan, Michael, "Militants Attack Indian Army Base in Kashmir," *Non-proliferation Review*, May 14, 2002.

Sundarji, K., "India's Nuclear Weapons Policy," in Jorn Gjelstad and Olav Njolstad, eds, *Nuclear Rivalry and International Order* (Oslo: International Peace Research Institute. 1996).

Swami, Praveen, "Failed Threats and Flawed Fences: India's Military Responses to Pakistan's Proxy War," *India Review*, 3(2), April 2004.

Tellis, Ashley J., C. Christine Fair, and Jamison Jo Medby, *Limited Conflicts Under the Nuclear Umbrella: Indian and Pakistani Lessons from the Kargil Crisis* (Santa Monica, Calif.: RAND, 2001).

Thomas, Raju G., ed., *Perspectives on Kashmir: The Roots of Conflict in South Asia*, (Boulder, Colo.: Westview Press, 1992).

Thorson, Stuart J., *Intractable Conflicts and Their Transformation* (Syracuse, NY: Syracuse University Press, 1989).

Tidwell, Alan C., *Conflict Resolved? A Critical Assessment of Conflict Resolution* (New York: Pinter Publishers, 1998).

Toynbee, Arnold, *A Study of History*, Vol. IX (London: Oxford University Press, 1954).

Varshney, Ashutosh, "India, Pakistan, and Kashmir: Antinomies of Nationalism," *Asian Survey*, 31, November 1991.

Vasquez, John A., "Distinguishing Rivals That Go to War from Those That Do Not: A Quantitative Comparative Case Study of Two Paths to War," *International Studies Quarterly*, 40, 1996.

Vasquez, John A., "The India–Pakistan Conflict in Light of General Theories of War, Rivalry, and Deterrence," in T. V. Paul, ed., *The India–Pakistan Conflict: An Enduring Rivalry* (Cambridge: Cambridge University Press, 2005).

Vasquez, John A. and Christopher Leskiw, "The Origins and War Proneness of Interstate Rivalries," *Annual Review of Political Science*, 4, 2001.

Vayrynen, R., "From Conflict Resolution to Conflict Transformation: A Critical Review," in H. W. Jeong, ed., *The New Agenda for Peace Research* (Aldershot: Ashgate, 1999).

Vayrynen, R., "To Settle or to Transform: Perspectives on the Resolution of National and International Conflicts," in R. Vayrynen, ed., *New Directions in Conflict Theory* (London: Sage Publications, 1991).

Vayrynen, R., ed., *The Quest for Peace: Transcending Collective Violence and War Among Societies, Cultures, and States* (London: Sage Publications, 1986).

Wallensteen, Peter, "The Resolution and Transformation of International Conflicts: A Structural Perspective," in Raimo Vayrynen, ed., *New Directions in Conflict Theory* (London: Sage, 1991).

Walt, Stephen M., "Containing Rogues and Renegades: Coalition Strategies and Counterproliferation," in Victor A. Utgoff, ed., *The Coming Crisis: Nuclear Proliferation, US Interests, and World Order* (Cambridge, Mass.: MIT Press, 2000).

Waltz, Kenneth N., "The Spread of Nuclear Weapons: More May be Better," *Adelphi Papers*, 171, Autumn 1981.

Wayman, Frank Whelon, "Recurrent Disputes and Explaining War," in John A. Vasquez, ed., *What Do We Know about War?* (London, Boulder, Colo., New York, and Oxford: Rowman & Littlefield, 2000).

Weinbaum, Marvin, *Pakistan and Afghanistan: Resistance and Reconstruction* (Boulder, Colo.: Westview Press, 1994).

Weltman, John J., "Nuclear Devolution and World Order," *World Politics*, 32(2), January 1980.

Wirsing, Robert G., *India, Pakistan, and the Kashmir Dispute: On Regional Conflict and its Resolution* (New York: St Martin's Press, 1994).

Wirsing, Robert G., *Kashmir in the Shadow of War: Regional Rivalries in a Nuclear Age* (New York and London: M. E. Sharp, 2003).

Wisner II, Frank G., Nicholas Platt, and Marshall M. Bouton, *New Priorities in South Asia: U.S. Policy Toward India, Pakistan, and Afghanistan* (New York: Council on Foreign Relations, 2003).

Wohlstetter, Albert, "Nuclear Sharing: NATO and the N+1 Country," in Richard N. Rosecrance, ed., *The Dispersion of Nuclear Weapons: Strategy and Politics* (New York: Columbia University Press, 1964).

Wright, Quincy, *A Study of War* (Chicago: University of Chicago Press, 1964).

Zehra, Nasim, "Anatomy of Islamabad's Kargil Policy," *Defense Journal*, 3(7), 1999.

## Other documents

"Bomb Controversy," *Muslim*, March 3, 1987.

"Can India and Pakistan Seize the Moment?," *South Asia Monitor*, 60, July 1, 2003.

"Conflict Transformation", www.beyondintractability.org/essay/transformation.

"Developing a Delivery System," *Frontline*, 16(9), April 24–May 7, 1999.

Economist Global Agenda, "Terror in India," December 19, 2001, www.economist.com.

Federation of American Scientists, September 9, 2000, www.fas.org/nuke/guide/India/missile/prithvi.htm.

*From Surprise to Reckoning: The Kargil Review Committee Report* (New Delhi: Sage Publications, 2000).

"Ghauri Missiles," September 9, 2000, http///www.pakmilitary.com/army/missiles/ghauri.html.

"Highway Beyond Agra," *Strategic Analysis*, Special Issue 25, October 25, 2001.

"If Pushed Beyond a Point by Pakistan, We Will Retaliate," *India Today*, April 30, 1990.

"India Bombs the Ban," *Bulletin of the Atomic Scientists*, 54(4), July/August 1998.

"India to Make 300 Prithvi Missiles," *Hindu*, September 8, 2000.

India–Pakistan Foreign Secretary level talks in 2006, January 17, 2006, http://www.mea.gov.in/pressbriefing/2006/01/17pb01.htm.

International Crisis Group Report, "Kashmir: Learning from the Past," *ICG Asia Report*, 70, Islamabad, New Delhi, and Brussels, December 4, 2003.

Joint Statement on Indian Pakistan Expert Level Talks on Nuclear CBMs, June 20, 2004, http://www.mea.gov.in/cgibin/db2www/meaxpsite/searchhome.d2w/searchstr?start=30&str=India–Pakistan&sectioncode=%20.

"Joint Statement, First Meeting of India–Pakistan Joint Study Group (JSG) on Trade and Economic Cooperation," http://www.mea.gov.in/speech/2005/02/23js01.htm.

"Kashmir: Learning from the Past," *ICG Asia Report*, 70 (Islamabad/New Delhi/Brussels, December 4, 2003).

"Maintaining Nuclear Stability in South Asia," *Adelphi Paper*, 312 (Oxford. Oxford University Press, 1997).

"Musharraf Desperate for Good Ties with India," *Times of India*, November 6, 2006.

"Not Doing Enough: The Prime Minister Will Tell Musharraf," *Times of India*, September 13, 2006.

Resolution 91, 1951, Concerning the India–Pakistan Question, United Nations Security Council. March 30, 1951, UN Doc.S/201/Rev.1 (March 30, 1951).

"Resolve Kashmir, then Sign No-War Pact: Musharraf," *Times of India*, May 5, 2003.

Special Media Briefing by Indian Foreign Secretary Shri Shyam Saran on India–Pakistan Foreign Secretary level talks, January 18, 2006, http://www.mea.gov.in/pressbriefing/2006/01/18pb01.htm.

United States, Code, Title 22, Section 2656f(d).

# Index

Locators in *italic* refer to figures.